My Journey with a Mystic

MY JOURNEY
WITH
A MYSTIC

FRITZ PETERS

PREFACE BY HENRY MILLER

TALE WEAVER
PUBLISHING

Typset by Laser-Set
Desktop Publishing Typesetting Software
Right to the Point Software
Huntington Beach, CA 92646

Tale Weaver Publishing
32395 Outrigger Way
Laguna Niguel, CA 92677
(714) 661-6276

This book is dedicated to the memory of Georges Gurdjieff, With an acknowledgment of a debt of thanks to:

Sheila Hodges
Lloyd L. Goff
Anne Raymond
Julia B. Tappan
and Victor Gollancz

without whose interest and enthusiasm it might never have been written.

PREFACE

Tᴴɪꜱ ɪꜱ ᴀ highly delectable book, and by delectable I do not mean a book to be taken lightly. Indeed, a more appropriate adjective to describe it would be *glorious*. Not only is it full of amazing anecdotes, it is also full of wisdom. The wisdom of life.

It is remarkable also in that it is an account of a boy's experience with an extraordinary human being whose remarks and observations could only have been partially comprehended at the time by the author. He frequently quotes Gurdjieff *verbatim*. His memory is absolutely astounding as well as his intuition. It must be borne in mind that when his mother put him in Gurdjieff's care—in the Institute for the Harmonious Development of Man at Fountainebleau—the boy had no idea who Gurdjieff was or what he was like as an individual. He learned fast. One opens this book and is instantly enchanted by the encounter of two very dissimiliar human beings. One realizes that this is no ordinary tale of childhood recollections.

To begin with, Gurdjieff was a thoroughly enigmatic figure. He was a living example of that Greek word, *Enantiodromos*, meaning the process by which a thing changes into its opposite. He could be tender, fierce, strict, indulgent, wise, clownish, utterly serious and a *farceur* all at one time. Even the author, then only eleven years old, who had been made Gurdieff's "slavey", did not know how to take him at times. Gurdjieff was a perpetual surprise. However, young as he was, and with no preparation for the ordeal, Fritz Peters, the boy, was astute enough to know that he was in the hands of a most unusual human being, a man who has been called a Master, a Guru, a Teacher, everything but a Saint.

Just as it is said that Jehovah showed his hind parts to Moses, so Peters reveals to us Gurdjieff's very real, very human aspects.

Much has been written about the scandalous behavior of Gurdjieff. And it is true that he seemed to care little for conventional behavior. In a sense, he was like a cross between the Gnostics of old and the latter day Dadaists.

Certainly, of him the Latin saying "nothing human is beneath me" was true. He was human to the core.

At times he reached sublime heights. And the author, imitating Gurdjieff's broken English, has given us these moments in Gurdjieff's own fantastic language. This broken English had frequently a "Satanic" character. If at moments Gurdjieff seemed to touch the hem of creation, at other moments one might say of him that he was an emissary of Satan himself, which is why this book is so utterly enjoyable. It will fascinate even those who have never heard of Gurdjieff. For one thing, this book debunks all the crackpot legends about Master-and-Devil. It is informative without ever being dull. It cuts capers without becoming shoddy. It delivers over to us one of the most enigmatic and controversial figures of our time, one unfortunately too little known by present day man.

I have read the book several times myself and each time with renewed interest. In a way of speaking I regard it as something on a par with *Alice in Wonderland,* a real treasure of our literature.

Henry Miller

Book One

BOYHOOD   WITH   GURDJIEFF

I

I MET AND talked to Georges Gurdjieff for the first time in 1924, on a Saturday afternoon in June, at the Château du Prieuré in Fontainebleau - Avon, France. Although the reasons for my being there were not very clear in my mind— I was eleven at the time—my memory of that meeting is still brilliantly clear.

It was a bright, sunny day. Gurdjieff was sitting by a small marble-topped table, shaded by a striped umbrella, with his back to the château proper, facing a large expanse of formal lawns and flower beds. I had to sit on the terrace of the château, behind him, for some time before I was summoned to his side for an interview. I had, actually, seen him once before, in New York the previous winter, but I did not feel that I had "met" him. My only memory of that prior time was that I had been frightened of him: partly because of the way he looked at—or through—me, and partly because of his reputation. I had been told that he was at least a "prophet"—at most, something very close to the "second coming of Christ".

Meeting any version of a "Christ" is an event, and this meeting was not one to which I looked forward. Facing the presence not only did not appeal to me—I dreaded it.

The actual meeting did not measure up to my fears. "Messiah" or not, he seemed to me a simple, straightforward man. He was not surrounded by a halo, and while his English was heavily accented, he spoke far more simply than the Bible had led me to expect. He made a vague gesture in my direction, told me to sit down, called for coffee, and then asked me why I was there. I was relieved to find that he seemed to be an ordinary human being, but I was troubled by the question. I felt sure that I was supposed to give him an *important* answer; that I should have some excellent reason. Having none, I told him the truth: That I was there because I had been brought there.

He then asked me why I wanted to be there, to study at his school. Once more I was only able to answer that it was all beyond my control—I had not been consulted, I had been, as it were, transported to that place. I remember my strong impulse to lie to him, and my equally strong feeling that I could not lie to him. I felt sure that he knew the truth in advance. The only question that I answered less than honestly was when he asked me if I wanted to stay there and to study with him. I said that I did, which was not essentially true. I said it because I knew that it was expected of me. It seems to me, now, that any child would have answered as I did. Whatever the Prieuré might represent to adults (and the literal name of the school was "The Gurdjieff Institute for the Harmonious Development of Man"), I felt that I was experiencing the equivalent of being interviewed by the principal of a high school. Children went to school, and I subscribed to the general agreement that no child would tell his teacher-to-be that he did not want to go to school. The only thing that surprised me was that I was asked the question.

Gurdjieff then asked me two more questions:

1. What do you think life is?

and

2. What do you want to know?

I answered the first question by saying: "I think life is something that is handed to you on a silver platter, and it is up to you (me) to do something with it." This answer touched off a long discussion about the phrase "on a silver platter", including a reference by Gurdjieff to the head of John the Baptist. I retreated—it felt like a retreat—and modified the phrase to the effect that life was a "gift", and this seemed to please him.

The second question (What do you want to know?) was simpler to answer. My words were: "I want to know everything."

Gurdjieff replied immediately: "You cannot know everything. Everything about what?"

I said: "Everything about man," and then added: "In English I think it is called psychology or maybe philosophy."

He sighed then, and after a short silence said: "You can stay. But your answer makes life difficult for me. I am the only one who teaches what you ask. You make more work for me."

Since my childish aims were to conform and to please, I
was disconcerted by his answer. The last thing I wanted to
do was to make life more difficult for anyone—it seemed to
me that it was difficult enough already. I said nothing in
reply to this, and he went on to tell me that in addition to
learning "everything" I would also have the opportunity to
study lesser subjects, such as languages, mathematics,
various sciences, and so forth. He also said that I would find
that his was not the usual school: "Can learn many things
here that other schools not teach." He then patted my
shoulder benevolently.

I use the word "benevolently" because the gesture was of
great importance to me at the time. I longed for approval
from some higher authority. To receive such "approval" from
this man who was considered by other adults to be a
"prophet", "seer", and/or a "Messiah"—and approval in such
a simple, friendly gesture—was unexpected and heartwarm-
ing. I beamed.

His manner changed abruptly. He struck the table with
one fist, looked at me with great intensity, and said: "Can
you promise to do something for me?"

His voice and the look he had given me were frightening
and also exciting. I felt both cornered and challenged. I
answered him with one word, a firm "Yes".

He gestured towards the expanse of lawns before us: "You
see this grass?"

"Yes."

"I give you work. You must cut this grass, with machine,
every week."

I looked at the lawns, the grass spreading before us into
what appeared to me infinity. It was, without any doubt, a
prospect of more work in one week than I had ever
contemplated in my life. Again, I said "Yes".

He struck the table with his fist for a second time. "You
must promise on your God." His voice was deadly serious.
"You must promise that you will do this thing no matter
what happens."

I looked at him, questioning, respectful, and with considerable awe. No lawn—not even these (there were four of them) — had ever seemed important to me before. "I promise," I said earnestly.

"Not just promise," he reiterated. "Must promise you will do no matter what happens, no matter who try stop you. Many things can happen in life."

For a moment his words conjured up visions of terrifying arguments over the mowing of these lawns. I foresaw great emotional dramas taking place in the future on account of these lawns and of myself. Once again, I promised. I was as serious as he was then. I would have died, if necessary, in the act of mowing the lawns.

My feeling of dedication was obvious, and he seemed satisfied. He told me to begin work on Monday, and then dismissed me. I don't think I realized at the time—that is, the sensation was new to me—but I left him with the feeling that I had fallen in love; whether with the man, the lawns, or me, did not matter. My chest was expanded far beyond its normal capacity. I, a child, an unimportant cog in the world which belonged to adults, had been asked to perform something that was apparently vital.

II

WHAT WAS "THE PRIEURÉ", which was the name most of us used, or "The Institute for the Harmonious Development of Man"?

At the age of eleven, I understood it to be simply some kind of special school, directed, as I have said, by a man who was considered by many people to be a visionary, a new prophet, a great philosopher. Gurdjieff himself once defined it as a place where he was attempting, among other things, to create a small world that would reproduce the conditions of the larger, outside world; the main purpose in creating such conditions being to prepare the students for future human, or life, experience. It was not, in other words, a school devoted to ordinary education which, generally, consists in the acquisition of various faculties such as reading, writing, and arithmetic. One of the simpler things that he was attempting to teach was a preparation for life itself.

It may be necessary to point out here, especially for the benefit of people who have had some contact with Gurdjieffian theory, that I am describing the "Institute" as I saw and understood it as a boy. I am not attempting to define its purpose or meaning for individuals who were interested in, or attracted to, Gurdjieff because of his philosophy. To me, it was simply another school—different from any school I had known, to be sure—and the essential difference was that most of the "students" were adults. With the exception of my brother and me, all the other children were either relatives —nieces, nephews, etc., of Mr. Gurdjieff—or his natural children. There were not many children in all: I can only remember a total of ten.

The routine of the school, for everyone except the smallest children, was the same. The day began with a breakfast of coffee and dry toast at six o'clock. From seven o'clock on, each individual worked at whatever task was assigned to him. The performance of these tasks was only interrupted during the day by meals: dinner at noon (usually, soup, meat, salad, and some kind of sweet pudding); tea at four in the afternoon; a simple supper at seven in the evening. After supper, at 8.30, there were gymnastics, or dances, in what was called the "study-house". This routine was standard for six days a week, except that on Saturday afternoons the women went to the Turkish bath; early Saturday evenings there were "demonstrations" of the dances in the study-house by the more competent performers, for the other students and for guests who frequently came to visit for weekends; after the demonstrations, the men went to the Turkish bath, and when the bath was over, there was a "feast" or special meal. The children did not participate in these late meals as diners—only as waiters or kitchen help. Sunday was a day of rest.

The tasks assigned to the students were invariably concerned with the actual functioning of the school: gardening, cooking, house-cleaning, taking care of animals, milking, making butter; and these tasks were almost always group activities. As I learned later, the group work was considered to be of real importance: Different personalities, working together, produced subjective, human conflicts; human conflicts produced friction; friction revealed characteristics which, if observed, could reveal "self". One of the many aims of the school was "to see yourself as others saw you"; to see oneself, as it were, from a distance; to be able to criticize that self objectively; but, at first, simply to *see* it. An exercise that was intended to be performed all the time, during whatever physical activity, was called "self-observation" or "opposing I to it" — "I" being the (potential) consciousness, "it" the body, the instrument.

At the beginning, and before I understood any of these theories or exercises, my task and, in a sense, my world, was completely centred on cutting the grass, for my lawns—as I came to call them—became considerably more vital than I could have anticipated.

The day after my "interview" with him, Mr. Gurdjieff left for Paris. We had been given to understand that it was customary for him to spend two days a week in Paris, usually accompanied by his secretary, Madame de Hartmann, and sometimes others. This time, which was unusual, he went alone.

As I remember, it was not until sometime on Monday afternoon—Mr. Gurdjieff had left Sunday evening—that the rumour that he had been in an automobile accident filtered down to the children at the school. We heard first that he had been killed, then that he had been seriously injured and was not expected to live. A formal announcement was made by someone in authority Monday evening. He was not dead, but he was seriously injured and near death in a hospital.

It is difficult to describe the impact of such an announcement. The very existence of the "Institute" depended entirely on Gurdjieff's presence. It was he who assigned work to every individual—and up to that moment he had supervised, personally, every detail of the running of the school. Now, the imminent possibility of his death brought everything to a standstill. It was only thanks to the initiative of a few of the older students, most of whom had come with him from Russia, that we continued to eat regularly.

While I did not know what was going to happen to me, personally, the one thing that was still vivid in my mind was the fact that he had told me that I was to mow the lawns "no matter what happened". It was a relief to me to have something concrete to do; a definite job that he had assigned to me. It was also the first time that I had any feeling that he was, perhaps, extraordinary. It was he who had said "no matter what happens", and his accident had happened. His injunction became that much stronger. I was convinced that he had known beforehand that "something" was going to happen, although not necessarily an automobile accident.

I was not the only one who felt that his accident was, in a sense, foreordained. The fact that he had gone to Paris alone (I was told it was the first time he had done so) was sufficient proof for most of the students. My reaction, in any event, was that it had become absolutely essential to mow the grass; I was convinced that his life, at least in part, might depend on my dedication to the task he had given me.

These feelings of mine assumed special importance when,

a few days later, Mr. Gurdjieff was brought back to the Prieuré, to his room which overlooked "my" lawns, and we were told that he was in a coma and was being kept alive on oxygen. Doctors came and went at intervals; tanks of oxygen were delivered and removed; a hushed atmosphere descended over the place—it was as if we were all involved in permanent, silent prayer for him.

It was not until a day or so after his return that I was told —probably by Madame de Hartmann—that the noise of the lawn-mower would have to stop. The decision I was forced to make then was a momentous one for me. Much as I respected Madame de Hartmann, I could not forget the force with which he had made me promise to do my job. We were standing at the edge of the lawn, directly beneath the windows of his room, when I had to give her my answer. I did not reflect for very long, as I recall, and I refused, with all the force in me. I was then told that his life might actually depend on my decision, and I still refused. What surprises me now is that I was not categorically forbidden to continue, or even forcibly restrained. The only explanation that I can find for this is that his power over his pupils was such that no single individual was willing to take the responsibility of totally denying my version of what he had told me. In any case, I was not restrained; I was simply forbidden to cut the grass. I continued to cut it.

This rejection of authority, of anything less than the highest authority, was deadly serious, and I think the only thing that sustained me in it was that I was reasonably convinced that the noise of a lawn-mower would not kill anyone; also, less logically, I did feel, at the time, that his life might—inexplicably—depend on my performance of the task he had given me. These reasons, however, were no defence against the feelings of the other students (there were about one hundred and fifty people there at the time, most of them adults) who were at least equally convinced that the noise I continued to make every day could be deadly.

The conflict continued for several weeks, and each day when "no change" in his condition was reported, it became more difficult for me to begin. I can remember having to grit my teeth and overcome my own fear of what I might be doing every morning. My resolve was alternately strengthened and weakened by the attitude of the other students. I was ostracized, excluded from every other activity; no one would sit at the same table with me at meals—if I went to a table where others were sitting, they woukd leave the table when I sat down—and I cannot remember any one person who either spoke to me or smiled at me during those weeks, with the exception of a few of the more important adults who, from time to time, continued to exhort me to stop.

III

By mid-summer, 1924, my whole life was centred on grass. By that time, I was able to mow my four lawns in a total of four days. The other things I did: taking my turn as "kitchen boy" or as "gate keeper" at the small gate house which we called the "concierge", were unimportant. I have little memory for anything other than the sound of that mowing machine.

My nightmare came to an end suddenly. Early one morning, as I was pushing the lawn mower up towards the front of the château, I looked up at Gurdjieff's windows. I always did this, as if hoping for some miraculous sign. This particular morning, I saw it at last. He was standing in the open window, looking down at me. I stopped, and stared back at him, flooded with relief. For what seemed a long time, he did not do anything. Then, with a very slow movement of his hand and arm, he brought his right hand to his lips and made a gesture which I later learned had always been characteristic of him: with his thumb and index finger, he, as it were, parted his moustache from the centre, and then his hand fell to his side and he smiled. The gesture made him real—without it, I might have thought the figure standing there simply an hallucination or a figment of my imagination.

The sensation of relief was so intense that I burst into tears, gripping the lawn mower with both of my hands. I continued to watch him through my tears until he moved slowly away from the window. And then I started to mow again. What had been the dreadful noise of that machine now became joyous to me. I pushed the lawn mower up and down, up and down, with all my strength.

I decided to wait until noon to announce my triumph, but by the time I went in to lunch I realized that I had no proof, nothing to announce, and, with what now seems surprising wisdom, I did not say anything, although I was unable to contain my happiness.

By evening, it was generally known that Mr. Gurdjieff was out of danger, and the atmosphere at dinner-time was

one of gratitude and thankfulness. My part in his recovery—
I had become convinced that I, alone, would be responsible
in great part for whatever happened to him—was lost in the
general rejoicing. All that happened was that the animosity
which had been directed towards me disappeared as suddenly as it had arisen. If it had not been for the fact that I
had actually, some weeks before, been forbidden to make
any noise near his windows, I would have thought that the
whole thing had existed only in my mind. The lack of any
kind of triumph, of any recognition, was a blow.

The incident was not, however, completely closed even
then. Mr. Gurdjieff appeared, warmly dressed and walking
slowly, a few days later. He came to sit at the little table
where he had first interviewed me. I was, as usual, trudging
up and down with my lawn mower. He sat there, seemingly
oblivious of everything around him, until I finished the lawn
which I had been mowing that day. It was the fourth and,
thanks to the impetus of his recovery, I had shortened my
mowing time to three days. As I pushed the mowing
machine ahead of me, taking it back to the shed where it
was kept, he looked at me and motioned me to come over to
him.

I dropped the lawn mower and went to stand at his side.
He smiled, again I would say "benevolently", and asked me
how long it took me to mow the lawns. I answered, proudly,
that I could mow all of them in three days. He sighed,
staring ahead of him at the expanse of grass, and stood up.
"Must be able to do in one day," he said. "This important."

One day! I was appalled, and filled with mixed emotions.
Not only was I given no credit for my accomplishment—at
least for having, in spite of everything, kept my promise; I
was practically being punished for it.

Gurdjieff paid no attention to my reactions, which must
have been visible on my mobile face, but put one hand on my
shoulder and leaned rather heavily on me. "This important,"
he repeated, "because when can cut lawns in one day, have
other work for you." He then asked me to walk with him—to
help him walk — to a particular field, not far away,
explaining that he was unable to walk easily.

We walked together slowly, and with considerable difficulty, even with my help, we ascended a path by the field he had mentioned. It was a sloping hill, filled with rocks, near the chicken yard. He sent me into a tool shed near the chicken coops and told me to bring him the scythe, which I did. He then led me into the field, took his hand from my shoulder, took the scythe in both of his hands and made a sweeping cutting gesture with it. As I watched him, I felt that the effort he was making was very great; I feared his pallor and his obvious weakness. He then handed the scythe back to me and told me to put it away. When I had done so, I came back to stand beside him, and once more he leaned heavily on my shoulder.

"When can cut all lawns in one day, this will be new work. Scythe this field every week."

I looked up the slope at the long grass, the rocks and trees and bushes. I was also aware of my own size—I was small for my age, and the scythe had seemed very large. All I could do was to stare at him, amazed. It was only the look in his eyes, serious and pained, that prevented me from making an immediate, angry, tearful protest. I simply bowed my head and nodded, and then walked with him, slowly, back to the main house, up the stairs and to the door of his room.

At eleven, I was no stranger to self-pity, but this development was almost too much for me. In fact, self-pity was only a small part of my feelings. I also felt anger and resentment. Not only had I had no recognition, no thanks—I was practically being punished. What kind of place was this school—and what sort of man was he, after all? Bitterly, and rather proudly, I remembered that I would be going back to America in the fall. I would show him. All that I had to do was never to manage to mow the lawns in one day!

Curiously, when my feelings subsided and I began to accept what appeared to be the inevitable, I found that my resentment and anger, although I still felt them, were not directed against Mr. Gurdjieff personally. There had been a look of sadness in his eyes as I had walked with him, and I had felt concerned about him, about his health; once again, although there had been no admonitions to the effect that I *must* do this work, I felt that I had taken on some kind of reponsibility; that I would have to do it for his sake.

The following day there was another surprise in store for me. He summoned me to his room in the morning and asked me, sternly, if I was able to keep a secret—from everyone. The firmness and the fiery glance he gave me as he asked me the question were completely unlike his weakness of the day before. I assured him, valiantly, that I could. Once more I felt a great challenge—I would keep his secret no matter what!

He then told me that he did not want to worry the other students — and particularly his secretary, Madame de Hartmann—but that he was almost blind, and that I was the only one who knew this. He outlined an intriguing plot to me: He had decided to reorganize all the work then going on at the Prieuré. I was to go everywhere with him, carrying an armchair; the excuse for this being that he was still very weak, and would need to rest from time to time. The real reason, however, which was part of the secret, was that I was to follow him because he could not actually see where he was going. In short, I was to be his guide, and his caretaker; the keeper of his person.

I felt, finally, that my reward had come; that my conviction had not been a false one, and that the keeping of my promise had been as important as I had hoped. The triumph was solitary since I could not share it, but it was genuine.

IV

MY NEW WORK as "chair-carrier" or, as I thought of it then, "guardian", took a great deal of my time. I was excused from all other duties with the one exception of the never-ending lawns. I was able to keep up with my mowing, but I had to do most of it before Mr. Gurdjieff appeared in the morning, or after he had retired to his room in the latter part of the afternoon.

I have never known whether or not there was any truth to his story of partial blindness. I assumed it was true because I always believed him implicitly—he seemed unable to tell anything other than the truth, although his way of telling it was not always direct. It has been suggested to me, and it also occurred to me, that this job of chair-carrier and guide was invented on my account, and that he made up the story of blindness as an excuse. I doubt this if only because it would have given me an exaggerated importance, which is a thing that I cannot imagine Gurdjieff doing. I was important enough, simply because I had been selected, without any additional reasons.

In the weeks that followed—probably a month in all—I carried that armchair for miles each day, usually following him at a respectful distance. I was sufficiently convinced of his blindness because he frequently wandered from the path, and I would have to drop the chair, run to his side, warn him of whatever danger existed — such as the possibility, often imminent, of his walking directly into the little ditch that ran through the property—and then rush back to the armchair, pick it up, and follow him again.

The work that he directed at that time involved everyone at the school. There were several projects going on at once: building a road, which meant hammering stone with iron mallets to produce the proper size rocks; clearing an area of woodland by removing entire acres of trees as well as their stumps and roots with shovels and pick-axes. In addition to such special projects, the usual duties of gardening, weeding, picking vegetables, cooking, housekeeping, etc., continued incessantly. Whenever Mr. Gurdjieff inspected a given project for any length of time, I would join in with the other workers until he was ready to proceed to another one or to return to the house.

After about a month, I was relieved of my chair-carrying assignment and went back to regular lawn-mowing, and my turn at other regular duties: working in the kitchen one day a week, standing my regular day of duty at the concierge to open the door and answer the telephone.

During my period of following him, I had had to fit my lawn-moving in, as I have said, when I could, and it was with some consternation—since I had momentarily forgotten about the hill which I was eventually to scythe weekly—that I found that when I got back to regular work, I had, without perceptible effort, achieved the goal he had set for me. At the moment of this discovery, one evening after tea when I had finished the fourth lawn that day, Mr. Gurdjieff was seated conveniently on a bench—not at his usual table —facing the lawns. I put the lawn mower away, and came back to the terrace and walked in his direction disconsolately. While I had never loved the lawns, the prospect of my next job made me feel sentimental about them. I stopped at what I thought of as a respectful distance from him and waited. I was wavering between telling him, and putting it off until some future time.

It was some time before he turned in my direction, as if angry with my presence, and asked me sharply if I wanted something. I nodded and went up to stand beside him. I said, quickly: "I can mow all the lawns in one day, Mr. Gurdjieff."

He frowned at me, shook his head, puzzled, and then said: "Why you tell me this?" He still seemed angry with me.

I reminded him of my new "job" and then asked him, almost tearfully, if I should start on that the following day.

He stared at me for a long time then, as if unable to remember or even to understand what I was talking about. Finally, with a brusque, affectionate, gesture, he pulled me roughly towards him and forced me down on the bench next to him, keeping his hand on my shoulder. Once again he smiled at me with that distant, incredible smile—I have referred to it as "benevolent" before—and said, shaking his head, "Not necessary work in field. You have already done this work."

I looked at him, confused, and greatly relieved. But I needed to know what I was to do—continue with the lawns?

He thought about this for some time and then asked me how much longer I was going to be there. I told him that I was supposed to go back to America for the winter in about one month. He thought about this and then said, dismissing the subject as if it were unimportant now, that I would simply work in the group at the usual duties; gardening when I wasn't on kitchen or concierge duty. "Will have other work for you if you come back next year", he said.

Although I spent another month there that year, the summer seems to me to have ended at that moment. The rest of the time was like a void: uneventful and undramatic. Those of us, that is the children, who worked along with the adults in the gardens were able to make enjoyable games of picking fruit or vegetables, catching mole-crickets, slugs and snails, weeding here and there with little interest of devotion to our tasks. It was a happy place for children: we lived safely within the confines of a rigorous discipline with definite limits, and the framework—except for the long hours—was not hard on us. We managed to fit in a great deal of play and childish intrigue while the tireless adults looked at us indulgently with half-closed eyes.

V

We left the Prieuré in October, 1924, to return to New York for the winter. I was part of a rather "unusual family group" at that time. My brother, Tom, and I lived in a strange, errant world for several years. My mother, Lois, had divorced my father when I was about eighteen months old; we had had a stepfather for several years, but in 1923, when my mother was hospitalized for about a year, Jane Heap and Margaret Anderson (Margaret is my mother's sister), co-editors of the notorious, if not famous, *Little Review,* had taken charge of us both. To this day, I am not at all sure that I understand why Margaret and Jane took on this responsibility. It was a strange form of "planned parenthood" for two women neither of whom, it seemed to me, would have wished for children of their own, and a mixed blessing from any point of view. As Margaret had not returned from France with us, the real responsibility devolved on Jane.

I can only describe our household as it seemed to me at the time: Tom and I went to a private school in New York; we also had various chores at home, helping with the cooking, dishwashing, and so on, and while we were exposed to many unusual influences and experiences, they had less effect on me, at any rate, than might have been expected. In a household, if that is the proper word, where a magazine was edited, and which was visited exclusively by artists, writers, and—for want of a better word—intellectuals, I managed to live in my own private world. The daily routine of school was considerably more important to me — involving, as it naturally did, other children and ordinary, comprehensible activities—than the temperamental and "interesting" life which, actually, formed our background. The world of the arts was no substitute for childhood; even family life with my mother and stepfather was more "normal" to me than living in New York away from my *family,* which, basically, revolved around my mother.

The most important exterior event of that winter was the sudden appearance of my father. Jane had decided, for reasons which I have never fully understood, that she (or perhaps she and Margaret) should adopt Tom and me legally. The adoption proceedings were the reason that my father came back into the picture after a complete absence of some ten years. At first, he did not actually appear in person. We were simply told that he was going to resist the adoption and that he wanted to assume custody of both of us himself.

As I understood it at the time, Jane, aided by A. R. Orage and others who were "Gurdjieff people", and after consulting both of us, was able to talk my father out of this, and the adoption became a legal fact.

In many ways, it was a terrifying winter for me. I think it is probably impossible for any adult to understand the feelings of a child who is told, in perfectly clear language, that he may or may not be adopted by this or that person. I do not believe that children, when they are consulted about such things, have "opinions"—they naturally cling to the known, relatively safe, situation. My relationship with Jane, as I felt and experienced it, was highly volatile and explosive. There was, at times, a great deal of emotion, of love, between us, but the very emotionality of the relationship frightened me. More and more I tended to shut out everything that was outside of me. People, for me, were something I had to exist with, had to bear. As much as possible, I lived alone, day-dreaming in my own world, longing for the time when I could escape from the complex, and often totally incomprehensible, world around me. I wanted to grow up and be alone—away from all of them. Because of this, I was almost always in trouble. I was lazy about my work at home, I resented any demands that were made on me, and any duties that I was supposed to perform, any contribution I was expected to make. Obstinate and independent because of my feeling of aloneness, I was usually in trouble, frequently punished. That winter, I began, slowly at first, but firmly, to despise my surroundings, and to hate Jane and Tom—mostly because they were there and a part of the life in which I lived. I worked well at school, but because it was easy for me, I had little real

interest in what I was doing. More and more, I retreated
into a dreamworld of my own making.

In this world of my own, there were two people who were
not enemies, who stood out with the brilliance of light-
houses, and yet there was no way that I could communicate
with them. They were my mother and, of course, Gurdjieff.
Why "of course"? The simple reality of Gurdjieff as a human
being—the, to me, uncomplicated relationship which I had
had with him during those few months in the previous
summer—became like a raft to a drowning man.

When I was consulted about the possibility of being
"taken over" by my father (who was simply another hostile
adult in my mind) I voiced my opposition loudly, not that I
expected my voice to have any weight. My main fear was
that I did not feel I could face another new, strange,
unknown world. Also, and this was very important to me
then, such a change in my existence would, I felt sure,
preclude any possibility of my ever seeing either Gurdjieff or
my mother again.

To complicate matters even further, my mother arrived in
New York, with a man who was not my stepfather, and she
was summarily dismissed by Jane. I remember being
allowed to speak to her on the stairs of the apartment; no
more than that. It is impossible for me, now, to judge Jane's
motives or her purpose at that time. I am convinced that she
was motivated, in her own mind, by the best of intentions.
The result was that I thought of her at that moment as my
mortal enemy. The link between the average child and his
mother—especially when that mother has been the only
parent for many years—is, I think, strong enough. In my
case it was violent and obsessive.

Matters did not improve when, shortly before Christmas,
my father made his actual, physical appearance. It was a
difficult, uneasy meeting; there was very little communication—I speak for myself alone—with him. He did not know
how to communicate without self-consciousness, being a shy
and "well-brought-up" man. One thing that he did manage
to communcate was that before we made any final decision
about the adoption (I had been under the impression for

some time that it was final and that he had been disposed of
as a threat) he would like Tom and me to spend a weekend
with him and his wife.

I felt that it was only fair to give him a trial. If this
statement seems *cold-blooded,* I can only say that most
childish decisions are, in that sense, "cold-blooded" and
logical—at least mine were. It was decided, presumably by
Jane and my father (and agreed to by Tom and me), that we
would go to visit him on Long Island for a week.

The visit, from my point of view, was a disaster. It might
have been less calamitous had my father not announced,
almost immediately upon our arrival, that in the event we
should decide to come to live with him, we would not be able
to live in his house, we would be sent to live in Washington,
D.C., with two of his maiden aunts. I suppose that it is
inevitable that adults must explain to children the actual
facts or circumstances which are facing them. However, this
announcement, made without any *feeling,* any emotion
(there was no suggestion that he loved or wanted us, or that
the aunts in question needed two young boys in their
household), seemed both completely illogical and even,
finally, hilarious to me. I began to feel even more alone than
I had before—like a piece of unwanted luggage for which
storage space was needed. Since my gentle father constantly
seemed to be seeking our approval and asking us questions,
I stated firmly after two days at his house that I did not
want to live with him or his aunts and that I wanted to go
back to New York. Tom stayed for the balance of the week; I
did not. However, the condition of my leaving was that I
should at least consider coming out to Long Island again, for
Christmas. I agreed coldly, to consider it. I may have—I do
not remember now—agreed without any reservation. I
would have done anything to get away. Even Jane in spite of
her rejection of my mother, was familiar ground; and what I
feared was the unfamiliar, the unknown.

Somehow, the winter did pass. Somehow, although I
frequently had nightmares about the possibility that I
would never see the Prieuré again, it was decided—it was
actually true—that we would return the next Spring.

Gurdjieff, by this time, had become the only beacon on the horizon, the only island of safety in a fearful and unpredictable future.

During that winter, Gurdjieff's first question to me: "Why had I come to Fountainebleau" assumed tremendous importance. Retrospectively, in those few months, he assumed great stature in my heart and in my mind. Unlike any other adult I had ever known, he made absolute sense. He was completely positive—he had ordered me to do things and I had done them. He had not questioned me, forced me to make decisions which I was completely unable to make. I began to long for someone who would do something as simple as to "order" me to mow a lawn—make a demand on me that was, however incomprehensible his motives might be (after all, every adult was "incomprehensible"), a *demand*. I began to think of him as the only logical, grown-up individual I had ever known. As a child, I was not concerned with—in fact I did not want to know—*why* any adult did anything. I needed, desperately, and wanted above everything else, an authority. And an authority, at my age, was anyone who knew what he was doing. To be consulted, at eleven; to be asked to make vital decisions about my own future—and that seemed to me to have been going on all winter—was not only impossible to understand, but very frightening.

His question evolved into "Why did I want to go back to Fountainebleau" and was not difficult to answer. I wanted to go back and live near a human being who knew what he was doing—whether or not I understood what he was doing was of no importance whatsoever. I did not, however, dismiss the original wording of the question—one of the reasons it remained alive in my mind was that I had had nothing, directly, to do with going there in the first place. I could only thank whatever force (the idea of "God" was rather vague to me then) had made it possible for me to be there at all. One year earlier, the most attractive thing about going to Fountainebleau was that I would have to cross the ocean to get there, and I loved boats.

In the course of the winter, and because of the importance

Gurdjieff had assumed in my mind, I was greatly tempted by the feeling that my presence there had been "inevitable" —as if there had been some inexplicable, mystical, logic that had made it necessary for me, personally, to arrive at that particular place at that particular time—that there had been some real purpose in my having gone there. The fact that Gurdjieff was primarily associated—in the conversation of most of the adults surrounding me at the time—with metaphysical activities, religion, philosophy, and mysticism, seemed to increase the possibility of some sort of foreordination in our meeting.

But in the long run, I did not succumb to the idea that my association with him was "predestined". It was my memory of Mr. Gurdjieff himself that prevented me from giving in to such daydreams. I was in no position to deny the possibility that he was clairvoyant, mystical, a hypnotist, even a "divinity". The important thing was that none of those things mattered. What did matter about him was that he was a positive, practical, sensible, logical human being. In my small mind the Prieuré seemed the most sensible institution in the entire world. It consisted, as I saw it, of a place which housed a large number of people who were extremely busy doing the necessary physical work to keep it going. What could have been simpler and what could have made more practical sense? I was aware that, at least by repute, there were probably other benefits that could accrue from being there. But at my age, and in my terms, there was simply one aim, and a very simple one at that. To be like Gurdjieff. He was strong, honest, direct, uncomplicated—an entirely "no-nonsense" individual. I could remember, quite honestly, that I had been terrified of the work involved in mowing the lawns; it was equally apparent to me that one of the reasons for my terror was that I was lazy. Gurdjieff *made* me mow the lawns. He did not do this by threats, promises of rewards, or by asking me. He *told* me to mow the lawns. He told me it was important. I did it. One obvious result, obvious to me at eleven years of age, was that work— just plain ordinary physical work—lost a great deal of its horror for me. I also understood, although perhaps not intellectually, why I had not had to scythe the hill—why I had, as he had said, "already done it".

The total effect of the winter of 1924-25 in New York was to make me long to go back to France. The first visit there had "happened", the result of an aimless, unconnected, chain of events which had depended on my mother's divorce, her illness, the existence of Margaret and Jane and their interest in us. The return, in the spring of 1925, did seem to be foreordained. My feeling was that, if necessary, I would get there alone.

My disenchantment with, and lack of understanding of, the adult world had come to a kind of climax at Christmas-time. I became (I am describing my feelings) something like a bone fought over by two dogs. The contest of wills, since my mother had been eliminated as a contender, for the custody of Tom and me, was still waging between Jane and my father. I feel sure, now, that it was a " face-saving " operation on both sides; I cannot believe that either side wanted us for our special value—I was certainly behaving badly enough not to be particularly desirable at the time. In any case, I had agreed, or at least agreed to consider, to visit my father at Christmas. When the time for the actual decision arrived, I refused. Jane's counter-offer of an "adult" Christmas—glamorous, with parties, visits to the theatre, and so forth, was my ostensible and handy reason for refusing to visit my father. My real reason, however, remained what it had always been: Jane, however impossible our relationship might seem to me, was the passport to Gurdjieff, and I did my best to achieve some sort of harmony with her. On her side, since she was neither infallible nor inhuman, my decision—indicating an apparent preference for her—pleased her.

My father was very unhappy. I could not understand why, since I had been told that the decision was mine to make. He arrived in New York to pick up Tom—who had agreed to spend Christmas with him—and brought with him several large boxes of presents for me. I was embarrassed by the presents, but when he also asked me—and it seemed to me used the presents as bait—to reconsider, I was wounded and furious. I felt that the unfairness, the lack of "justice" in the adult world, was synthesized by this act. I told him, raging at him in tears, that I could not be bought and that I would always hate him for what he was doing to me.

For the sake of the memory of my father, I would like to digress just long enough to say that I am fully conscious of his good intentions, and that I appreciate the horrible emotional shock he received from me at the time. What was sad, perhaps even heart-breaking for him, was that he had no conception of what was really happening. In his world, children did not reject their parents.

The winter did end, finally, although I still think of it as interminable. But it did end, and with the spring my longing for the Prieuré intensified. It was not until we were actually on a ship bound for France that I believed I would really get back. And it was not until I went through the gate of the Prieuré once more that I was able to stop dreaming, believing and hoping.

When I saw him again, Gurdjieff put his hand on my head, and I looked up at his fierce moustache, the broad, open smile underneath the shining, bald head. Like some large, warm animal, he pulled me to his side, squeezing me affectionately with his arm and hand, and said: "So . . . you come back?" It was phrased as a question, something a little more than a statement of fact. All I was able to do was to nod my head against him and contain my explosive happiness.

VI

THE SECOND SUMMER — the summer of 1925 — was a homecoming. I found, as I had dreamed I would, that nothing, essentially, had changed. There were some people missing from the summer before, and some new people, but the comings and goings of individuals were of little importance. Once again, I was absorbed into the place, becoming a cog in the functioning of the school. With the exception of the mowing of the lawns, which had become some other person's task, I went back to the customary, routine chores, along with everyone else.

The great security of the Institute for a child, as opposed to the usual boarding school, for example, was the immediate feeling of belonging. It may be true that the purpose of working with other people in the maintenance of the school proper—which is what all our tasks amounted to—had a higher aim. On my level, they made me feel that I, however unimportant I might be as an individual, was one of the small, essential links that kept the school going. It gave each of us a feeling of value—of worth; I find it hard now to imagine any single thing that would be more encouraging to the ego of a child. We all felt that we had a place in the world—we were needed for the simple reason that we performed functions that had to be performed. We did not just do anything, such as study for our own benefit. We did things that had to be done for the general welfare.

In the usual sense, we had no lessons, we did not "learn" anything at all. However, we did learn to do our own washing and ironing, to cook, to milk, to chop wood, to scrape and polish floors, to paint houses, to repair roofs, to mend our clothing, to take care of animals; all these things in addition to working, in large groups, on the customary major projects: road-building, clearing wooded areas, planting and harvesting, etc.

There were two major changes at the Institute that summer, although they were not immediately apparent to me. Gurdjieff's mother had died during the winter, which had made a subtle, emotional change in the feeling of the place—she had never taken an active part in the running of the school, but we had all been aware of her presence—and, much more important, Gurdjieff had begun to write.

I had only been there about a month, when it was announced that a complete reorganization was to be made in the way the Institute was to function and, alarming to everyone, it was also announced that for various reasons, mostly because Gurdjieff would no longer have the time or energy to supervise his students personally, not everyone would be allowed to stay on. We were also told that, in a period of the two or three days following this announcement, Gurdjieff would interview every student personally and decide whether or not they would be allowed to stay on and, if so, what they would do.

The general reaction was to drop everything and wait until each person's individual fate had been decided. After breakfast the following morning, the buildings echoed with gossip and speculation; everyone expressed his or her doubts and fears about the future. To many of the older students, the announcement seemed to mean that the school would no longer have value for them since Gurdjieff's energies would be concentrated on his writing and not on individual teaching. The speculation and the expression of fears made me nervous. Since I had no conception of what Gurdjieff might decide about my personal fate, I found it simpler to go on with my particular job of the moment—working in the clearing, removing tree stumps. Several of us had been assigned to this work, but only one or two of us went to work that morning. By the end of the day, there had been a good many interviews, and a number of students had been told to leave.

The following day, I went to work as usual, but when I was going to return to work after lunch, my turn for an interview came.

Gurdjieff was sitting out of doors, on a bench near the main building, and I went to sit next to him. He looked at me as if surprised to find that I existed. He asked me what I had been doing, and, more particularly, what I had done since the announcements had been made. I told him, and he

then asked me if I wanted to stay on at the Prieuré. I said,
of course, that I did. He said, very simply, that he was glad I
did because he had new work for me. Beginning the
following day, I was to take care of his personal quarters—
his room, dressing-room, and bathroom. He handed me a
key, impressing upon me firmly that I was the only one—
other than himself—who had a key, and he explained that I
would have to make his bed, sweep, clean, dust, polish,
wash, and generally maintain order. When the weather
required, I would be responsible for making fires and
keeping them going; an additional responsibility was that I
would also be required to be his "server" or "waiter"—which
meant that if he wanted coffee, liquor, food, or anything,
brought to him at any hour of the day or night, I was to
bring it. For this reason, he explained, a buzzer would be
installed in my room.

He also explained that I would not participate in general
projects any longer, but that my additional chores would
include the usual work in the kitchen and concierge except
that I would be relieved of these duties long enough to
perform my housekeeping chores. One other piece of new
work was that I was to take care of the chicken yard—feed
the chickens, collect the eggs, slaughter the chickens and/or
ducks when required, etc.

I was very proud to have been selected as his "care-taker",
and he smiled at my joyful reaction. He informed me, very
seriously, that my selection had been made on the spur of
the moment—he had dismissed a student who had already
been doing this work, and when I had appeared to be
interviewed, he had realized that I was not essential in any
other general function and was available for this work. I felt
somewhat ashamed of my pride, but was no less happy for
that, I still felt that it was an honour.

At first, I had no more contact with Gurdjieff than I had
before. In the early morning, I would release the chickens
from their coops, feed them and collect the eggs and bring
them to the kitchen. By that time, Gurdjieff was usually
ready for his morning coffee, after which he dressed and
went to sit at one of the small tables near the terrace where

he would spend the morning writing. During that time, I cleaned the room. This took a fairly long time. The bed was enormous and always in great disorder. As for the bathroom! What he could do to his dressing-room and bathroom is something that cannot be described without invading his privacy; I will only say that, physically, Mr. Gurdjieff, at least so I gathered, lived like an animal. The mere cleaning of these two rooms was a major project every day. The disorder was frequently so great that I had visions of great, hygienic dramas transpiring nightly in the dressing-room and bathroom. I often felt that he had some conscious aim to destroy these rooms. There were times when I would have to use a ladder to clean the walls.

It was not until later that summer that my care-taking chores began to assume really major proportions. Because of his writing, there were many more visitors to his room—people who were working on immediate translations of his books—as he wrote them—into French, English, Russian, and possibly other languages. I understood that the original was in a combination of Armenian and Russian; as he said that he could not find any single language which gave him sufficient freedom of expression for his complicated ideas and theories. My additional work was mostly in the form of "serving"—everyone who interviewed him did so in his room. This meant the serving of coffee and Armagnac, and also meant that the room would have to be at least straightened up after these conferences. Gurdjieff preferred to go to bed during such meetings. In fact, unless he was entering or leaving the room, I hardly remember ever seeing him in his room when he was not in the great bed, lying in state. Even the drinking of coffee could produce a holocaust —there would be coffee all over the room and usually in the bed, which, of course, would have to be re-made with fresh linen each time.

There were rumours at the time, and I am in no position to deny them, that a great deal more went on in his rooms other than drinking coffee and Armagnac. The normal state of his rooms after one night indicated that almost any human activity could have taken place there the night

before. There is no doubt that his rooms were lived in, in the
fullest sense on the word.

I have never forgotten the first time that I was involved
in an incident in his room that was something more than
the usual performance of my housekeeping chores. He had a
distinguished visitor that day—A. R. Orage—a man who
was well-known to all of us, and accepted as an accredited
teacher of Gurdjieffian theory. After luncheon that day, the
two of them retired to Gurdjieff's room, and I was
summoned to deliver the usual coffee. Orage's stature was
such that we all treated him with great respect. There was
no doubt of his intelligence, his dedication, his integrity. In
addition, he was a warm, compassionate man for whom I
had a great personal affection.

When I reached the doorway of Gurdjieff's room with my
tray of coffee and brandy, I hesitated, appalled at the violent
sounds of furious screaming — Gurdjieff's voice — from
within. I knocked and, receiving no reply, entered. Gurdjieff
was standing by his bed in a state of what seemed to me to
be completely uncontrolled fury. He was raging at Orage,
who stood impassively, and very pale, framed in one of the
windows. I had to walk between them to set the tray on the
table. I did so, feeling flayed by the fury of Gurdjieff's voice,
and then retreated, attempting to make myself invisible.
When I reached the door, I could not resist looking at both of
them: Orage, a tall man, seemed withered and crumpled as
he sagged in the window, and Gurdjieff, actually not very
tall, looked immense - a complete embodiment of rage.
Although the raging was in English I was unable to listen to
the words—the flow of anger was too enormous. Suddenly,
in the space of an instant, Gurdjieff's voice stopped, his
whole personality changed, he gave me a broad smile—
looking incredibly peaceful and inwardly quiet—motioned
me to leave, and then resumed his tirade with undiminished
force. This happened so quickly that I do not believe that
Mr. Orage even noticed the break in the rhythm.

When I had first heard the sound of Mr. Gurdjieff's voice
from outside the room I had been horrified. That this man,
whom I respected above all other human beings, could lose

his control so completely was a terrible blow to my feelings of respect and admiration for him. As I had walked between them to place the tray on the table, I had felt nothing but pity and compassion for Mr. Orage.

Now, leaving the room, my feelings were completely reversed. I was still appalled by the fury I had seen in Gurdjieff; terrified by it. In a sense, I was even more terrified when I left the room because I realized that it was not only *not* "uncontrollable" but actually under great control and completely conscious on his part. I still felt sorry for Mr. Orage, but I was convinced that he must have done something terrible—in Gurdjieff's eyes—to warrant the outburst. It did not cross my mind that Gurdjieff could have been, in any sense at all, wrong. There was no question but that I believed in him with my whole being, absolutely. He could do no wrong. Oddly enough, and I find this hard to explain to anyone who did not know him personally, my devotion to him was not fanatical. I did not believe in him as one believes in a god. He was right, always, to me, for simple, logical reasons. His unusual "mode of life", even such things as the disorder of his rooms, calling for coffee at all hours of the day or night, seemed far more logical than the so-called normal way of living. He did whatever he did when he wanted or needed to. He was invariably concerned with others, and considerate of them. He never failed, for example, to thank me and to apologize to me when I had to bring him coffee, half-asleep, at three o'clock in the morning. I knew instinctively that such consideration was something far more than ordinary, acquired courtesy. And, perhaps this was the clue, he was interested. Whenever I saw him, whenever he gave me an order, he was fully aware of me, completely concentrated on whatever words he said to me; his attention never wandered when I spoke to him. He always knew exactly what I was doing, what I had done. I think we must all have felt, certainly I did, when he was with any of us, that we received his total attention. I can think of nothing more complimentary in human relations.

VII

It was in the middle of that busy summer that Gurdjieff asked me one morning, rather brusquely, whether or not I still wanted to study. He reminded me, rather sardonically, of my desire to learn "everything", and asked me if I had changed my mind. I told him I had not.

"Why you not ask about this then, if not change mind?"

I said, embarrassed and uncomfortable, that I had not mentioned it again for several reasons. One was that I had already asked him and that I assumed that he had not forgotten it, second that he was already so busy writing and conferring with other people that I did not think he would have time.

He said that I would have to learn about the world. "If want something, must ask. You must work. You expect me to remember for you; I already work hard, much harder than you can even imagine, you wrong if also expect me always remember what you want." He then added that I made a mistake in assuming that he was too busy. "If I busy, this my business, not your affair. If I say I teach, you must remind me, help me by asking again. This show you want learn."

I agreed, sheepishly, that I had been mistaken, and asked when we would start the "lessons". This was on a Monday morning, and he told me to meet him at his room at ten o'clock the following morning, Tuesday. When I got there the next morning, I listened at the door to be sure that he was up, knocked and went in. He was standing in the middle of the room, fully dressed. He looked at me, as if astonished. "You want something?" he asked, not unkindly. I explained that I was there for my lesson. He looked at me, as he sometimes had on other occasions, as if he had never seen me before. "You supposed to come this morning?" he asked, as if he had completely forgotten. "Yes," I said, "at ten o'clock."

He looked at the clock on his bed table. It read about two minutes after ten and I had been there at least a full minute. Then he turned to me, looking at me as if my explanation had greatly relieved him: "This morning, I remember was something at ten o'clock, but forget what. Why you not here at ten o'clock?"

I looked at my own watch and said that I had been there at ten o'clock.

He shook his head. "You ten seconds late. Man can die in ten seconds. I live by my clock, not yours. If want to learn from me must be here when my clock say ten o'clock. Today, no lesson."

I did not argue with him, but did gather my courage enough to ask him if that meant I would never have any "lessons" from him. He waved me away. "Certainly have lessons. Come next Tuesday ten o'clock. If necessary can come early and wait—is way not to be late," then he added, and not without malice, "unless you too busy to wait for Master."

The following Tuesday I was there by quarter past nine. He came out of his room as I was about to knock—a few minutes before ten—smiled and told me he was glad I was on time. Then he asked me how long I had been there. I told him, and he shook his head, irritated. "I tell last week," he said, "that if not busy can come early and wait. I not tell to waste almost hour of time. Now we go." He told me to get a thermos bottle of coffee from the kitchen and to meet him at his car.

We drove a very short distance on a narrow, lightly travelled road, and Gurdjieff stopped the car. We descended and he told me to bring the coffee with me, and went to sit on a fallen tree near the edge of the road. He had stopped a hundred yards or so beyond a group of workmen who were laying a stone water-ditch at the side of the road. Their work consisted in bringing stones from either one of two large piles at the side of the road, carrying them to the unfinished section of the ditch, where other men were placing them in the dirt. We watched them silently, while Gurdjieff drank coffee and smoked, but said nothing to me. After a long time, at least half an hour, I finally asked him when the lesson would begin.

He looked at me with a tolerant smile. "Lesson begin at

ten o'clock," he said. "what you see? Notice anything?"

I said that I had been watching the men, and that the only unusual thing I had noticed was that one of the men always went for the pile that was furthest from the actual work.

"Why you think he do this?"

I said I didn't know but that he seemed to be making work for himself because he had to carry the heavy stones further each time. He could just as easily have gone to the nearer pile of rock.

"Is true," Gurdjieff then said, "but must always look at all sides before make judgment. This man also have pleasant short promenade in shade along road when he return for next stone. Also, he not stupid. In one day he not carry so many stones. Always logical reason why people do thing certain way; necessary find all possible reasons before judge people."

Gurdjieff's language, although he paid very little attention to the proper tenses, was always unmistakably clear and definite. He did not say anything more, and I felt that he was, partly by his own concentration, forcing me to observe whatever was going on around me with as much concentration as I could. The rest of the hour went by rapidly, and we returned to the Prieuré; he to his writing and I to my housekeeping. I was to return the following Tuesday at the same time for the next lesson. I did not dwell on what I had—or had not—learned; I was beginning to understand that "learning" in Gurdjieff's sense did not depend on sudden or obvious results, and that one could not expect any immediate spurts of knowledge or understanding. More and more I began to have the feeling that he scattered knowledge as he lived, oblivious of whether or not it was accepted and put to any use.

The next lesson was completely unlike the first one. He told me to clean the room, everything except making the bed, while he lay in bed. He watched me all the time, making no comment until I made the fire—it was a rainy, damp summer morning and the room was cold—and when I had lighted the fire, it smoked relentlessly. I added dry wood, blew on the coals industriously, but with little success. He did not continue to watch my efforts for very long. He got out of bed suddenly, picked up a bottle of Cognac, pushed me to one side and poured a stream of Cognac on to the small flame; the fire burst out into the room and then settled into a steady flame. Without any comment he then went into his dressing-room and dressed while I made his bed. It was not until he was ready to leave the room that he said, casually: "If want immediate, necessary result, must use any means." Then he smiled. "When I not here, you have time; not necessary use fine old Armagnac."

And that was the end of that lesson. The dressing-room, which he had demolished silently in a few minutes, took me the rest of the morning to clean.

VIII

As PART OF the "complete reorganization" of the school, Mr. Gurdjieff told us that he was going to appoint a "director" who would supervise the students and their activities. He made it clear that this director would report regularly to him, and that he would still be fully informed concerning everything that took place at the Prieuré. However, his personal time would be devoted almost entirely to his writing and he would spend a much larger proportion of his time in Paris.

The director turned out to be a certain Miss Madison, an English bachelor lady (as the children all called her) who had, up to that time, been mainly in charge of the flower gardens. To most of us—children that is—she had always been a slightly comical figure. She was tall, of uncertain age, a bony, angular shape topped off by a somewhat untidy nest of fading reddish hair. She had, up to that time, stalked about the flower gardens, usually carrying a trowel and decorated with strands of raffia, knotted to her belt and flowing in streams from her waist as she walked. She took to the directorship with zeal and relish.

Although Gurdjieff had told us that we were to accord Miss Madison every respect—"as if she were me"—I at least wondered whether she quite deserved that respect; I also suspected that he would not be as fully informed as when he had personally supervised the work. In any case, Miss Madison became a highly important figure in our lives. She began by setting up a series of rules and regulations—I have often wondered whether she had not come from an English Army family—which, ostensibly, were to simplify the work and, in general, to introduce efficiency into what she called the haphazard functioning of the school.

Since Mr. Gurdjieff was now absent at least half of each week, Miss Madison felt that I did not have enough to do simply taking care of the chickens and cleaning his room. Among other things, I was assigned to take care of our one horse and one donkey, and also to do a certain amount of work on the flower beds, under Miss Madison's immediate, personal supervision. In addition to these specific chores, I was—as was everyone else—subject to a great many general, groundrules. No one was to leave the grounds without specific permission from Miss Madison; our rooms were to be inspected at regular intervals; in short, a general military-style discipline was to be enforced.

A further change caused by the "reorganization" of the school was the discontinuing of the nightly demonstrations of the dances or gymnastics. There were still classes in these gymnastics, but they only lasted for an hour or so during the afternoon, and it was on rare occasions, when Gurdjieff brought weekend guests to the Prieuré, that we gave "demonstrations". Because of this, our evenings had been free all that summer, and many of us went to the town of Fountainebleau — a walk of about two miles — in the evenings. There was nothing much for children to do in town, except to go to an occasional movie or sometimes to a small country fair or carnival. This previously unsupervised —in fact, unmentioned—privilege was important to all of us. Up to that time, no one had bothered about what any of us did in our free time as long as we were present in the morning and ready to go to work. Confronted with the order that we were to have what amounted to "passes" in order to go to town—we were told that we would have to give a "good reason" for any excursion off the grounds of the school proper—we rebelled. There was no common agreement to rebel or to disregard this particular rule. As individuals, no one obeyed it; no one ever asked for a "pass".

Not only did we not ask for permission to leave the ground, but we went to town even when we had no reason or desire to go. We did not, of course, leave by the front gate where the "passes" would have to be shown to whoever was on duty as concierge, we simply climbed the walls going and coming. There was no immediate reaction from Miss Madison but we soon learned, although we could not imagine how it was possible, that she had an accurate record of each person's absence. We learned of the existence of this record from Mr. Gurdjieff when, on one of his returns to the Prieuré after an absence of several days, he announced to all of us that Miss Madison had "a little black book" in which she had recorded all the "misdemeanours" of the students. He also told us that he was, for the time being, reserving his own opinion about our behaviour, but reminded us that he had appointed Miss Madison as director and that we were supposed to obey her. While it seemed to be a technical victory for Miss Madison, it was also a hollow one; he had done nothing to help her enforce her discipline.

My first difficulty with Miss Madison arose because of the chickens. One afternoon, just after Gurdjieff had left for Paris, I learned from one of the other children—I was cleaning his room at the time—that my chickens, at least several of them, had found some way out of the chicken yard and were happily tearing up Miss Madison's flower gardens. When I arrived at the scene of the destruction, Miss Madison was furiously chasing chickens all over the garden and, together, we managed to get them all back into their pen. There had not been much damage done to the flowers and I helped Miss Madison, on her orders, to repair such damage as there was. She then told me that it was my fault that the chickens had escaped because I had not kept the fences in proper order; also that I would not be allowed to leave the grounds of the Institute for a week. She added that if she found another chicken in the gardens, she would, personally, kill it.

I did repair the fences, but apparently I did not do a very good job. One or two chickens escaped the next day and went back to the flower gardens. Miss Madison kept her promise and wrung the neck of the first chicken she was able to catch. Since I had become very fond of the chickens— I had a personal relationship with each one of them and had even given them names—I took revenge on Miss Madison by destroying one of her favourite plants. In addition, for purely personal satisfaction, I also left the grounds and went to Fountainebleau that night.

Miss Madison took me seriously to task the next morning. She said that if we could not come to an understanding together, she would have to take the matter up with Mr. Gurdjieff; that she knew that he would not tolerate any flaunting of her authority. She also said that I, by this time, led the list of offenders in her little black book. My defence was to tell her that the chickens were useful and that the garden was not; that she had no right to kill my chicken. She said that I was in no position to judge what she had a right to do, and also that Mr. Gurdjieff had made it very clear that she was to be obeyed.

Since we had come to no truce or agreement, the incident was brought to Mr. Gurdjieff's attention when he returned from Paris later that week. Immediately upon his return, he was, as it were, pounced upon by Miss Madison, and closeted in his room with her for a long time. I did become anxious during that time. After all, whatever my reasons had been, I had disobeyed her, and I had no assurance that Gurdjieff was going to see things my way.

He called for coffee later that evening after supper and when I brought it to his room, he told me to sit down. Then he asked me how I was getting along and how I liked Miss Madison. Not knowing what she had told him, I replied carefully that I was getting along all right, but that the Prieuré was very different when she was in charge.

He looked at me seriously: "How different?" he asked.

I replied that Miss Madison made too many rules, that there was too much discipline.

He did not say anything about this remark but then he told me that Miss Madison had told him about the fracas in the flower gardens and that she had killed a chicken, and he wanted to know my version of the story. I told him how I felt about it and that I felt, particularly, that Miss Madison had no right to kill the chicken.

"What you do with dead chicken?" he asked me.

I said that I had cleaned it and taken it to the kitchen to be eaten.

He considered this, nodded, and said that I should understand, then, that the chicken after all had not been wasted; also that, while the chicken, although dead, had been useful, the dead flower that I had uprooted in anger could serve no purpose—could not, for instance, be eaten. Then he asked me if I had repaired the fences. I said that I had repaired them a second time after the chickens had escaped again and he said that was good, and sent me to get Miss Madison.

I went for her, feeling crestfallen. I could not deny the logic of what he had said to me, but I still felt, resentfully, that Miss Madison had not been entirely in the right. I found her in her room, and she gave me an all-knowing, superior look, and followed me back to Gurdjieff's room. He told us both to sit down and then told her that he had talked to me about the problem of the chickens and the garden and that he was sure—he looked at me as he said this—that there would be no more difficulty. Then he said, unexpectedly, that we had both failed him. That my failure had been in not helping him by obeying Miss Madison, since he had put her in charge, and that she had failed by killing the chicken, which was, incidentally, *his* chicken; not only was it his chicken but it was my responsibility, which he had delegated to me, and that while I should have kept it in its pen, she had no right to take its killing upon herself.

Then he told Miss Madison to leave, but added as she was leaving that he had now spent a long time, when he was already very busy, on the discussion of this matter of the chicken and the garden, and that one of the functions of a director was to relieve him of such time - consuming, unimportant problems.

Miss Madison left the room—he had indicated that I was to stay—and he asked me if I felt I was learning anything. I was surprised by the question and did not know how to answer it, except to say that I did not know. It was then, I think, that he first mentioned, directly, one of the basic purposes and aims of the Institute. He said, disregarding my unsatisfactory response to his question about learning, that, in life, the most difficult thing to achieve for the future, and perhaps the most important, was to learn to live with the "unpleasant manifestations of others". He said that the story we had both told him was, of itself, completely unimportant. The chicken and the plant did not matter. What was important was the behaviour of me and of Miss Madison; that if either one of us had been "conscious" of our behaviour, and not simply reacting to one another, the problem would have been solved without his intervention. He said that, in a sense, nothing had happened except that Miss Madison and I had given in to our mutual hostility. He did not explain this any further, and I was confused, and told him so. He told me that I would probably understand this later in life. Then he said that I would have my lesson the following morning, although it was not a Tuesday; and apologized for the fact that he was unable to keep my lessons on a regular schedule because of his other work.

IX

WHEN I WENT for my lesson the following morning, Gurdjieff looked very tired. He said that he had been working very hard—most of the night—that writing was very hard work. He was still in bed, and he stayed there throughout the lesson.

He began by asking me about the exercise that had been given to all of us to do, and which I referred to previously as "self-observation". He said that it was a very difficult exercise to do and that he wanted me to do it, with my entire concentration, as constantly as possible. He also said that the main difficulty with this exercise, as with most exercises that he did—or would in the future—give to me or to any of his students, was that to do them properly it was necessary not to expect results. In this specific exercise, what was important was to see oneself, to observe one's mechanical, automatic, reactionary behaviour without comment, and without making any attempt to change that behaviour. "If change," he said, "then will never see reality. Will only see change. When begin to know self, then change will come, or can make change if wish—if such change desirable."

He went on to say that his work was not only very difficult, but could also be very dangerous for some people. "This work not for everyone," he said. "For example, if I wish to learn to become millionaire, necessary to devote all early life to this aim and no other. If wish to become priest, philosopher, teacher, or businessman, should not come here. Here only teach *possibility* how become man such as not known in modern times, particularly in western world."

He then asked me to look out of the window and to tell him what I saw. I said that, from that window, all I could see was an oak tree. And what, he asked, was on the oak tree? I told him: acorns.

"How many acorns?"

When I replied, rather uncertainly, that I did not know, he said impatiently: "Not exactly, not ask that. *Guess* how many!"

I said that I supposed there were several thousand of them.

He agreed and then asked me how many of the acorns would become oak trees. I answered that I supposed only five or six of them would actually develop into trees, if that many.

He nodded. "Perhaps only one, perhaps not even one. Must learn from Nature. Man is also organism. Nature make many acorns, but possibility to become tree exist for only few acorns. Same with man—many men born, but only few grow. People think this waste, think Nature waste. Not so. Rest become fertilizer, go back into earth and create possibility for more acorns, more men, once in while more tree—more real man. Nature always give—but only give possibility. To become real oak, or real man, must make effort. You understand this, my work, this Institute, not for fertilizer. For real man, only. But must also understand fertilizer necessary to Nature. Possibility for real tree, real man also depend just this fertilizer."

After a rather long silence, he continued: "In west—your world—is belief that man have soul given by God. Not so. Nothing given by God, only Nature give. And Nature only give possibility for soul, not give soul. Must acquire soul through work. But unlike tree, man have many possibilities. As man now exist he have also possibility grow by accident —grow wrong way. Man can become many things, not just fertilizer, not just real man: can become what you call 'good' or 'evil', not proper things for man. Real man not good or evil—real man only conscious, only wish acquire soul for proper development."

I had listened to him, concentrated and straining, and my only feeling—I was twelve then—was one of confusion, incomprehension. I sensed and felt the importance of what he was saying, but I did not understand it. As if aware of this (as he surely was), he said: "Think of good and evil like right hand and left hand. Man always have two hands—two sides of self—good and evil. One can destroy other. Must have aim to make both hands work together, must acquire third thing: thing that make peace between two hands, between impulse for good and impulse for evil. Man who all 'good' or man who all 'bad' is not whole man, is one-sided. Third thing is conscience; possibility to acquire conscience is already in man when born; this possibility given—free—by Nature. But is only possibility. Real conscience can only be acquired by work, by learning to understand self first. Even your religion—western religion—have this phrase 'Know thyself'. This phrase most important in all religions. When begin know self already begin have possibility become genuine man. So first thing must learn is know self by this exercise, self-observation. If not do this, then will be like acorn that not become tree—fertilizer. Fertilizer which go back in ground and become possibility for future man."

X

As IF BY some settling process, Miss Madison's directorship
became, automatically, something that we managed to live
with without further difficulty. There was too much work to
be done, ordinary labour to keep the school functioning, for
anyone to care very much about the rules and regulations,
or about how the work was accomplished. Also, there were
too many people there, and the physical set-up was too big,
for Miss Madison (who had not given up her never-ending
gardening) to be able to observe each of us constantly and
individually. The only other incident in which Miss Madison
and I found ourselves in conflict that summer—sufficient
conflict to come to Mr. Gurdjieff's attention—was the
incident of the Japanese garden.

At some time in the past, long before I had been at the
Prieuré, one of Mr. Gurdjieff's projects had been to build
what he had called a "Japanese Garden". An island had
been created in the wood, using water from the ditch that
ran through the property. A small, six- or eight-sided
oriental-looking pavilion had been built on the island, and a
typical Japanese, arched bridge led to the island proper. It
looked rather typically oriental, and was a pleasant place to
retire to on Sundays when we were not on duty at one of our
usual tasks. One of the students—an adult American man—
went there with me one Sunday afternoon; he was a recent
arrival at the Prieuré and, if I remember correctly, our
reason for being there was that I was serving as his guide to
the physical layout of the school. It was the usual practice at
that time for one of the children to walk all over the
seventy-five acres of the grounds with new arrivals, showing
them the various vegetable gardens, the Turkish bath, the
location of current projects, and so on.

My companion and I stopped to rest at the Japanese
garden and he, as if sneering at the garden, told me that
while it might be "Japanese" in intention, it was completely
ruined by the presence, just in front of the door to the little
pavilion, of two plaster busts, one on either side of the door,
of Venus and Apollo. My reaction was immediate and angry.

Also, in some curious way, I felt that the criticism of the busts was a personal criticism of Gurdjieff's taste. With mixed motives and considerable daring, I told him that I would remedy the situation and promptly threw the two busts into the water. I remember feeling that, in some obscure way, I was defending Gurdjieff's honour and his taste by doing so.

Miss Madison, whose sources of information had always been a puzzle to me, learned of this. She told me, horrified, that this wilful destruction of the busts could not pass unnoticed and that Mr. Gurdjieff would be informed of what I had done immediately upon his return from Paris.

As his next return from Paris was on a weekend, he was accompanied by several guests who came with him in his car, plus a good many additional guests who had come in their own cars or by train. As was customary on the days that he returned from his trips, the entire student-body assembled after dinner in the main salon of the Château. In the presence of everyone (it was rather like a stockholders' meeting) he received a formal report from Miss Madison covering the general events that had transpired during his absence. This report was then followed by a summary, from Miss Madison, of whatever problems had arisen that she felt needed his attention. She sat beside him, on this occasion, little black book firmly open on her lap, and talked to him earnestly, but not loudly enough for us to hear, for a short time. When she had finished, he waved her to a chair and asked whoever had destroyed the statues in the Japanese garden to step forward.

Embarrassed by the presence of all of the students as well as a number of distinguished guests, I stepped forward with a sinking heart, furious with myself for my abandoned gesture. At that moment, I could think of no justification for what I had done.

Gurdjieff, of course, asked me why I had committed this crime, and also whether I realized that the destruction of property was, in fact, criminal? I said that I realized that I should not have done it but that I had done it because the statues were of the wrong period and civilization, historically, and that they should not have been there in the first place. I did not involve the American in my explanation.

With considerable sarcasm, Gurdjieff informed me that while my knowledge of history might be impressive, I had, nonetheless, destroyed "statues" that had belonged to him; that he, personally, had been responsible for placing them there; that, in fact, he liked Greek statues in Japanese gardens—at any rate in that particular Japanese garden. In view of what I had done, he said that I would have to be punished, and that my punishment would consist of giving up my "chocolate money" (his term for any child's "spending money" or "allowance") until the statues were replaced. He instructed Miss Madison to find out the cost of equivalent replacements and to collect that amount from me, however long it might take.

Mostly because of my family situation — Jane and Margaret had almost no money at the time, and certainly none to give to us—I had no so-called "chocolate money"; at least, I had none on what could be called a regular basis. The only spending money I ever had at that time was occasional money that my mother would send to me from America—for my birthday or for Christmas, or sometimes for no obvious reason. At that particular moment, I had no money at all, and I was also sure that the statues would be hideously expensive. I foresaw an eternity of handing over whatever money might come my way in order to pay for my rash act. It was a horrible prospect, particularly as I had had a birthday only a few months earlier and Christmas was several months in the future.

My dismal, moneyless future came to an abrupt end when I received a completely unexpected cheque for twenty-five dollars from my mother. Before turning the cheque over to Miss Madison, I learned from her that the "statues" were common, plaster casts, and would only amount to about ten dollars. Even that amount was not easy for me to part with. The twenty-five dollars might have to last me at least until Christmas.

At the next assembly, Miss Madison informed Mr. Gurdjieff that I had given her the money for the new "statues"—he refused even to understand the word "bust"—and asked whether she should replace them.

Gurdjieff thought this question over for some time and then, finally, said "No". He called me over to him, handed me the money which she had given to him, and said that I could keep it, on the condition that I would share it with all the other children. He also said that while I had been wrong in destroying his property, he wanted me to know that he had thought about the whole question and that I had been right about the impropriety of those particular "statues" in that place. He suggested that I could have—although I was not to do so now—replaced them with the proper type of statue. The incident was never mentioned again.

XI

Towards the end of the summer, I learned that Mr. Gurdjieff was making plans to go to America for an extended visit—probably the entire winter of 1925-26. The question of what was going to happen to Tom and me automatically came to my mind, but this was quickly solved: to my great relief, Jane told us that she had decided that she would have to go back to New York but that Tom and I would stay on at the Prieuré that winter. She took us to Paris with her one weekend and introduced us to Gertrude Stein and Alice B. Toklas; Jane had somehow persuaded Gertrude and Alice to, as it were, watch over us during her absence.

On our occasional visits to Paris, we had met many controversial and distinguished people: James Joyce, Ernest Hemingway, Constantin Brancusi, Jaques Lipschitz, Tristan Tzara, and others—most of whom had been contributors at one time or another to *The Little Review*. Man Ray had photographed both of us; Paul Tchelitchev, after two or three consecutive days of work on a pastel portrait of me, threw me out of his studio, telling me that I was unpaintable. "You look like everyone," he had said, "and your face is never quiet."

I was either too young or too self-involved at that time to be fully conscious of the privilege, if that is the word, of knowing or meeting such people. In general, they did not make a very strong impression on me; I did not understand their conversation, and was aware of their importance only because I had been told they were important.

Of all such people, Hemingway and Gertrude Stein did stand out as genuinely impressive to me. At our first meeting with Hemingway, whose *A Farewell to Arms* had not yet been published, he impressed us with his stories of bull-fighting in Spain; with a great exuberance he ripped off his shirt to show us his "battle-scars" and then fell to his hands and knees, still stripped to the waist, to play at being a bull with his first child, still only a baby at that time.

But it was Gertrude Stein who made the greatest impact

on me. Jane had given me something of hers to read—I do not know what it was — and I had found it totally meaningless; for that reason I was vaguely alarmed at the prospect of meeting her. I liked her immediately. She seemed uncomplicated, direct, and enormously friendly. She told us—she, too, had a "no-nonsense" quality about her that appealed to me as a child—that we were to visit her every other Thursday during the coming winter, and that our first visit would be on Thanksgiving Day. Although I was worried about Gurdjieff's absence—I felt that the Prieuré could not possibly be the same without him—my immediate liking of Gertrude and the knowledge that we would be seeing her regularly was considerable consolation.

* * *

Gurdjieff only spoke to me directly about his forthcoming trip on one occasion. He said that he was going to leave Miss Madison in full charge and that it would be necessary for me —as well as for everyone else—to work with her. Miss Madison no longer troubled or frightened me, I was getting used to her, and I assured him that I would do my best. He then said that it was important to learn to get along with people. Important in one way only—to learn to live with all kinds of people and in all kinds of situations; to live with them in the sense of not reacting to them constantly.

Before his departure, he called a meeting of certain of the students and Miss Madison; only those students, mostly Americans, who were going to stay at the Prieuré during his absence—excluding his own family and a few of the older students, or followers, who had been with him for many years and who, apparently, were not subject to Miss Madison's discipline. I had the feeling that Gurdjieff's immediate family, his brother, sister-in-law and their children, were not so much "followers" or "students" as simply "family" that he supported.

At this gathering, or meeting, Miss Madison served tea to all of us. It seems to me now that this was her idea, also that she was making an attempt to "put her best foot forward" with those students who would be in her charge during the winter to come. We all listened as she and Mr.

Gurdjieff discussed various aspects of the functioning of the Institute—mostly practical problems, work assignments, and so forth, but the one outstanding memory of that meeting was the serving of the tea by Miss Madison. Instead of sitting in one place, pouring the tea, and handing it to us, she poured each cup, standing, and then brought it to each person. She had, unfortunately for her, a physical habit—it was sufficiently delicate, actually, to seem to be a kind of refinement—of faintly passing wind each time that she stooped over, which she had to do as she handed each person his or her cup of tea. Inevitably, there would be a rather faint, single report at which she would immediately say "Pardon me" and stand up.

We were all amused and embarrassed by this, but no one was more amused than Gurdjieff. He watched her attentively, the faint beginning of a smile on his face, and it was impossible not to watch him as we all "listened" to Miss Madison. As if unable to control himself any longer, he began to talk. He said that Miss Madison was a very special person, with many qualities that might not be immediately apparent to the casual onlooker (he could be very verbose and flowery in the English language when he chose). As an example of one of her qualities, he cited the fact that she had a particularly exceptional manner of serving tea with the accompaniment of a small, sharp report, like that of a toy gun. "But so delicate, so refined,." he said, "that it is necessary to be alert, and highly perceptive, even to be aware of this." He went on to remark that we should notice her extreme politeness: that she unfailingly excused herself after each report. He then compared this "grace" of hers with other social graces, stating that it was not only unusual but, to him, even with his wide experience, completely novel.

It was impossible not to admire Miss Madison's composure during this merciless, lengthy comment on her unfortunate habit. While it was obviously "farting", none of us could bring ourselves, even in our own minds, to the use of that gross word. As Gurdjieff talked about it, the habit became practically "endearing" to us, making us feel sympathetic and tender towards Miss Madison. The "end result" as someone punned mercilessly, was that we all felt a spontaneous, genuine liking for Miss Madison that none of us had felt before. I have often wondered since then whether or not Gurdjieff was not making use of a minor weakness in Miss Madison's seemingly impervious "armour" for the very purpose of bringing her down from the level of strict "director" to a more human conception in the minds of those of us who were present. It was certainly impossible for us to take Miss Madison too seriously from that time on; it was also equally impossible to dislike her with any great intensity—she seemed, from then on, far too human, and too fallible. For my own part, I have never heard a delicate "fart" in my life since then, without it being accompanied, in my mind, by a rather tender memory of Miss Madison.

I will not now state that Miss Madison's wind-passing made me learn to actually love her, but it certainly came close to achieving that goal. There were times when we were able to work together without difficulty or animosity, and I attribute all of those periods to her habit, or at least to my memory of it. It was and is impossible for me to whole-heartedly despise anyone who is, for any reason, a comic figure. There was a pathetic aspect to this "farting", and since the habit is relatively universal, we were inevitably laughing at ourselves, as well, when we poked fun at her behind her back. Even the phrase, as we were always doing things "behind her back", had immediate, hilarious connotations. In fact nothing could have been more appropriate for her. Even her "reports", or the mention of them, was enough to send us off into gales of laughter. And as children, we, of course, made up elaborate, merciless jokes about the possibility of the walls of her room collapsing from a constant barrage.

For her own part, Miss Madison continued to direct the activities of the school, busy, stern, and dedicated; and with occasional sharp reports, like punctuation, always accompanied by a bland apology.

XII

WITHOUT GURDJIEFF, THE Prieuré was a different place; but it was not only his absence that made it so. The very winter changed the tempo and the routine. We all settled into what seemed, in comparison with the busy active summer, a kind of hibernation. There was little or no work at all on outside "projects" and most of our duties were confined to such things as working our turns in the kitchen—much more frequent because there were so many fewer people there—in the concierge, chopping wood and transporting it to our rooms, keeping the house clean, and, in my case, finally some studies in the usual sense of the word. One of the students who had remained for the winter was an American recently graduated from college. Almost every evening, sometimes for several hours at a time, I studied the English language with him and also mathematics. I read voraciously, as if I had been starving for that kind of learning, and we went through all of Shakespeare as well as such books as the Oxford books of English Verse and English Ballads. On my own, I read Dumas, Balzac, and great many of the other French writers.

The outstanding experiences of the winter, however, were all due to Gertrude Stein and, in a lesser way, to Alice Toklas.

Our first visit to Paris to see Gertrude was a memorable one. While we were happy enough to be at the Prieuré, there was still no question but that Tom and I both missed many things that were essentially American. That first visit was on Thanksgiving Day, a holiday that, of course, meant nothing to the French or to the students at the Prieuré. We arrived at Gertrude's apartment on the rue de Fleurus at about ten o'clock in the morning. We rang the bell, but there was no answer. Alice, apparently, had gone somewhere, and Gertrude, we learned shortly, was in the bath on the second floor. When I rang the second time, Gertrude's head appeared above me, and she tossed a bunch of keys out of the window. We were to make ourselves at home in the salon until she had had her bath. As this occurred every time we went to Paris, it was obvious that Gertrude took a bath every day at just that hour, or at least every other Thursday.

A large part of the day was spent in a thoroughly enjoyable, long talk with Gertrude. I realized, later, that it was really a cross-examination. She asked us about our entire lives, our family history, our relationship with Jane and with Gurdjieff. We answered in full detail and Gertrude, patiently and without comment, never interrupted except to ask another question. We talked until late in the afternoon when Alice suddenly appeared to announce dinner—I had by that time forgotten that it was Thanksgiving —and Gertrude put us to work setting the table.

I have never known such a Thanksgiving feast in my life. It must, I suppose, have been enhanced by the fact that it was completely unexpected, but the amount and quality of the food amounted to a spectacle. I was very moved when I learned that most of the traditional, American foods— including sweet potatoes, pumpkin pie, marshmallows, cranberries, all unheard of in Paris—had been specially ordered from America for this dinner and for us.

In her usual direct, positive way, Gertrude said that she felt that American children needed to have an American Thanksgiving. She also voiced some rather positive doubts about the way we were living. She was suspicious of both Jane and Gurdjieff as "foster parents" or "guardians" of any children, and told us forcefully that she was going to take a hand in our upbringing and education, beginning with our next visit. She added that life with "mystics" and "artists" might be all very well, but that it amounted to nonsense as a steady diet for two young American boys. She said that she would work out a plan for our future visits with her that would, at least in her mind, make more sense. We left Paris that evening, late, to return to Fountainebleau and I can still recall the warmth and happiness I felt in the experience of the day, and particularly my strong feelings of affection for both Gertrude and Alice.

Gertrude's plan, as she outlined to us on our next visit, was an exciting one. She said that I was doing enough studying and reading and that while there might be some vague rewards for us in meeting intellectuals and artists, she felt very strongly that we had one opportunity that we must not neglect: the chance to get to know, intimately, the City of Paris. She made it clear that she thought this was important for many reasons, among them that exploring and getting to know a city was a comprehensible activity for children of our age, and something that would leave its mark on us forever, also that it had been neglected shamefully. She felt that there would be time enough for us in the future, when we were at least more grown up, to delve into more nebulous pursuits, such as the arts.

We began on a series of expeditions which continued throughout the whole winter—barring days when weather prevented, which were few. We piled into Gertrude's Model-T Ford—Gertrude at the wheel and Alice and Tom squeezed into the front seat with her, while I sat next to Gertrude on the tool box on the left running board of the car. My job on these expeditions was to blow the horn at Gertrude's command. This required my full attention because Gertrude drove her little, old car majestically, approaching intersections and corners unhesitatingly and with repeated announcements (by me) on the horn.

Little by little, we did Paris. The monuments came first: Nôtre-Dame, Sacré-Coeur, the Invalides, the Tour Eiffel, the Arc de Triomphe, the Louvre (from the outside at first—we had seen enough paintings for a while in Gertrude's opinion), the Conciergerie, the Sainte Chapelle.

When we visited any monument or building that did, or could, involve climbing, Gertrude invariably handed me a red silk scarf. I was instructed to climb (in the case of the Eiffel Tower I was allowed to take the elevator) to the top of the given monument of the day and then wave to Gertrude from its summit with the red scarf. There was no question of lack of trust. She said, unequivocally, that children were all lazy. She would be able to prove to her own conscience that I had actually made the climb when she saw the red scarf fluttering from some tower or other. During these climbs, she and Alice remained seated in the Ford in some conspicuous place below us.

From buildings, we graduated to parks, squares, boulevards, important streets and on special occasions longer excursions to Versailles and Chantilly—any place that could be fitted into a comfortable one-day journey. Our days were always climaxed by a fabulous meal which had always been prepared by Alice. Generally, she managed to prepare something for us in advance, but there were times when her dedication to culinary art was such that she felt she was unable to accompany us. In her way, Alice was giving us a gastronomic education.

From these excursions I have retained a feeling about, and a flavour of, Paris that I would never have experienced otherwise. Gertrude would lecture us about each place we visited, giving us the highlights of its history, bringing to life the famous people of the past who had created, or lived in, the places we visited. Her lectures were never over-long, never boring; she had a particular talent for re-creating the feeling of a place as she talked—she could bring buildings to life. She taught me to look for history as I lived, and urged me to explore Fountainebleau on my free days from the Prieuré. She told me much of its history before I went there, and, sensibly, said that there was no reason for her to accompany me there since it was in our backyard.

I have never forgotten that winter. The long evenings of reading and study in our warm rooms, the more or less casual day-to-day living at the Prieuré, the continual looking forward to my visits to Paris with Gertrude and Alice. The one sombre, harsh note during the winter was the occasional reminder, by Miss Madison, of the fact that I was, somehow, shirking at least some of my duties. She warned me that I was again heading the list in the black book she still kept relentlessly, but I was heedless of her warnings. Thanks primarily to Gertrude, and secondarily to my reading, I was living in the past—walking with history and Kings and Queens.

XIII

IN ADDITION TO the group of children, Mr. Gurdjieff's
relatives, and a few adult Americans, the only people who
had not gone to America with Mr. Gurdjieff were older
people—mostly Russians—who did not seem to fit into the
category of students. I did not know why they were there
except that they appeared to be what might be called
"hangers-on", practically camp-followers. It was difficult, if
not impossible, to imagine that they were in any sense
interested in Gurdjieff's philosophy; and they constituted,
along with Gurdjieff's family, what we called simply "The
Russians". They seemed to represent the Russia that no
longer existed. Most of them, I gathered, had escaped from
Russia (they were all "White" Russians) with Gurdjieff, and
they were like an isolated remnant of a prior civilization,
justifying their existence by working, without any apparent
purpose, at whatever chores were given them, in return for
which they received food and shelter.

Even during the active summers, they led their own,
private existence: reading the Russian newspapers, discussing Russian politics, gathering together to drink tea in the
afternoons and evenings, living like displaced persons in the
past, as if unaware of the present or the future. Our only
contact with them was at meals and at the Turkish baths,
and very occasionally they did participate in some of the
group work projects.

Notable among these "refugees" was one man, sixty years
of age, by the name of Rachmilevitch. He was distinguished
from "The Russians" because he was inexhaustibly curious
about everything that took place. He was a mournful, dour
type, full of prophecies of disaster, dissatisfied with everything. He complained, continually, about the food, the
conditions in which we lived—the water was never hot
enough, there was not enough fuel, the weather too cold or
too hot, people were unfriendly, the world was coming to an
end; in fact anything at all—any event, or any condition—
was something that he seemed to be able to turn into a
calamity or, at least, an impending disaster.

The children, filled with energy, and without enough to occupy them during the long winter days and evenings, seized on Rachmilevitch as a target for their unused vitality. We all mocked him, aped his mannerisms, and did our best to make his life one long, continuous, living hell. When he would enter the dining-room for a meal, we would begin on a series of complaints about the food; when he attempted to read his Russian newspaper, we would invent imaginary political crises. We withheld his mail when we were on concierge duty, hid his newpapers, stole his cigarettes. His unending complaints had also irritated the other "Russians" and, subversively, they not only did nothing to restrain us, but, subtly and without ever mentioning his name directly, approved, and urged us on.

Not content with badgering him during the day, we took to staying up at night at least until he had turned off the light in his room; then we would gather in the corridor outside his bedroom door and have loud conversations with each other about him, disguising our voices in the hope that he would not be able to pick out any individuals among our group.

Unfortunately, and understandably, he was not able to disregard our activities—we never gave him a moment's peace. He would appear at meals, enraged by our night-time excursions in the halls, and complain in a loud voice about all of us, calling us devils, threatening to punish us, vowing to get even with us.

Seeing that no other adults—not even Miss Madison— sympathized with him, we felt emboldened, and were delighted with his reactions to us. We "borrowed" his glasses, without which he was unable to read—when he hung out his clothes to dry, we hid them, and we waited for his next appearance and his violent, raging, frustrated reactions with great anticipation and delight, moaning in a body with him as he complained about and raged at us.

The torture of Rachmilevitch came to a climax, and an end, when we decided to steal his false teeth. We had often mimicked him when he was eating—he had a way of sucking on these teeth, which made them click in his mouth

—and we would imitate his habit to the great amusement of most of the other people present. There was something so whole-heartedly mischievous about our behaviour that it was difficult for anyone not to participate in our continually high, merry, malicious spirits. Whenever poor Rachmile-vitch was present in any group, invariably his very presence would make all the children begin to giggle, irresistibly and infectiously. His very appearance was enough to start us laughing uncontrollably.

Whether I volunteered for the teeth-stealing mission or whether I was chosen, I no longer remember. I do remember that it was a well-planned group project, but that I was the one who was to do the actual stealing. To accomplish this, I was secreted in the corridor outside his room one night. A group of five or six of the other children proceeded to make various noises outside his room: wailing, blowing through combs which had been wrapped in toilet paper, pretending we were ghosts and calling out his name mournfully, predicting his immediate death, and so on. We kept this up interminably and as we had foreseen, he was unable to contain himself. He came tearing out of the room, in the dark, in his nightshirt, screaming in helpless rage, chasing the group down the corridor. This was my moment: I rushed into his room, seized the teeth from the glass in which he kept them on the table by his bed, and rushed out with them.

We had no plan as to what to do with them—we had not gone so far as to think that we might keep them forever— and after a long consultation, we decided to hang them on the gas fixture above the dining-room table.

We were, of course, all present the following morning, eagerly awaiting his appearance and squirming in anticipation. No one could have been a more satisfactory target for our machinations: as expected, he came into the dining-room, his face shrunken around the mouth by his lack of teeth, the very living embodiment of frustrated rage. He lashed out at us verbally and physically, until the dining-room was in an uproar as he chased us around the table, demanding in high-pitched screams the return of his teeth.

All of us, as if unable to stand the combination of suspense
and delight, began casting glances upward, above the table,
and Rachmilevitch finally calmed down for long enough to
look up and see his teeth, hanging from the gas fixture.
Accompanied by our triumphant shouts of laughter, he got
up on the table and removed them and replaced them in his
mouth. When he sat down again, we realized that we had—
for once—gone too far.

He managed to eat his breakfast with a certain cold,
silent, dignity, but although we continued, as if our motors
were running down, to poke fun at him rather listlessly, our
hearts were not in it any longer. He looked at us coldly, with
a feeling that was even beyond hatred—the look in his eyes
was like that of a wounded animal. He did not, however, let
it go at that. He took the matter up with Miss Madison, who
then cross-questioned us unendingly. I finally admitted to
the actual theft, and although we all received black marks
in her little black book, she informed me that I now led the
list by an enormous margin. She kept me on in her room
when she had dismissed the other children, to enumerate
the list of things which she had marked up against me. I did
not keep the stables sufficiently clean; I did not sweep the
courtyard regularly; I did not keep Gurdjieff's room properly dusted; the chicken yard was a general mess; I was
careless about my own room, my clothes and my appearance. In addition, she felt sure that I was the ring-leader in
all the offences that had been committed against poor old
Mr. Rachmilevitch.

As it was already early in the spring and Gurdjieff's
arrival from America was imminent, I did pay some
attention to her words. I cleaned up the chicken-yard, and
made at least a small improvement in most of my jobs
generally, but I was still living in some sort of dreamworld
and I put off as many things as I could. When we learned
that Gurdjieff was going to arrive on a particular day—it
was told to us in the morning of the very day that he was to
reach the Prieuré—I surveyed the condition of my various
chores and I was horrified. I realized that it would be
impossible for me to get everything in order before he

arrived. I concentrated on cleaning his rooms thoroughly, and sweeping the courtyard; my most "visible" projects. And, filled with guilt, instead of dropping my work when I knew he was arriving, I continued sweeping the courtyard, and did not go to greet him as everyone else had done. To my horror, he sent for me. I went to join the group, shamefacedly, expecting some immediate retribution for my sins, but he only embraced me warmly and said that he had missed me and that I was to help take his baggage up to his room and bring him coffee. It was a temporary reprieve, but I dreaded what was to come.

XIV

THE SATURDAY EVENING after Gurdjieff's return from America, which had been in the middle of the week, was the first general "assembly" of everyone at the Prieuré, in the study-house. The study-house was a separate building, originally an airplane hangar. There was a linoleum-covered raised stage at one end. Directly in front of the stage there was a small, hexagonal fountain, equipped electrically so that various coloured lights played on the water. The fountain was generally used only during the playing of music on the piano which was to the left of the stage as one faced it.

The main part of the building, from the stage to the entrance at the opposite end, was carpeted with oriental rugs of various sizes, surrounded by a small fence which made a large, rectangular open space. Cushions, covered by fur rugs, surrounded the sides of this rectangle in front of the fence, and it was here that most of the students would normally sit. Behind the fence, at a higher level, were built-up benches, also covered with Oriental rugs, for spectators. Near the entrance of the building there was a small cubicle, raised a few feet from the floor, in which Gurdjieff habitually sat, and above this there was a balcony which was rarely used and then only for "important" guests. The cross-wise beams of the ceiling had painted material nailed to them, and the material hung down in billows, creating a cloud-like effect. It was an impressive interior—with a church-like feeling about it. One had the impression that it would be improper, even when it was empty, to speak above a whisper inside the building.

On that particular Saturday evening, Gurdjieff sat in his accustomed cubicle, Miss Madison sat near him on the floor with her little black book on her lap, and most of the students sat around, inside the fence, on the fur rugs. New arrivals and "spectators" or guests were on the higher benches behind the fence. Mr. Gurdjieff announced that Miss Madison would go over all the "offences" of all the students and that proper "punishments" would be meted out to the offenders. All of the children, and perhaps I, especially, waited with bated breath as Miss Madison read from her book, which seemed to have been arranged, not alphabetically, but according to the number of offences committed. As Miss Madison had warned me, I led the list, and the recitation of my crimes and offences was a lengthy one.

Gurdjieff listened impassively, occasionally glancing at one or another of the offenders, sometimes smiling at the recital of a particular misdemeanour, and interrupting Miss Madison only to take down, personally, the actual number of individual black marks. When she had completed her reading, there was a solemn, breathless silence in the room and Gurdjieff said, with a heavy sigh, that we had all created a great burden for him. He said then that he would give out punishments according to the number of offences committed. Naturally, I was the first one to be called. He motioned to me to sit on the floor before him and then had Miss Madison re-read my offences in detail. When she had finished, he asked me if I admitted all of them. I was tempted to refute some of them, at least in part, and to argue extenuating circumstances, but the solemnity of the proceedings and the silence in the room prevented me from doing so. Every word that had been uttered had dropped on the assemblage with the clarity of a bell. I did not have the courage to voice any weak defence that might have come to my mind, and I admitted that the list was accurate.

With another sigh, and shaking his head at me as if he was very much put upon, he reached into his pocket and pulled out an enormous roll of bills. Once again, he enumerated the number of my crimes, and then laboriously peeled off an equal number of notes. I do not remember exactly how much he gave me—I think it was ten francs for each offence—but when he had finished counting, he handed me a sizeable roll of francs. During this process, the entire room practically screamed with silence. There was not a murmur from anyone in the entire group, and I did not even dare to glance in Miss Madison's direction.

When my money had been handed to me, he dismissed me and called up the next offender and went through the same process. As there were a great many of us, and there was not one individual who had not done something, violated some rule during his absence, the process took a long time. When he had gone through the list, he turned to Miss Madison and handed her some small sum—perhaps ten francs, or the equivalent of one "crime" payment—for her, as he put it, "conscientious fulfilment of her obligations as director of the Prieuré."

We were all aghast; we had been taken completely by surprise, of course. But the main thing we all felt was a tremendous compassion for Miss Madison. It seemed to me a senselessly cruel, heartless act against her. I have never known Miss Madison's feelings about this performance; except for blushing furiously when I was paid, she showed no obvious reaction to anything at all, and even thanked him for the pittance he had given her.

* * *

The money that I had received amazed me. It was, literally, more money than I had ever had at one time in my life. But it also repelled me. I could not bring myself to do anything with it. It was not until a few days later, one evening when I had been summoned to bring coffee to Gurdjieff's room, that the subject came up again. I had had no private, personal contact with him—in the sense of actually talking to him, for instance—since his return. That evening—he was alone—when I had served him his coffee, he asked me how I was getting along; how I felt. I blurted out my feelings about Miss Madison and about the money that I felt unable to spend.

He laughed at me and said cheerfully that there was no reason why I should not spend the money any way I chose. It was my money, and it was a reward for my activity of the past winter. I said I could not understand why I should have been rewarded for having been dilatory about my jobs and having created only trouble.

Gurdjieff laughed again and told me that I had much to learn.

"What you not understand," he said, "is that not everyone can be troublemaker, like you. This important in life—is ingredient, like yeast for making bread. Without trouble, conflict, life become dead. People live in status-quo, live only by habit, automatically, and without conscience. You good for Miss Madison. You irritate Miss Madison all time—more than anyone else, which is why you get most reward. Without you, possibility for Miss Madison's conscience fall asleep. This money should really be reward from Miss Madison, not from me. You help keep Miss Madison alive."

I understood the actual, serious sense in which he meant what he was saying, but I said that I felt sorry for Miss Madison, that it must have been a terrible experience for her when she saw us all receiving those rewards.

He shook his head at me, still laughing. "You not see or understand important thing that happen to Miss Madison when give money. How you feel at time? You feel pity for Miss Madison, no? All other people also feel pity for Miss Madison, too."

I agreed that this was so.

"Think necessary talk all time, that learn through mind, through words. Not so. Many things can only learn with feeling, even from sensation. But because man talk all time —use only formulatory centre—people not understand this. What you not see other night in study-house is that Miss Madison have new experience for her. Is poor woman, people not like, people think she funny—they laugh at. But other night people not laugh. True, Miss Madison feel uncomfortable, feel embarrassed when I give money, feel shame perhaps. But when many people also feel for her sympathy, pity, compassion, even love, she understand this but not right away with mind. She feel, for first time in life, sympathy from many people. She not even know then that she feel this, but her life change; with you, I use you like example, last summer you hate Miss Madison. Now you not hate, you not think funny, you feel sorry. You even like Miss Madison. This good for her even if she not know right away —you will show; you cannot hide this from her, even if you wish, cannot hide. So she now have friend, when used to be enemy. This good thing which I do for Miss Madison. I not concerned she understand this now—someday she understand and make her feel warm in heart. This unusual experience—this warm feeling—for such personality as Miss Madison who not have charm, who not friendly in self. Someday, perhaps even soon, she have good feeling because many people feel sorry, feel compassion for her. Someday she even understand what I do and even like me for this. But this kind learning take long time."

I understood him completely and was very moved by his words. But he had not finished.

"Also good thing for you in this," he said. "You young, only boy still, you not care about other people, care for self. I do this to Miss Madison and you think I do bad thing. You feel sorry, you not forget, you think I do bad thing to her. But now you understand not so. Also, good for you, because you feel about other person—you identify with Miss Madison, put self in her place, also regret what you do. Is necessary put self in place of other person if wish understand and help. This good for your conscience, this way is possibility for you learn not hate Miss Madison. All people same— stupid, blind, human. If I do bad thing, this make you learn love other people, not just self."

XV

GURDJIEFF'S TRIP TO the United States had been made, according to him, for various reasons—one of the most important ones being to make enough money to keep the Institute going at the Prieuré. Mr. Gurdjieff did not own the property, but rented it on a long-term lease, and since very few of the students were "paying guests", money was needed to make the various rental payments as well as to provide the food that we were unable to grow or produce on the land; to pay the light and gas and coal bills. And Mr. Gurdjieff's own expenses were also heavy at that time: he maintained an apartment in Paris, and had had to pay for the passage of all the students he had taken to America with him— enough, for instance, to be able to put on a demonstration of his gymnastics while he was there.

On his return, he frequently regaled us with stories about his adventures in America, about the American habit of embracing with open arms any new "movement", "theory", or "philosophy", simply in order to divert themselves, and about their gullibility in general. He would tell us how it was almost impossible for them not to give him money—the very act of giving him money made them feel important, and he called this "extortion" of them "shearing sheep". He said that most of them had pockets that were so full of green folding "stuff" that it gave them itchy fingers and they could not wait to part with it. Nevertheless, in spite of his stories about them and the way he made fun of them, he genuinely liked the Americans and, on occasions when he was not making fun of them, he would point out that, of all the peoples of the Western World, they were distinguished by various characteristics: their energy, ingenuity and their real generosity. Also, though gullible, they were good-hearted and eager to learn. Whatever their attributes or their faults, he had managed, during his stay in America, to collect a very large sum of money. I doubt that any one of us knew exactly how much, but it was generally believed to be in excess of $100,000.

The first obvious show of spending after his return to

France was the sudden and unexpected delivery of literally scores of bicycles to the Prieuré. They arrived by the truckload, and Gurdjieff personally distributed them to everyone there, with only a few exceptions: himself, his wife, and one or two of the smallest children. We were all amazed, and a great many of the Americans were appalled at this seeming waste of the money which many of them had helped to contribute to his "cause". Whatever his reasons for the acquisition of bicycles, the results were shatteringly colour-ful.

There were incredibly few people, considering the number of students living at the Prieuré at the time, who could actually ride a bicycle. But they had not been purchased idly —they were to be ridden. The entire grounds became a sort of enormous training-ground for bicycle riders. For days, and in the case of many of us, weeks, the grounds rang with the sound of bicycle bells, crashes, shouts of laughter and pain. In large groups we rode, teetering and collapsing to our assigned work on projects in the gardens and the woodlands. Anyone who had some valid reason or excuse for walking soon learned to beware of what had formerly been footpaths; for like as not, a bicycle would come careening at them, its rider frozen in horror and totally out of control, as he or she crashed into the unfortunate pedestrian or another equally helpless rider.

I suppose that most of us learned to ride quickly enough, although I seem to remember having bruised knees and elbows most of the summer. However long the process actually took, it seemed a very long time before it was safe to either ride or walk on the Prieuré grounds without genuine danger from almost any angle in the form of some novice bicyclist.

Another project that was initiated that same summer was equally colourful, although it did not involve the spending of any great sums of money. Everyone, with the sole exception of a skeleton group who had to work in the kitchen or on duty at the concierge, was put to work on the re-making of the lawns—the same lawns that I had mowed so arduously that first summer. No one escaped this duty, not even those so-called "distinguished" guests: persons who came for short visits, presumably to discuss Mr. Gurdjieff's theories with him, and who, up to that time, had not participated in work projects. Every available tool was put to use and the lawns were littered with people digging up the grass, raking, re-seeding, and rolling the new seed into the ground with heavy iron rollers. People worked so closely together that it sometimes seemed as if there was barely room for them all. During this activity, Gurdjieff would march up and down among the workers, criticizing them individually, goading them on, and helping to contribute a feeling of furious, senseless activity to the whole proceedings. As one of the more recent American students remarked, surveying this ant-like activity, it was as if the entire student body, and perhaps particularly Gurdjieff, had at least temporarily taken leave of their senses.

At intervals, and sometimes for several hours at a time, Gurdjieff would suddenly cease his supervision of us, and go to sit at his small table from which he could watch all of us, and write steadily on his books. This only added to the comical aspect of the whole project.

It was on the second or third day that one voice rose in a protest against the whole project. It was Rachmilevitch. In a towering rage, he laid down whatever implement he had been using, marched straight up to Gurdjieff and told him that what we were doing was insane. There were so many people working on the lawns, according to him, that the new grass-seed might better be thrown away than sown under our feet. People were digging and raking aimlessly, wherever they could find a vacant spot, paying no attention to what they were doing.

In what seemed to be equal fury, Gurdjieff protested against this uncalled for criticism—he knew better than anyone in the world how to "rebuild" lawns, he was an expert, he was not to be criticized, and so on, ad infinitum. After several minutes of this raging argument, Rachmile-vitch turned on his heels and strode away. Everyone—we had all been impressed with his standing up to the "master" in this way—stopped their work and watched him until he disappeared into the woods beyond the furthest lawns.

It was not until an hour or so later, when we were about to pause for our usual afternoon tea, that Mr. Gurdjieff called me over to him. At some length he told me that it was essential that Mr. Rachmilevitch be found and brought back. He said that in order to save Rachmilevitch's face it was necessary to send for him, that he would never return of his own accord, and he instructed me to harness the horse and go and find him. When I protested that I did not even know where to begin to look, he said that he was sure that if I followed my own instincts I would locate him without difficulty and that, perhaps, even the horse would help.

In an attempt to put myself in Rachmilevitch's place, when I had harnessed the horse to the wagon, I set off towards the woods beyond the main, formal gardens. It seemed to me that he could only have gone to one of the distant vegetable gardens—a walk of at least a mile, and I headed for the furthest one, at the very end of the property. On the way I was troubled about what I would do if and when I did find him, particularly since I had been the chief culprit in the conspiracy against him during the winter. Nothing had ever been said about that to me—at least not by Gurdjieff—and I felt that I had been selected only because I was in charge of the horse, and that Gurdjieff could not have picked any less suitable candidate for this errand.

I was not very surprised when my hunch proved to be right. He was in the garden, as I had hoped he might be. But, as if to lend a dreamlike quality to the affair, he was not in what I would have thought a normal, usual place. He was, of all things, sitting up in an apple tree. Concealing my astonishment—I really did think he was mad—I drove the horse and wagon directly underneath the tree and stated my errand. He looked at me distantly and refused to go back. I did not know of any arguments—I could not think of any good reasons—with which to persuade him to come back, so I said that I would wait there as long as he did; that I could not return without him. After a long silence, during which he occasionally glared at me, he suddenly, without a word, dropped quietly into the wagon from the tree and then sat on the seat next to me as I drove back to the main house. Tea had been saved for us and we sat across from each other at the table as we drank our tea, while Gurdjieff watched us from a distant table. Everyone else had gone back to work.

When we had finished, Gurdjieff told me to unharness the horse, thanked me for finding Rachmilevitch, and said that he would see me later.

Gurdjieff came to the stable before I was through with the horse and asked me to tell him exactly where I had found Mr. Rachmilevitch. When I told him that I had found him sitting in a tree in the "far garden" he looked at me, incredulous, made me repeat this—asked me if I was absolutely sure—and I assured him that he had been in a tree and that I had had to sit there for a long time, under the tree, before he had consented to come back with me. He asked me what arguments I had used and I confessed that I had not been able to think of anything except to say that he had to come back and that I had said I would wait there for as long as he would. Gurdjieff seemed to find this whole story very amusing and thanked me profusely for telling it to him.

Poor Mr. Rachmilevitch. When everyone was assembled in the salon that evening, he was still an object of interest to us all. It was the first time that any of us could remember one single individual defying Gurdjieff in the presence of everyone else. But the incident was not over. After the customary playing of music on the piano by M. de Hartmann, Mr. Gurdjieff told us that he had a very amusing story to tell us, and proceeded to reconstruct, in elaborate details, and with a great many new embellishments of his own, the story of Rachmilevitch's defiance of the afternoon, his disappearance, and my "capture" of him. Not only was the story highly embellished, but he also acted out all the parts—himself, Rachmilevitch, the interested spectators, me, even the horse. Amusing as it was to all of us, it was more than Rachmilevitch could bear. For the second time that day, he strode away from Gurdjieff after a furious outburst, vowing that he would leave the Prieuré for ever;

he had, finally, had enough.

I do not believe that anyone took him seriously at the time, but, to our surprise and consternation, he actually did leave the following day for Paris. He had been so much a part of the place, so conspicuous because of his never-ending complaints, that it was like the end of an era—as if some essential property of the school had suddenly vanished.

XVI

Jane Heap had returned to France at the same time as Gurdjieff, and had, of course, been to the Prieuré to see us. With her return, and to my regret, the visits to Paris to see Gertrude Stein and Alice Toklas had come to an end. I was very surprised when I was sent for one afternoon by the concierge, and told that I had a visitor. I was very pleased to learn that it was Gertrude and was very happy to see her, but my happiness was dispelled almost at once. Gertrude took a short walk with me in the grounds of the school, gave me a box of candy which she told me was a "farewell" gift for both of us from herself and Alice. She did not give me any opportunity to remonstrate with her, and said that she had made the trip to Fountainebleau especially to see us (I do not remember now whether she actually saw Tom or not) because she did not want to part from us by simply writing a letter.

When I asked her what she meant, she said that because of some difficulty she was having with Jane, and also because she still thought that we were not being properly brought up, she had decided that she could no longer go on seeing us. Any relationship with her, because of her disagreement with Jane—and, I gathered, with Gurdjieff as well—would inevitably only make trouble for us. There was nothing that I could say to this. Gertrude cut my protests short, said that she was very sorry to have to do what she was doing, but that there was no other way out.

I was shocked and saddened by this sudden, unexpected end to what had been a very happy, exciting and rewarding relationship, and, perhaps mistakenly, I think I blamed Jane for it. I cannot remember whether I ever mentioned it to Jane, or whether she explained it to me, but I do remember feeling, perhaps mistakenly, that she — not Gurdjieff — was the cause. Whatever the cause, my relationship with Jane deteriorated steadily from that time on, and while she was still my legal guardian, I rarely saw her. Looking back on my behaviour at that time, it now seems to me that I was being uncivilized to a high degree—I don't know about Jane. Jane made her usual periodic visits to the Prieuré on weekends but while I actually did see her —that is, I saw her with my eyes from a distance—we hardly spoke to each other for a period of about two years. She did, of course, see Tom and Gurdjieff, and I knew from the general gossip at the school and from Tom that the "problem of Fritz" was frequently discussed and also that Gurdjieff had been brought into these discussions; however, during that entire time, when I was still in very close contact with Gurdjieff because of my room-cleaning duties, he never mentioned Jane to me, and his behaviour towards me never altered. Not only did it not alter, but, partly because of the break with Jane, my feelings of respect and love for him only increased.

* * *

When Gurdjieff returned from his first trip to Paris after the "Rachmilevitch affair", to our surprise, he brought Rachmilevitch back with him. In the short period that he had been absent from the Prieuré he seemed to have changed a great deal. He now appeared to be resigned instead of contentious and quarrelsome, and in the course of time we even began to feel a certain affection for him. I was very curious about his return and while I did not have the temerity to bring up the subject directly when I was with Gurdjieff, he brought it up himself. He simply asked me, unexpectedly, if I were not surprised to see Rachmilevitch back at the Prieuré, and I told him that I was very surprised and admitted that I was, also, curious as to how it had happened; his resolve to leave for ever had been very definite.

Gurdjieff then told me the story of Rachmilevitch. According to this tale, Rachmilevitch had been a Russian refugee who had located in Paris after the Russian revolution and had become a prosperous merchant dealing in such merchandise as teas, caviar, and various other products for which there was, primarily, a demand among displaced Russian persons. Gurdjieff had apparently known him for a long time—he may have been one of the people who came to France with Gurdjieff from Russia some years before—and had decided that his personality was an essential element in the school.

"You remember," he said, "how I tell you that you make trouble? This true, but you only child. Rachmilevitch grown man and not mischievous, like you, but have such personality that he constantly cause friction whatever he do, wherever he live. He not make serious trouble, but he make friction on surface of life, all the time. He cannot help this—he too old to change now.

"When I tell you that though Rachmilevitch is already rich merchant I pay him to stay here, you are surprised, but this so. He very old friend and very important for my purposes. I cannot pay him what he can already make, all by self, in tea business in Paris; so when I go to see him I humble self, have to beg him to make sacrifice for my sake. He agree to do this, and I now have obligation to him for life. Without Rachmilevitch, Prieuré is not same; I know no one person like him, no person who just by existence, without conscious effort, produce friction in all people around him."

I had by this time acquired the habit of always assuming that in anything that Gurdjieff did there was always "more than meets the eye"; I was also familiar with his theory that friction produced conflicts which, in turn, agitated people and, as it were, shocked them out of their habitual, routine behaviour; also I could not help but wonder what rewards were in this for Rachmilevitch, besides money, that is. Gurdjieff's only answer to this was to say that it was also a privilege for Rachmilevitch to be at the Prieuré. "Nowhere else can his personality perform such useful work." I was not particularly impressed by this answer, but I did have a picture in my mind of Rachmilevitch's every move being of great importance. It seemed, at best, a curious destiny—he must, I assumed, live in a constant state of cataclysm, creating havoc incessantly.

There was no question that his presence not only created trouble, but also seemed to attract it. Very shortly after his return, he and I were again the focal points in another "incident".

It was my day on kitchen duty. As was customary for the

"kitchen-boy" I got up at four-thirty in the morning. Since I was lazy by nature and also at that age, the only way I could be sure of awakening on time for kitchen duty was to drink as many glasses of water as I could before I went to bed at about eleven the night before. Alarm clocks were unheard of at the Prieuré, and this recipe for early rising (which someone had suggested to me) never failed to work. As the nearest toilet was at a considerable distance from my room, there was no doubt of my actual waking up and I did not fall asleep again. The only difficulty was in regulating the amount of water. Too often I awakened at three, instead of four-thirty. Even on those mornings I did not dare to go back to bed again, and could not face drinking another quantity of water sufficient to waken me in another hour or so.

The kitchen boy's first duties were to build the fires in the coke stoves, fill the coal scuttles, make the coffee and heat the milk, slice and toast the bread. The water for the coffee took a long time to come to a boil as it was heated in twenty-five litre enamelware pots, which were also used to make the soup for the midday meal. The cook—there was usually a different cook every day, but the menus were written down, with recipes, in advance for each day of the week— normally was not required to appear in the kitchen until breakfast was over. On this particular day, the cook had not appeared by nine-thirty and I began to worry. I looked at the menu, and the recipe for the soup of the day, and since I had often seen the various cooks prepare the meal that was scheduled for that day, I made the necessary preliminary preparations.

When the cook had still not appeared by about ten o'clock I sent some child to find out what had happened to her and was told that she was sick and would not be able to come to the kitchen. I took my dilemma to Gurdjieff, and he said that since I had already started the meal I might as well return to the kitchen and finish it. "You be cook today," he said grandly.

I was very nervous about the responsibility, as well as rather proud of being entrusted with it. My greatest difficulty was in having to move the enormous soup kettles around the top of the large coal stove when I had to add coal to the fire, which was frequently necessary in order to keep the soup cooking. I worked hard all the morning and was reasonably proud of myself when I managed to finish the meal and deliver it, intact, to the serving table. The cook being absent, it was also necessary for me to serve it.

Habitually, the students formed a line, each person with his soup plate, silver, etc., in his hands, and as they passed by the serving table the cook would serve them one piece of meat and a ladleful of soup. Everything went well for a time. It was not until Rachmilevitch appeared—among the last to be served—that my difficulties began. The soup pot was almost empty by the time he reached me and I had to tilt it in order to fill the ladle. When I served him—it seemed to me that it was decreed by our mutual fates—the ladle also brought up a fair-sized lump of coke. It was a thick soup and I did not see the coke until it was deposited, with a hard, clanking sound, in his soup plate.

Judging by Rachmilevitch's reaction, his world came to an end at that instant. He started in on a tirade against me that I thought would never end. Everything that all of the children had done to him during the past winter was brought up, hashed over in detail; and as he cursed and raged I stood helplessly behind the soup kettle, silent. The tirade came to an end with Gurdjieff's appearance. He did not usually appear at lunch—he did not eat lunch—and he explained his appearance by saying that we were making so much noise that he was unable to work.

Rachmilevitch turned on him immediately, beginning his recital of woes and wrongs all over again from the beginning. Gurdjieff watched him steadily, unblinking, and this seemed to have a calming effect. Rachmilevitch's voice gradually lowered in tone, and he seemed to run down. Without saying anything to him, Gurdjieff picked the lump of coke out of Rachmilevitch's soup plate, threw it on the ground, and asked for a plate of soup himself. He said that since there was a new cook today, he felt that it was his responsibility to taste his cooking. Someone went for a plate for him, I served him what remained in the soup pot and he ate it, silently. When he had finished, he came over to me, congratulated me loudly, and said that the soup—this particular soup—was a favourite of his and was better than he had ever tasted.

He then turned to the assembled students and said that he had great experience and training in many things, and that in the course of his life he had learned a great deal about food, chemistry, and proper cooking, which included, of course, the taste of things. He said that while this particular soup was one that he had, personally, invented and which he liked very much, he now realized that it had always lacked one element to make it perfect. With a sort of obeisance in my direction, he praised me saying that I, by a fortunate accident, had found the perfect thing—the one thing that this soup needed. Carbon. He ended this speech by saying that he would instruct his secretary to change the recipe to include one piece of coke—not to be eaten, but to be added for flavour only. He then invited Rachmilevitch to have after-dinner coffee with him, and they left the dining area together.

XVII

ALTHOUGH THERE WERE many people at the Prieuré who were considered important for one reason or another, such as Madame de Hartmann, his secretary, and her husband, the pianist and composer, M. de Hartmann, who arranged and played the various pieces of music which Gurdjieff composed on his small "harmonium", the most impressive permanent resident was his wife, who was always known to us as Madame Ostrovsky.

She was a very tall, big-boned, handsome woman, and she seemed to be ever-present, moving almost silently along the corridors of the buildings, supervising the operation of the kitchens, the laundry-rooms and the general housekeeping work. I never knew exactly how much, or what authority she had. On the few occasions when she actually said anything to us, which were rare, there was no question in our minds but that her word was law. I remember being particularly fascinated by the way she moved; she walked without any perceptible movement of her head and without the slightest jerkiness in her movements; she was never hurried, but at the same time she worked at incredible speed; every movement she made in whatever she was doing was absolutely essential to that particular activity. During the first summer at the Prieuré she usually prepared Gurdjieff's meals and took them to his room, and it was when she was in the kitchen that we had an opportunity to observe her at work. She rarely spoke, in fact, she did not seem to use words as a means of communication unless it was absolutely essential, and when she did speak, she never raised her voice. She seemed surrounded by an aura of gentle firmness; everyone regarded her with a certain awe, and she inspired a very real feeling of devotion, although it was hardly ever expressed outwardly, among all the children.

Although most of us had no contact with her in the usual sense—for example, I doubt that she ever even addressed me personally—when we learned that she was seriously ill, it was a matter of concern to all of us. We missed the feeling of unspoken authority that she had always carried with her, and the lack of her presence gave us a feeling of definite, if indefinable, loss.

Her illness, in addition, made a great change in Gurdjieff's routine. Once she was confined to her room—which faced his room and was of equal size, but at the opposite end of the main building—Gurdjieff began to spend several hours with her each day. He would go to her room for a short visit each morning, supervise the persons who were delegated to taking care of her—his two eldest nieces and, on occasion, others—and would then return after lunch, usually to spend the entire afternoon with her.

During this period, our contact with Gurdjieff was rare, except for the evenings in the salon. He was preoccupied and withdrawn and left almost all of the details of the running of the Prieuré to others. We occasionally saw him when we were on kitchen duty as he would come to the kitchens to supervise, personally, the preparation of her food. She was on a diet which included a large amount of blood, pressed in a small hand press from meat which had been especially selected and purchased for her.

At the beginning of her illness, she did make occasional appearances on the terrace, to sit in the sun, but as the summer went on she finally took to her room permanently. Gurdjieff informed us, one evening, that she was incurably ill with some form of cancer and that the doctors—some two months before—had given her only two weeks to live. He said that although it might take all his strength, he was determined to keep her alive for as long as possible. He said that she was "living through him" and that it took almost all of his daily energy, but that he hoped to keep her alive for another year, or at least for six months.

As I was still in charge of his rooms, I necessarily had a certain amount of contact with him. He would often send for coffee during the night, which was now the only time he gave to his writing—often staying up until four or five in the morning, having worked from about ten o'clock the night before.

In addition to the chickens, the donkey, the horse, a

number of sheep, and for a time one cow, there were a number of cats and dogs around the Prieuré. One of the dogs, a rather ugly black and white mongrel, had always tended to follow Gurdjieff around, but not to such an extent that he could have been called Gurdjieff's dog. At this period, with Gurdjieff rarely absent from the Prieuré—he had cut his trips to Paris to an absolute minimum—this dog, named Philos by Gurdjieff, became his constant companion. He not only followed him everywhere, but also slept in Gurdjieff's room unless Gurdjieff put him out personally, which he usually did, telling me that he did not like anyone or anything sleeping in the same room with him. Upon being put out of the room, Philos would curl up directly in front of the door, and then go to sleep against it. He was a reasonably fierce watchdog and became very protective of Gurdjieff. He was, however, extremely tolerant of me as I was — obviously with Gurdjieff's permission — constantly coming and going to and from Gurdjieff's room. When I would enter it late at night with my tray of coffee, he would glare up at me, yawn and permit me to step over him and enter the room.

One night, it was very late and the entire Prieuré was silent and dark with the exception of Gurdjieff's room, Gurdjieff set aside his work when I came in and told me to sit on the bed beside him. He talked at some length about his work, how hard his writing was, how exhausting his daily work with Madame Ostrovsky, and then, as usual, asked me about myself. I recapitulated the various things that I was doing, and he commented that since I had a great deal to do with animals—I took care of the chickens, the horse, the donkey, and recently had been feeding Philos, too —he would like to know what I thought of them. I said that I thought of them all as my friends and told him, to his amusement, that I even had names for all the chickens.

He said that the chickens were not important—very stupid creatures—but that he hoped that I would take good care of the other animals. The donkey did not matter too much, but he was concerned with the horse and the dogs. "Horse and dog, and sometimes also true of cow," he said, "are special animals. Can do many things with such animals. In America, in Western world, people make fools of dogs—make learn tricks, other stupid things. But these animals truly special—no longer just animals." He then asked me if I had ever heard of reincarnation and I said that I had. He said that there were people, some Buddhists for example, who had many theories about reincarnation, some "even believe animal can become man—or sometimes that in next reincarnation can become animal." He laughed when he said this, and then added: "Man do many strange things with religion when learn a little—make up new things for religion, sometimes things that have little truth, but usually come from original thing that was true. In case of dogs, they not all wrong," he said. "Animals have only two centres— man is three-centred being, with body, heart, and mind, all different. Animal cannot acquire third brain and become man; but just because of this, because of this impossibility to acquire third brain, is necessary always treat animals with kindness. You know this word, 'kindness'?"

I said that I did, and he said: "Never forget this word. Very good word and not exist in many languages. Not in French, for instance. French say 'gentil' but this not mean same thing. Not *kind,* kind come from kin, like family, like same thing. Kindness mean to treat like self."

"Reason for necessity treat dog and horse with kindness," he went on, "is because unlike all other animal, and even though he know cannot become man, cannot acquire third brain like man, in his heart all dog and horse who associate with man *wish* become man. You look at dog or horse and you always see, in eyes, this sadness because know not possible for them, but even so, they wish. This very sad thing to wish for impossible. They wish this because of man. Man corrupts such animals, man almost try to make dog and horse human. You have heard people say 'my dog almost like human'—they not know they speak near-truth when say this, because is almost truth, but still impossible. Dog and horse seem like human because have this wish. So, Freets," — as he always pronounced my name — "you remember this important thing. Take good care of animals;

always be kind."

He then spoke about Madame Ostrovsky. He said that his work with her was extremely tiring and very difficult "because I try to do thing with her which is almost not possible. If she alone, already she be long time dead. I keep alive, make stay alive, with my strength; very difficult thing. But also very important — this most important moment in life for her. She live many lives, is very old soul; she now have possibility ascend to other world. But sickness come and make more difficult, make impossible for her to do this thing alone. If can keep alive few months more will not have to come back and live this life again. You now part of Prieuré family—my family—you can help by making strong wish for her, not for long life, but for proper death at right time. Wish can help, is like prayer when for other. When for self, prayer and wish no good; only work good for self. But when wish with heart for other, can help."

When he had finished, he looked at me for a long time, patted my head in that affectionate animal way, and sent me to bed.

XVIII

ALTHOUGH GURDJIEFF WAS always set apart from everyone else at the Prieuré, unquestioned, and accorded great respect which was combined with a proper element of fear, his "dictatorship" was also very benevolent. There was a side of his nature that was not only physically magnetic and animal-like, but extremely earthy. His sense of humour was often very subtle, in an oriental sense, but also had a broad, crude side, and he was a very sensual man.

He manifested this side of himself particularly when he was alone with the men and boys—in the Turkish bath or, during the summer, at the swimming pool. Our swimming pool was at the far end of the formal lawns and gardens, facing the château beyond the expanse of lawns. Contrary to popular belief, there was no mingling of the sexes in any "immoral" sense. The men and women bathed separately at the bath, and different hours were allotted for male or female use of the swimming pool. There was, in fact, a very strict code of morality in this purely physical sense, and we were highly amused when people sent us clippings from the Sunday supplements of various newspapers which "proved" that the Institute was a nudist colony, or a "free-love" group —some sort of crack-pot organization tinged with a certain licentiousness. Actually the nearest thing to "nudity" was the common habit—for some of the men only, of course—of working out of doors stripped to the waist. And, while it was true that we swam without bathing suits, the swimming pool was equipped with curtains which were always drawn whenever anyone went in swimming. It was forbidden, in fact, for even the small children to swim without drawing the curtains.

In spite of Gurdjieff's many preoccupations—especially his wife's illness—that summer, he frequently joined the other men and the boys at their allotted hour before lunch at the swimming pool. When everyone had stripped, Gurdjieff would, inevitably, begin to joke about their bodies, their sexual prowess, their various physical habits. The jokes were usually what would be called "dirty" or at least "lewd" and he found all such stories highly amusing, whether he told them or whether they were told by the other men who were quick to join in the spirit of such joking. One of his favourite amusements or diversions at the swimming pool was to line all the men up facing in one direction and then compare their sunburns. This became a ritual of what Gurdjieff called the "white ass" club. He would look at all of us from the rear, remarking on the various shades of tan or sunburn, and the glowing whiteness of our buttocks. He would then make us all turn around and make additional comments on the size and variety of male genitalia exposed to him. Finally, we would, each time he appeared to swim, be rated, as members in good standing of his "white ass" club. Tom and I usually rated high—in addition to deeply tanned backs and chests, since we were children and wore shorts, our legs were also deeply tanned, and because of this he would make some comment, usually to the effect that our small buttocks were "asses that shine with whiteness, like stars."

A good many of the older men, particularly the Russians, not only did not expose themselves to the sun, but rather disliked any form of nudity and were usually embarrassed by these proceedings. They, of course, rated very low on the list, but Gurdjieff, himself, was the lowest. So low, as he said, that he actually belonged to a different club. Since he always wore a hat—winter and summer—although his face was dark, his bald head was glistening white. His club, of which he was the president and sole member, was called something like the "white crown" club, and he would compare the whiteness of his bald pate with the whiteness— he made elaborate comparisons of the degree of white always—of our behinds.

One of his favourite stories on these occasions was a long, involved tale about a farmhand who was having an affair with the farmer's wife. The farmer, suspecting his wife and the farmhand, went searching for them with his rifle, and discovered them when he perceived, in the moonlight, the farmhand's white ass, bouncing rhythmically through the darkness, shining in the reflected light of the moon.

Although these stories were often repeated and many of them were not, in the first place, particularly funny, his own immense enjoyment in telling them made us all laugh. He was a superb storyteller, spinning out even the dullest tales to such fantastic lengths, embellishing them with such ornamentation and detail, accompanied by pointed, significant gestures and expressions, that it was impossible not to listen to him with total absorption.

The subtler side of his humour—which was always complicated and involved—expressed itself very differently. Early that summer, a group of us, for our own amusement, had been exploring the cellars of the main building and we had come across a tunnel. While we did follow it for almost half a mile, the rats, cobwebs, and mouldy dankness, and the complete darkness, kept us from trying to reach its end. There was a rumour that, since the Prieuré had been reputedly built by Louis XIV for Madame de Maintenon, this was an underground passage to the Palace of Fountainebleau. Be that as it may, Gurdjieff was greatly interested in our discovery of this tunnel, and went to examine it personally.

A week or so after this discovery, he told me that he had an important job for me. He talked at some length about the tunnel, and then asked me to take a bottle of the ordinary red wine which we drank at meals, and bought at that time for about eight cents a litre, open it, pour out half of it and then refill the bottle by the addition of half a bottle of sparkling Perrier water. I was then to recork the bottle, seal it with sealing wax, cover it with sand and cobwebs— "wonderful cobwebs for this purpose in tunnel"—and bring it to him when he called for it.

I must have looked puzzled, and he went on to explain that two very distinguished guests were scheduled to visit him the following week. This wine was being prepared especially for them. He would call me and when he asked for "one of the bottles of the special old wine" I was to bring this bottle with a cork-screw and two glasses. He smiled a good deal during these instructions and I made no comment about them, although I knew that he was "up to something"

—a phrase he often used when he was planning anything.

The two visitors arrived. They were well-known to me, in fact they were well-known, by reputation, to everyone there, and they elicited the automatic admiration and respect that is generally accorded to "famous" people, whether actually deserved or not. I ushered the visitors—both women—to Gurdjieff's room and then retired to my waiting post near the bell (there were two bells for me—one in the kitchen and one in my room). When I heard the expected ring I ran to his room and was told to bring "the special old, rare wine that we had found during a recent project of excavating the ruins of the original monastery". This colourful exaggeration had a basis in fact. The Prieuré had been, in the 12th century, a monastery and there were a few ruins to substantiate this. Those ruins, of course, had nothing at all to do with the tunnel from the cellars. The original monastery building had been at a completely different location on the property.

I brought the wine as I had been instructed with only two glasses, the bottle completely covered with dirt, sand and cobwebs, plus a napkin with which to hold it—my personal touch of elegance. Before telling me to open the bottle (he simply told me to wait there for a few minutes) he told them the story of the wine that was about to be served.

He began with a long, and highly inaccurate, account of the founding of the Prieuré (in 900) by some order of monks who, among other things, like all monks, made wine. "These special monks; very intelligent. Monks like this no longer exist on earth. With such intelligence," he continued, "naturally such monk make also very wonderful wine."

He then said, with a quick, stern glance at me, as if to silence any possible laughter from me, "I have many projects, all very important, at Prieuré. One project this year is excavation of old ruins." He then described, at great length, the number of people and the great energy involved in this project and how, miraculously, we had come across eleven bottles of wine . . . wine that had been made by these self-same intelligent monks. "Now come problem for me . . . who I know worthy to drink such wine; wine that no longer exist anywhere in world except here at Prieuré?

This wine too good for me. I already ruin stomach with drinking Armagnac. Then I think of just you ladies, who, as if by Act of God, plan to visit me. Just most suitable to first taste this wine."

I was then ordered to open the bottle. I wrapped it in the napkin, uncorked it and poured a little of the "wine" into the two glasses. Gurdjieff watched me with great intensity, and when I passed the wine to the two ladies, he turned his equally intense attention to them; he appeared to be burning with anticipation, unable to wait for their reaction.

The ladies, properly impressed and suiting their reactions to the momentous occasion, lifted their glasses gingerly in his direction and sipped, delicately. Gurdjieff was unable to restrain himself. "Tell!" he commanded them. "How taste this wine?"

The ladies, as if overcome, were momentarily unable to speak. At last, one of them, with half-closed eyes, murmured that it was "superb"; the other adding that she had never tasted anything to compare with it.

Puzzled, and embarrassed on their account, I started to leave the room but Gurdjieff stopped me with a firm gesture and indicated that I was to refill their glasses. I stayed with them until they had finished the bottle, with continued appropriate exclamations of rapture and ecstasy. He then told me to take the bottle and glasses, to prepare their rooms—on the very same floor as his—one room in which Napoleon had slept, the other having been occupied at some point by some King's mistress—and to let him know when the rooms were ready.

The rooms, of course, had been ready that morning, but I laid fires in the fireplaces, waited a suitable time and then returned to his room. He told me to take them to their rooms, and then instructed them that they must rest after the experience of having tasted this marvellous wine, and must prepare for the feast of the evening—a great feast which was being prepared, especially in their honour.

When I saw him later, alone, his only mention of the wine-drinking episode was to congratulate me on the appearance of the bottle. I gave him a significant, knowing look as if to tell him that I had understood what he was doing, and he said, rather seriously, but with a faint, mocking smile on his face: "Way you look, I know you already make judgment of this ladies; but remember what I tell before, necessary look all sides, all directions before make judgment. You not forget this."

XIX

I sometimes thought of Gurdjieff as a clever fisherman or trapper; the incident of the ladies and the "famous old wine" was only one of many instances in which he, to my mind at least, laid a trap or baited a hook and then sat back to watch, with great amusement, the prey reveal themselves, their weaknesses, when caught. Although I sensed an element of malice in this, the saving grace seemed to lie in the fact that, in most cases, the "prey" was unaware of what had happened. At times, it seemed to me that this kind of "playing" with people was literally nothing more than a diverson for him, something to take his mind off the continuous pressures under which he worked. When speaking of such experiences, he would frequently refer to them as "bubble-pricking", which I did not find especially apt since the "deflating" was frequently unnoticed by the particular target of the moment.

In the normal course of time, Gurdjieff acquired numerous reputations, including that of a sort of "faith-healer" or, on a somewhat simpler level, "miracle-worker". It was perhaps inevitable that he was, therefore, frequently consulted about day-to-day "life" or "mundane" problems, in spite of the fact that he had frequently reiterated that his work had nothing to do with the solution of such problems. Nevertheless, and even though forewarned, a great many people insisted on consulting him about just such problems, which seemed to me surprising and, usually, embarrassing, particularly since the people who did consult him were generally considered, or at least considered themselves, intellectual, intelligent people.

I remember one woman who, at great expense to herself (which was perhaps not pertinent, since she had money), made a trip from America to the Prieuré, for one week, to consult him about the very kind of problem which he had so often stated was not in his province. When she arrived, she demanded an immediate interview, but was told that Gurdjieff would be unable to see her until sometime that evening. She was assigned to a comfortable room and, through his secretary, told that she would have to pay a large sum, daily, for the use of the room. She was also warned that there would be an additional, large fee for her "consultation".

He did not see her alone, but met and welcomed her at dinner that evening in the presence of everyone. In the course of his preliminary conversation with her, he said that he understood she had an important problem to discuss with him, and he behaved as if he were enormously impressed that she should have made such a long, expensive trip just to consult him. She said that the problem was one that had troubled her for a long time, and that she had felt—when she had met him in America the previous winter—that he was, unquestionably the only person who could help her to solve it. He said that he would try to help her, and that she could make an appointment for an appropriate time for such a consultation by speaking to his secretary. She went on to say, in front of the entire assembled company, that it was very urgent. He said that he would see her as soon as possible but that, for now, the important business of the day was to have dinner.

At the dinner table, the woman gave every appearance of great nervousness, smoked one cigarette after another, and coughed a great deal—to such an extent that everyone at the table was aware of her. Giving up any attempt at conversation because of her constant coughing, Gurdjieff remarked that she seemed to have a bad cough. She responded at once, pleased with his attention, and said that it was part of the problem about which she wished to consult him. He frowned at her, but before he had an opportunity to say anything more, she plunged ahead. She said that she was having trouble with her husband and that her cigarette-smoking and her coughing were simply "exterior manifestations", in her opinion, of this difficulty. We were all listening (I was waiting on table) by this time. Gurdjieff frowned at her again, but she went on relentlessly. She said that cigarettes, as everyone knew, were a phallic symbol, and that she had discovered that her excessive smoking and the resultant coughing were "manifestations" which always occurred when she was having the aforesaid difficulty with her husband, adding that, of course, her troubles were sexual.

Gurdjieff had listened to her, as he always did, with undivided attention, and after a thoughtful pause he asked her what kind of cigarettes she smoked. She named an American brand which she said she had smoked for years. He nodded, very thoughtfully, at this disclosure, and after a suspenseful silence said that he thought the cure, or the solution, was very simple. He suggested that she change her brand of cigarettes, that perhaps "Gauloises Bleues" would be a good brand to try. For the time being that ended the conversation.

It was only later, in the salon, during the rather ceremonious coffee-drinking, that she was heard to praise him extravagantly and say that he had, of course, given her the solution—that his way of solving problems was never obvious, but that she had understood him.

She stayed at the Prieuré for a day or two longer, bought an enormous supply of "Gauloises Bleues"—as many as the law allowed her to take out of the country—and without demanding any further consultations, and having informed Gurdjieff that she had understood him, returned to America. It was only after her departure that Gurdjieff referred to her as "one of those God-given accidents who have unconscious good-will for me." He had charged her a large fee and she had paid it gladly.

Although I did not mention it to Mr. Gurdjieff at the time, I did refer to that incident and others like it, some time later. At that time, he told me that many people—people with "middle-class western world morality" had questions about, and objections to, his methods of procuring money, which he always needed for the support of the Prieuré and also of many of the students who were not able to pay him anything. He said, almost angrily, that our kind of morality was based on money; that the only thing that troubled us about such occurrences was the fact that he had, apparently, extracted money without having given anything in return.

"All my life," he said forcefully, "I tell people this work not for everyone. If can solve problems with religion or with your American psychiatrist, this good. But people not listen what I say; always find other meaning—interpret what I say in own way, make self feel good. So must pay for this good feeling. Many times I tell that my work cannot help with ordinary life problems: sex, illness, unhappiness; such things. If cannot solve such problems alone, then my work, which not have to do with such problems, no good for them. But such people come here no matter what I tell, to have good feeling; woman who smoke many cigarettes can now tell everyone, but particularly her 'self' that she consult me about problem and that I give answer, even though I not give answer. So just such people can justify existence by helping me with many money problems. Even with their stupidity they help good thing—my work. This already enough reward for such people."

"Is unfortunate weakness in people today; they ask advice but not wish help, wish only find out what already want. They not listen words I say—I always say what I mean, my words always clear—but they not believe this, always look for other meaning, meaning which exist only in their imagination. Without such woman, such people, you and many other people at Prieuré not eat. Money this woman pay is money for food." It was one of the few times that I had ever heard him "explain" or "justify" such activity on his part.

XX

In the natural course of events, since Mr. Gurdjieff was engaged in writing books, it was necessary for him to employ a typist. He did not set about this in any ordinary manner, but he employed, with great fanfare, a young German woman he had discovered somewhere in his travels. For several days before her arrival we heard about her. Elaborate preparations were made for her coming, including finding the proper room for her, the acquisition of a typewriter, arrangements for suitable working space, and so on. Gurdjieff praised her attributes to all of us, told us how lucky he had been to find this perfect person "for my purposes", and we awaited her arrival with great anticipation.

When she did arrive, she was introduced to all of us, a dinner was served in her honour, and the process was very festive—she was given what we called the "royal treatment", and she responded to it whole-heartedly, taking herself as seriously as Gurdjieff seemed to take her. It turned out that her major, magnificent accomplishment was that she could type, as Gurdjieff repeatedly told us in complete amazement, "without even looking at key on typewriter."

No secretary or typist has, I feel sure, ever been accorded such treatment because of her ability to use the touch system. As if to prove to us all that this ability actually existed, the young woman installed herself at a table on the terrace, in full view of all of us as we came and went to and from work, and remained there — typing merrily — all summer long, except on rainy days. The clicking of her typewriter resounded in all of our ears.

My first contact with her, and in fairness to her I must admit to a strong anti-German prejudice, having grown up on stories of German atrocities during World War I, was one evening when I was doing my own washing in the courtyard in back of the house after work. She did not know me, except by sight, and, assuming that I was French, called to me from a window overlooking the courtyard, asking me in heavily accented French where she could obtain what she called some "Savon Lux"; she managed to convey to me that she needed this to wash her stockings. I said, in English, which I knew she understood and spoke much better than French, that I assumed she could buy it at the local *épicerie* about half a mile distant. Her response was to toss some coins down to me and to tell me that she would appreciate my getting her some at once.

I picked up the money, went up the stairs and handed it to her. I said that I thought I should explain to her that there were no errand boys at the Prieuré and that no one had, so far, told me that she was any exception to the general rule that everyone did their own personal work, which included personal shopping. She said, with a "charming" smile, that she was sure that no one would have any objections to my performing this errand for her since she was, as perhaps I did not yet realize, engaged on very important work for Mr. Gurdjieff. I explained that I, too, was engaged on similar work; that I took care of him and his rooms and did my own errands as well.

She seemed amazed, and after a moment's reflection said that she would straighten out the matter with Mr. Gurdjieff —that there must be some misunderstanding, at least on my part, concerning her function at the school. I did not have to wait very long for further developments. A "coffee summons" came from his room only a few minutes later.

When I arrived at his room with the coffee, the typist, as I had expected was sitting with him. I served the coffee and then Mr. Gurdjieff turned to me with one of his "winning" smiles: "You know this lady?" he asked.

I said that, yes, I knew her.

He then said that she had spoken to him and that he understood that she had asked me to perform an errand for her and that I had refused. I said that it was true and that, besides, everyone else performed their own errands.

He agreed that this was so, but said that he had not had time to instruct her about everything and that he would appreciate it very much if, on this one occasion and as a favour to him, because she was very important to him, I would be kind enough to do what she asked. I was baffled

and even angry, but I said, of course, that I would. She
handed me the money and I went to the store and bought
her soap. I assumed that, however I might feel, he had good
reason for asking me to do the errand for her and decided
that the incident was closed. Perhaps she was actually
"special" in some way that I had not realized; Gurdjieff, at
least, appeared to think she was.

I was furious, however, when after I had given her the
soap and her change, she gave me a tip and said that she
was sure that I now realized that she had been right in the
first place, and that she hoped Mr. Gurdjieff's action had
made it clear to me. I smouldered, but managed to hold my
tongue. I also managed not to mention it to Mr. Gurdjieff
when I saw him, but I continued to smoulder.

Several days later, on a weekend, a number of guests
arrived. Gurdjieff welcomed them at his usual little table
near the lawns, in front of the terrace where the typist was
at work. I brought coffee for all of them and served it. He
indicated with a gesture, that I was not to leave, and then
proceeded to tell the assembled guests that he could hardly
wait to show them his new marvels, his two wonderful new
acquisitions: an electric icebox and a "touch typist". He then
told me to lead the way to the pantry where the new
refrigerator had been installed, and the guests were properly mystified upon being shown an ordinary model Frigidaire
which, as Gurdjieff put it, "all by self can make ice", even,
"without my help"—a true product of the genius of the
western world. This inspection completed, we all went back
to the terrace to inspect the second marvel who, also
"without my help and even without looking at keys", was
able to type his book. The typist stood up to greet him but
Gurdjieff, without introducing her, told her to sit down.
Then, at his command, she typed "without even looking at
keys" but gazing triumphantly off into space.

Gurdjieff stood among his guests, gazing at her with
unbounded admiration, speaking of her as another product
of the "genius" of the western world. I was, actually,
fascinated by the ability to use the touch system on a
typewriter and my own interest and admiration were

unfeigned. Gurdjieff, suddenly, looked in my direction and smiled an enormous, broad smile, as if we shared some huge joke together, and then told me to collect the coffee cups.

It was not until much later that evening, in his room, that he referred to the typist once more. He spoke first of the "electric icebox"—"only have to put in plug and instantly box make noise of humming and begin produce ice." He smiled at me again, conspiratorially. "Is so with German lady. I like plug—I tell type, and she also begin make noise and produce not ice, but book. Wonderful American invention."

I almost liked her then, and would have been happy to do her errands from that time on. I could not refrain from saying so, and Gurdjieff nodded at me, looking pleased. "When you help typing lady, you help me, like giving oil to machine which keep working; this wonderful thing."

XXI

ONE OF THE pleasures and challenges of "concierge duty"
was a competition among all the children—this duty was
almost exclusively the work of the children — to be
sufficiently alert on this job to have the gates, through
which the automobiles had to pass, opened in time for Mr.
Gurdjieff to drive through them without having to stop his
car and blow the horn as a signal to the gatekeeper.

One difficulty with this was that the entrance to the
Prieuré was at the foot of a long hill which descended from
the railway station; the streetcar to Samois also passed
directly in front of the gate where the highway made a wide
turn in the direction of Samois, away from the Prieuré.
Frequently the noise of the "tramway" obscured the sound of
cars coming down the hill, and interfered with our game.
Also, once Mr. Gurdjieff became aware of the competition,
he would usually coast down the hill so that we would not be
aided by the sound of the motor.

It was mostly thanks to Philos, the dog, who often
followed me around during Mr. Gurdjieff's absences, that I
was usually able to get the gates opened in time for him to
sail through them, a big smile on his face. By watching
Philos, whose ears would prick up at the sound of any
passing car, but who would jump to his feet at the sound of
Mr. Gurdjieff's car, I was almost always successful.

Amused by this game of ours, Mr. Gurdjieff once asked
me how it was that I was able to, practically unfailingly,
have the gates open in time, and I told him about Philos. He
laughed and then said that this was a very good example of
cooperation. "Show that man have much to learn, and can
learn from many unexpected places. Even dog can help. Man
very weak, need help all time."

Late that summer, I was on concierge duty when Mr.
Gurdjieff was to leave on a trip. For some reason, it was a
particularly important departure, and everyone was gathered around his automobile when he was about ready to
leave. I was among the leave-takers, and when he had
finally started the motor of the car, I ran to the big gates to

open them. In my haste, I stumbled and fell, and one of my knees hit the heavy iron catch, just above the level of the ground, which served to hold one of the gates open. It was rusty and, as I had fallen hard, it penetrated rather deeply. As Gurdjieff was about to drive through the gates, he looked at me, saw the blood running down my leg, stopped, and asked me what had happened. I told him and he told me to wash it off, which I did as soon as he had left.

By the middle of the afternoon—he had left about noon—my leg was very painful, my knee swollen, and I had to stop work. The work I was assigned to that afternoon was cleaning the parquet floors of the salons, which meant scraping the floors with heavy steel wool to remove the old wax and accumulated dirt; this was done by standing on the steel wool and pushing it back and forth, with the grain of the wood, with one's foot.

By evening, my knee had swollen alarmingly, and I was not well enough to eat dinner. I was put to bed and various treatments began. Different people had different ideas about the treatments, but it was decided that the knee was badly infected and that the proper remedy was a hot onion poultice. Baked or perhaps boiled onions were placed on the open wound, which was then wrapped in heavy, transparent oiled cloth, and then wrapped again with a bandage. The purpose, of course, was to draw the poison out of the infected knee.

Although I received constant attention and the best of care—there was a resident doctor at the Prieuré who had supervised the treatments given me—my leg did not improve. By the following day it was enormous and small boils began to appear on my body, extending from well below my knee almost to my waist. I was delirious all day, coming out of my delirium occasionally when additional and more frequent poultices were applied. But nothing seemed to help.

It was late that afternoon when Gurdjieff returned from his trip. Some time after his arrival, when he inquired about me, he was told about my condition and he came to see me in my room. He removed the bandage and poultice and sent someone to the local pharmacy at once. They brought back a remedy, then called "Ouata-plasme", apparently also some form of poultice, and Gurdjieff had them build a fire in the stove in my room on which he could boil water. When the water was boiling, he dipped a small square of this impregnated cotton into the water, and then applied it immediately to the affected knee, again wrapping it in the oiled cloth and a bandage. He insisted that it be applied at once, directly from the boiling water, and I remember these applications as being excruciatingly painful. Instructions were given to someone to stay the night in my room and to apply these new poultices every four hours or so; which was done.

By the following afternoon, I was much better, and the poultices, when removed, where black with gelatinous, infected matter. That evening, Mr. Gurdjieff came to visit me again. As it was a Saturday and there was to be a demonstration in the study-house, he insisted that I should attend along with all the others, and had his nephew carry me there and back "piggy-back". When we arrived at the study-house, he placed me in the small cubicle, where I sat behind him, during the demonstration. When it was over, I was carried back to my room. There was nothing very spectacular about the treatment or the cure, but Gurdjieff had something to say to me about it when I was on my feet again.

He asked to look at my leg, on which I was still wearing a small bandage, and when he had pronounced it cured, he asked me if I remembered what he had said about Philos helping me to identify his car when he arrived at the Prieuré gates. I said that I did, of course, and he said that these two things—the help of the dog, and the infection in my knee—had one thing in common. They were proof, of a kind, of man's dependence on other creatures. "To dog, you owe thanks, because he help you with small thing; to me you owe more than this, perhaps owe life to me. They try when I not here, even doctor try, fix your leg, but only get worse. When I come, I fix leg, because only I know about this new medicine which have in France now. I know this because I

interested in everything, because necessary know all things
for self in life. Just because I know this thing, and because I
come back in time, you now well. You all right."

I said that I realized this and I thanked him for what he
had done. He smiled, indulgently, and said that it was
impossible to thank him for what he had done for me.
"Cannot give thanks for life, not possible give enough
thanks; also perhaps will be times when you wish I not save
life. You young now, you glad not die—this serious thing,
because illness like you have very dangerous, can even kill.
But when you grow, you not always like life, and maybe you
not thank me, but make curse on me because I not let die.
So do not thank now."

He went on, then, to say that life was a " . . . two-edged
sword. In your country, you think life is only for pleasure.
You have saying in your country: 'pursuit of happiness', and
this saying show that people not understand life. Happiness
is nothing, is only other side of unhappiness. But in your
country, in most of world now, people only want happiness.
Other things also important: suffering important because is
also part of life, necessary part. Without suffering man
cannot grow, but when you suffer, you think only of self, you
feel sorry for self, wish not to suffer because this make you
feel not comfortable, make you wish escape from thing that
make you feel bad. When man suffer, he feel only self-pity.
Not so if real man. Real man also sometimes feel happiness,
real happiness; but when he also feel real suffering, he not
try to stop this thing in self. He accept this because he know
is proper to man. Must suffer to know truth about self; must
learn suffer with will. When suffering come to man must
make *intentional* suffering, must feel with all being; must
wish with such suffering that it will help make conscious;
help to understand."

"You have only physical suffering, suffering of body
because of pain in leg. This suffering also help if you know
how to use for self. But this is suffering like animal, not
important suffering. With other suffering, suffering in all
self, is possibility understand that all people suffer this way,
is possibility also understand how depend on Nature, on

other people, on everything, for help in life. Cannot live life alone. Aloneness—not loneliness, which is bad thing—but *aloneness* can be good thing for man, very necessary for life, but also necessary learn not live alone because real life depend on other human being and not just on self. Now, you still boy, cannot understand what I talk—but remember this thing; remember for time when you not thank me because I save life."

XXII

As that summer came to an end, many of the visiting Americans prepared to leave the Prieuré, probably never to see it again. They had been allowed to stay on even though the school had been reorganized, but it was not expected that they would be back the following year. It had again been decided, to my great relief, that we would not return to America that year, and I looked forward to the winter because Mr. Gurdjieff also was not planning to go away. Except for his occasional absences when it had been necessary for him to go to Paris on business, he had been in Fountainebleau constantly. His wife's condition, as he had predicted, was steadily worse all the time and we began to expect her imminent death.

In the several months that she had been confined to her room, I had only seen her once, when I had been sent to her room on some errand or other for Mr. Gurdjieff. The change in her had shocked and appalled me. She was incredibly thin, and although she did look at me with the semblance of a smile, even that small effort had seemed to exhaust her.

As the gardening and most of the outdoor projects came to an end for the winter, we began to make our usual preparations: drying fruit and vegetables, preparing meat for storage in large barrels in the cellars, cutting and splitting wood for all the stoves and fireplaces. Some of the floors of the school were closed off for the winter and some of the students even doubled up, sharing rooms to save on fuel. With the diminished number of students, most of our work was indoors as it had been the winter before; most of the available manpower was needed for general housekeeping and in the kitchens, stables and the concierge.

The one event that loomed enticingly ahead of us, as the fall came to an end, was Christmas. It would be the first Christmas I had spent at the Prieuré when Mr. Gurdjieff was also there, and we had heard many stories about the elaborate Christmas ceremonies—there were always two celebrations, one for the "English" calendar and one for the "Russian" calendar which came two weeks later—and there

would also be two New Years to celebrate as well as
Gurdjieff's birthday which was, appropriately, on the first
day of January by one or the other of these two calendars.

As the time approached, we began to make elaborate
preparations. Various traditional holiday candies were
made, cakes were baked and stored, and all the children
were allowed to help in the preparation of what were called
"guest presents", usually gaily coloured paper sacks of
candies to be hung on the Christmas tree. The tree itself
was huge. We cut it in the forest on the grounds of the
Prieuré and it was set up in the main salon, so tall that it
touched the very high ceiling. A day or so before Christmas,
everyone helped with the trimming of the tree, which
consisted mostly of hanging presents on the tree and also
decorating it with hundreds of candles. A special, long pole
was cut, to stand by the tree, to be used to put out any
candles that threatened to set the tree on fire.

It was late on Christmas eve afternoon by the time that
all the preparations had been made, and there was to be a
feast that evening, after which everyone would join together
in the salon for the distribution of presents, sometime that
night. It was beginning to get dark when Mr. Gurdjieff sent
for me. He talked to me about Christmas, asked me about
previous Christmases in America and how I felt about that
holiday, and when I had given him the expected answers,
told me that, unfortunately, it was always necessary for
some people to work on holidays in order that the others
should be able to enjoy themselves. He mentioned the people
who would be working in the kitchens, waiting on tables,
cleaning up, and so forth, and then he said that someone
would also, of course, have to be on duty at the concierge
that evening. He was expecting a long distance telephone
call and there would have to be someone there to answer it.
He had chosen me because he knew that I could be trusted;
also I spoke English, French and enough Russian to be able
to deal with any telephone call that might come.

I was thunderstruck and could hardly believe what I was
hearing. I could not remember ever having looked forward
to any single celebration as I had looked forward to that one.

He saw the disappointment in my face, of course, but said simply that while I would not be able to participate in the general festivities that night, I could look forward to Christmas that much longer, as I would get my presents on the following day. There was obviously no way in which I felt I could get out of this assigned duty, and I left him with a heavy heart. I had my supper early, in the kitchen, and then reported to relieve whomever had been assigned to the concierge that particular day. Normally, no one was on duty in the concierge at night. A Russian family lived on the upper floor of the building and answered the telephone or unlocked the gate on the few occasions when it might be necessary.

It had snowed the day before, and the front courtyard, between the concierge house and the main building, was covered with snow, glistening white, and lighted by the brilliant lamps in the long corridor and the main salon, both of which faced the courtyard. It was dark when I reported for duty, and I sat glumly, filled with self-pity, inside the small concierge house, staring at the lights of the big house. There was no activity there now, the rest of the students, at this time, would be about to go in to dinner.

It seemed an interminable time before I began to see people filing into the big salon. Someone began to light the candles on the tree, and I was unable to contain myself. I left the door to the concierge open, and approached as close to the main house as I could and still be reasonably certain that I would be able to hear the telephone if it should ring. It was very cold—also I was uncertain about just how far away I would be able to hear the telephone bell—and from time to time, as the tree was being lighted, I would run back to the concierge to warm myself and to stare angrily at the telephone. I was praying for it to ring, so that I would be able to join the others. All it did was to stare back at me, stern and silent.

When the distribution of the presents began, starting with the smallest children, I was unable to control myself, and, forgetting all my responsibilities, I went right up to the windows of the main salon. I had not been there more than a minute when Gurdjieff's eye caught me and he stood up and strode across the salon. I left the window and, as if he had sent for me, went directly to the entrance of the château instead of back to the concierge. He arrived at the door at almost the same time as I did, and we stood, momentarily, looking at each other through the glass door. Then he opened it with a sudden, harsh movement. "Why not at concierge? Why you here?" he demanded angrily.

I made some half-tearful protest about having to be on duty when everyone else was celebrating Christmas, but he cut me short. "I tell you do this thing for me, and you not do. Impossible hear telephone from here, maybe ring now and you stand here and not hear. Go back." He had not raised his voice, but there was no question that he was very angry with me. I went back to the concierge, hurt and overflowing with self-pity, determined that I would not leave my post again, no matter what might happen.

It must have been close to midnight when the family who lived on the upper floor returned and I was allowed to leave for the night. I went back to my room, hating Gurdjieff, hating the Prieuré, and by this time almost feeling proud of my "sacrifice" for him. I vowed that I would never mention that evening to him or to anyone else; also, that Christmas would never mean anything to me again. I expected, however, that something would be done for me the following day, that Gurdjieff would explain it to me, or in some way "make it up to me". I still fancied myself as a sort of "favourite" because of my work in his rooms—my special position.

The following day, to my further chagrin, I was assigned to work in the kitchen, since they would need extra help; I would have enough time off to clean his rooms, and would be able to deliver coffee to him at any time he might want it. I saw him several times, briefly, during the day, but always with other people, and no reference was made to the previous evening. At some point during the afternoon, someone, who said they had been delegated by Gurdjieff, gave me some Christmas presents, small things plus a copy of Jules Verne's *Twenty Thousand Leagues Under the Sea;*

and that was the end of Christmas, except for the interminable waiting on table that night at the Christmas dinner for all the students and various guests. Since I was, this time, not alone as a waiter, I was unable to feel that I had, once again, been singled out or "punished" as I felt I had been the night before.

While Gurdjieff never at any time made any reference to that evening, it did mark a change in my relationship with him. He no longer spoke to me as if I were a child, and my private "lessons" came to an end; nothing was said about this by Gurdjieff, and I felt too intimidated to bring up the question of the lessons. Even though there had been no telephone call of any kind on Christmas eve, I had a lurking suspicion that there might well have been one during one of the periods when I had stayed away from the concierge house, and it preyed on my conscience. Even if there had not been a telephone call at all, I knew that I had "failed" in the duty that had been assigned to me, and I could not forget it for a long time.

XXIII

VERY EARLY ONE spring morning, I awakened while it was still dark, with only the very faint light of the sun beginning to be visible on the horizon. Something troubled me that morning, but I could not imagine what it was; I had a vague feeling of restlessness, a sensation that something unusual was happening. In spite of my usual, lazy, comfortable habit of staying in bed until the very last moment—which was about six o'clock—I got up with the dawn and went down to the still-silent, cold kitchens. As much for my comfort as to help whomever was assigned to kitchen-boy duty that day, I began to build the fire in the big iron cook-stove, and while I was stoking it with coke, my buzzer rang (it rang simultaneously in my room and in the kitchen). It was early for Gurdjieff, but the ring fitted my sense of uneasiness, and I raced to his room. He was standing in the open doorway to the room, Philos at his side, and he looked at me urgently. "Go bring Dr. Schernvall right away," he commanded, and I turned to leave, but he stopped me, saying: "Madame Ostrovsky is dead. Better tell."

I raced out of the building, and ran to the house where Dr. Schernvall lived; a small house, (not far from the chicken yard), which was named, probably by the French years before, "Paradou". Dr. and Mme. Schernvall, together with their young son, Nikolai, lived on the top floor of this building. The rest of the building housed Mr. Gurdjieff's brother, Dmitri, and his wife and four daughters. I awakened the Schernvalls and told them the news. Mme. Schernvall burst into tears, and the doctor began to dress hastily, and told me to go back and tell Mr. Gurdjieff that he was on his way.

When I got back to the main house, Mr. Gurdjieff was not in his room, so I went down the long hall to the opposite end of the building and knocked, timidly, on the door of Madame Ostrovsky's room. Mr. Gurdjieff came to the door, and I told him the doctor was on his way. He looked impassive, very tired, and very pale. He told me to wait near his room and tell the doctor where he was. The doctor appeared a few

minutes later and I directed him to Mme. Ostrovsky's room.
He had only been there a few minutes when Mr. Gurdjieff
came out of the room. I was standing in the corridor,
undecided, not knowing whether to wait for him or not. He
looked at me without surprise and then asked me if I had
the key to his room. I said that I did, and he said that I was
not to come in and also that I was not to let anyone else in
the room until he sent for me. Then, followed by Philos, he
went down the long hall to his room, but did not allow
Philos to go in with him. The dog, looking angrily at me,
settled himself against the door as Mr. Gurdjieff locked it,
and growled at me for the first time.

It was a long, sad day. We all performed our assigned
tasks but a heavy cloud of sorrow hung over the school. It
was one of the first real spring days that year, and even the
sunshine and the unaccustomed warmth of the day seemed
inappropriate. All our work was done in a hushed silence;
people spoke to each other in whispers, and an air of
uncertainty spread through all the buildings. Presumably,
the necessary arrangements for the funeral were being
handled by someone, Dr. Schernvall, or Madame de Hartmann, but most of us were unaware of them. Everyone
waited for Mr. Gurdjieff to appear, but there was no sign of
life from his room, he had not had breakfast, did not ring for
lunch or for dinner, or for coffee at any time during the
entire day.

The following day, in the morning, Madame de Hartmann
sent for me and said that she had knocked on Mr.
Gurdjieff's door and had received no answer and asked me
to give her my key. I said I could not give it to her and told
her what Mr. Gurdjieff's instructions had been. She did not
argue with me, but said that she was worried because they
were going to move Madame Ostrovsky's body to the study-
house where it would remain overnight until the funeral the
following day; she thought that Mr. Gurdjieff should know
about this, but in view of what he had told me she decided
that she should not disturb him.

Late that afternoon, when there had still been no sign
from Mr. Gurdjieff, I was sent for again. This time, Mme. de

Hartmann said she would have to have the key. The Archbishop, presumably from the Greek Orthodox Church in Paris, had arrived, and Mr. Gurdjieff would have to be notified. After an inner struggle with myself, I finally gave in. The Archbishop's appearance was almost as forbidding as Gurdjieff's could be at times, and I could not stand up against his apparent importance.

A short while later, she found me again. She said that even with the key she was unable to get into the room. Philos would not let her come close enough to the door to get the key in the lock; that I would have to go, since Philos knew me well, and tell Mr. Gurdjieff that the Archbishop had arrived and must see him. Resigned and fearful of the consequences, I went up to his room. Philos looked at me without friendliness when I approached. I had tried to feed him the day before and also that morning, but he had refused to eat or even to drink water. Now, he watched me as I got the key out of my pocket, and seemed to decide that he would allow me to pass. He did not move, but as I opened the door he did allow me to step over him into the room.

Mr. Gurdjieff was sitting in a chair in his room—the first time I had ever seen him sitting in anything other than the bed—and looked at me without surprise. "Philos let you in?" he asked.

I nodded, and said that I was sorry to disturb him and that I had not forgotten his instructions but that the Archbishop had arrived and that Madame de Hartmann . . . He interrupted me with a wave of his hand. "Is all right," he said quietly, "must see Archbishop." Then he sighed, stood up, and said: "What day today?"

I told him that it was Saturday and he asked me if his brother, who was in charge of the fires at the Turkish bath, was preparing for the baths as usual. I said that I did not know, but that I would find out. He told me not to let him know, simply to tell Dmitri to have the baths ready as usual, and also to tell the cook that he would be down for dinner that night and that he wanted a very special meal to honour the Archbishop. Then he told me to feed Philos. I said that I had tried to feed him but that he had refused to eat. Gurdjieff smiled "When I leave room, will eat. You feed again." Then he left the room, walking slowly and thoughtfully down the stairs.

This was my first experience with death and while Gurdjieff had changed—he seemed unusually pensive and extremely tired—more so than I had ever seen him—he did not fit my preconceived notions of grief. There were no manifestations of sorrow, no tears, just an unusual heaviness about him, as if it required great effort for him to move.

XXIV

THE TURKISH BATH consisted of three rooms, and a small
furnace room in which Mr. Gurdjieff's brother, Dmitri,
stoked the fires. The first room, into which one entered, was
for dressing and undressing; the second room was a large,
circular room, equipped with a shower and several water
faucets, benches along all the walls, and a massage table in
the centre of the room; the third room was the steam-room,
with wooden benches on several levels.

In the first room there were two long rows of benches
along one side of the room and opposite them a large, higher
bench where Mr. Gurdjieff always sat, facing and looking
down on the other men. Because of the number of men at
the Prieuré the first summer I was there, Mr. Gurdjieff had
told Tom and me to climb up on his bench behind him,
where we would sit, peering over his shoulders at the
assembled company. Any "important" guests always sat
directly in front of him. Now, even though the baths were no
longer crowded since there were not as many students at the
Prieuré since the reorganization of the school, Tom and I
still occupied our places behind Mr. Gurdjieff; this had
become a part of the ritual connected with the Saturday
bathing.

Once we had all undressed, it was customary to spend
about half an hour, most of the men smoking and talking,
while Gurdjieff urged them on to tell him stories; the
stories, as at the swimming pool, were generally ribald or
off-colour, at his insistence. Inevitably, before we proceeded
to the steam-room, he would tell any newcomers a long,
involved story about his exalted position as the head of the
Prieuré, and founder of the Institute, and the story always
included references to Tom and me as his "Cherubim" and
"Seraphim".

Conventionally, because of my preconceptions about
death, and since Mme. Ostrovsky had died only about
thirty-six hours previously, I expected the ritual of the bath
that particular Saturday night to be a mournful and
lugubrious one. I could not have been more mistaken. When

I arrived at the bath that evening, somewhat later than most of the others, I found everyone still wearing their underwear and Mr. Gurdjieff and the Archbishop were involved in a lengthy argument about the problem of undressing. The Archbishop insisted that he could not take a Turkish bath with no covering of any kind, and refused to participate in the bath if the other men were to be completely naked. The argument must have gone on for about fifteen minutes after I arrived, and Gurdjieff seemed to be enjoying it immensely. He made numerous references to the Scriptures, and generally poked fun at the Archbishop's "false modesty". The Archbishop remained adamant, and someone was despatched back to the main house to find something we could all wear. Apparently, the problem had come up before, since the messenger returned with a large number of muslin breech-cloths which had been unearthed somewhere. We were all instructed to wear them, and to undress as modestly as possible. When we finally went into the steam - room, feeling uncomfortable and embarrassed in our unaccustomed attire, Gurdjieff, as if he now had the Archbishop at his mercy, gradually removed his breech-cloth, and one by one the rest of us did the same. The Archbishop made no further comments, but stubbornly kept his breech-cloth around his waist.

When we left the steam-room and went into the middle room to wash, Mr. Gurdjieff again directed a long harangue at the Archbishop. He said that not only was this partial clothing a form of false modesty but that it was psychologically and physically harmful; that ancient civilizations were aware that the most important cleansing rituals had to do with the so-called "private parts" of the body, which could not be properly cleaned if any garment was worn over them, and that, in fact, many religious ceremonies in former civilizations had stressed such cleanliness as a part of their religious and sacred rites. The result was a compromise: the Archbishop did not object to his arguments and agreed that we could do as we wished, but that he would not, and he did not, remove his covering.

After the bath, the argument continued in the first room,

the dressing-room, during the "cooling-off" period which also lasted for about half an hour; Gurdjieff was determined about not venturing into the night air after a steam bath. A cold shower was essential, but cold air was forbidden. In the course of the discussion in the dressing-room, Mr. Gurdjieff brought up the question of funerals and said that one important measure of respect even for the dead was to attend their obsequies fully cleansed, in mind and body. His tone, which had been ribald in the beginning, serious in the washing room, had become conciliatory and persuasive and he reiterated that he had in no way intended to show disrespect to the Archbishop.

Whatever the differences between them, they apparently respected one another; at dinner, which was almost a banquet, the Archbishop turned out to be a convivial and well-mannered hard drinker, which pleased Mr. Gurdjieff, and they seemed to enjoy one another's company.

* * *

After dinner, although it was very late by that time, Mr. Gurdjieff had everyone assemble in the main salon and told us a long story about funeral customs in various civilizations. He said that since Mme. Ostrovsky wished it, she would have a proper funeral, as decreed by her Church, but he added that other customs which had existed in great civilizations in the distant past, civilizations that were literally unknown to modern man, were pertinent and important. He described one such funeral rite where it was the prevailing custom for all of the relatives and friends of the deceased to gather together for three days after the death of an individual. During this period they thought of, and told the assembled company, everything that had been considered an evil or harmful act—in short, a sin—that had been committed by the deceased during his or her lifetime; the purpose of this being to create opposition which would force the soul to fight its way out of the body of the deceased and make its way to another world.

During the funeral the following day, Mr. Gurdjieff remained silent and withdrawn from the rest of us, as if only his body were actually present among the mourners.

He only intervened at one point in the ceremonies, at the moment when the body was to be removed from the study-house and placed on the hearse. At that moment, with the pall-bearers assembled, a woman who had been very close to his wife threw herself on the coffin, hysterically, literally wailing and sobbing with grief. Gurdjieff went over to her and removed her from the coffin, speaking to her quietly, and the funeral proceeded. We followed the coffin to the cemetery, on foot, and each one of us threw a small handful of earth on the coffin when it had been lowered into the open pit near the grave of his mother. After the services, Mr. Gurdjieff and all the rest of us paid our silent respects at the graves of his mother and of Katherine Mansfield, who was also buried there.

XXV

During the time of Mme. Ostrovsky's illness and Mr. Gurdjieff's daily sessions with her, one person, who had been a close friend of his wife for many years, seriously objected to what Mr. Gurdjieff was doing; her argument was that Mr. Gurdjieff was prolonging his wife's sufferings interminably and that this could not possibly serve any worthy or useful purpose—no matter what he had said about it. This woman was Mme. Schernvall, the doctor's wife, and her anger against Mr. Gurdjieff had reached such a pitch that, while she did continue to live at the Prieuré, she never appeared in his presence and refused to speak to him for several months. She would argue her case against him to anyone who happened to be within earshot, and even once told me a long story to illustrate his perfidy.

According to her, she and her husband, the doctor, were two of the original group who had come with Gurdjieff from Russia some years before. We had heard about the incredible difficulties they had encountered escaping the various forces involved in the Russian revolution and how they had finally made their way to Europe through Constantinople. One of the things which Madame Schernvall now brought up against Mr. Gurdjieff, as proof of his unreliability and even of his evil nature, was that it was largely thanks to her that they had finally been able to make their escape. Apparently, by the time they had reached Constantinople they were entirely out of funds and Mme. Schernvall made it possible for them to continue to Europe by lending a pair of very valuable earrings to Mr. Gurdjieff, which enabled them to hire a boat and cross the Black Sea. Even Madame Schernvall admitted, however, that she had not offered the earrings spontaneously. Mr. Gurdjieff had known of their existence and, as a last resort, had asked her for them, promising that he would leave them in Constantinople in good hands and that he would, on his honour, return them to her someday—as soon as he could raise the necessary money to redeem them. Several years had passed and, even though Mr. Gurdjieff had, in the meantime, raised large amounts of money in the Unites States, she had never seen the earrings again. Not only was this proof of his lack of good intentions; in addition she always brought up the question of what he had done with the money he had raised —had he not, for instance, purchased all those bicycles with money that could have been used to buy back her jewels?

This story had been told to most of us at different times, and at the time of Mme. Ostrovsky's death I had completely forgotten it. A few weeks after the funeral, Gurdjieff asked me one day if I had seen Mme. Schernvall recently and inquired as to her health. He expressed his regret at the fact that he never saw her any more and said that it made his relations with the doctor very difficult, and that it was not a good situation. He gave me a long lecture about the vagaries of women and said that he had finally decided that it was up to him to make an effort to win back Mme. Schernvall's affection and her goodwill. He then handed me part of a chocolate bar, in a torn box, as if someone had already eaten the other half, and told me to take it to her. I was to tell her how he felt about her, how much he did respect her and value her friendship, and to say that this chocolate was an expression of his esteem for her.

I looked at the torn wrapping and thought, privately, that this was hardly the way to win back her friendship, but I had learned not to express such reactions. I took it from him and went to see her.

Before handing her the small package, I gave her his messages, quoting him as exactly as I could, which took some time, and then handed her the little, torn package. She had listened to me with obviously mixed emotions and by the time I handed her the package she was eager to receive it. When she saw it, however, her features assumed a look of disdain. She said that he was never serious about anything, and that he had forced me to give her this long, elaborate message just as a preliminary joke to giving her a half-eaten piece of chocolate, which she did not like in any case.

I then said that I was surprised because he had told me that she liked this particular brand of chocolate above anything else in the world. She gave me an odd look when I said this and then opened the package hastily. He had chosen the right messenger; I had so completely forgotten her tale about the jewels that I was as astonished as she when she found, of course, the earrings. She burst into tears, hugged me, became almost hysterical; she made up her face, put on the earrings, and then proceeded to tell me the entire story all over again, but this time with the significant difference that this was proof of what a wonderful man he was, and how she had always known that he would keep his promise to her. I was as surprised by her switch of feelings as I had been when I saw the earrings.

I went back to him, as he had instructed me, and told him the whole story in detail. He was greatly amused by it, laughed a great deal, and then told me, at least in part, his story. He said that her facts were correct, but that she had no conception of the difficulties he had experienced in trying to get the earrings back. He had "pawned" them for a very large sum of money to a trusted friend in Constantinople and when he had, finally, been able to return the money, together with the proper interest, he had learned that his friend was dead. It had taken him, from then on, several years of unflagging effort to located the jewels and to persuade the present owner, apparently a usurer, to return them for a sum far exceeding their value.

I could not help but blurt out my obvious reaction: Why had he done this? Were any jewels worth such a price, and, in addition, did Mme. Schernvall fail to realize that whatever the value of the jewels, the very lives of Gurdjieff's group at that time had probably depended on them?

He told me then that the value of the jewels was not an important element in the story. One reason he had redeemed them was because of his wife's friendship for Mme. Schernvall; that friendship could not be evaluated, and that it was necessary to do this for the sake of the memory of his wife. Further, he said that any man had an obligation to keep any promise that was made truthfully and solemnly, as he had made that particular promise. "I not do this for her only," he said, "also do for sake of my soul."

"You remember," he said then, "how I tell about good and evil in man—like right hand, left hand? In other sense, this also true of man and woman. Man is active, positive, good in Nature. Woman is passive, negative, evil. Not evil in your American sense like 'wrong', but very necessary evil; evil that make man good. Is like electric light—one wire passive or negative; other wire active, positive. Without such two elements not have light. If Mme. Schernvall not evil for me, perhaps I forget promise, serious promise, I make to her. So without her help, because she not let me forget what I promise, I not keep promise, not do good for my soul. When give back earrings I do good thing: good for me, for memory of wife, and good for Mme. Schernvall who now have great remorse in heart for bad things she say about me. This important lesson for you."

XXVI

Mr. Gurdjieff's relationship with me, although it continued in a surface sense to be the same, had undergone a definite change which I felt had begun with the previous Christmas. I continued to clean his rooms, bring him coffee, and do his errands, but the easy, affectionate feeling that had existed between us—almost like that of a father and son —seemed to be disappearing; it was as if he had set out to create a certain distance and reserve between us.

When he had talked to me before, whatever the subject of our conversations, he had often referred to the fact that I was still a child and that much of what he was saying was something that I could not, at the time, understand. But with the change, while he still talked to me frequently, his tone was more serious and he no longer referred to me as a boy. I felt that he was beginning to expect me to fend for myself, to use my own mind—that he was, in fact, urging me to grow up.

He often discussed human relations in general, the specific roles of male and female, and human destiny; as often as not these discussions were not directed to me exclusively, but to a group of which I was a member. He took pains to make it clear to us that whenever he addressed anyone on any subject in the hearing of others, it would or could be beneficial for everyone present to listen to what he was saying. Many of us had the feeling that when he addressed one individual he was often talking not so much to that person as to anyone in the group who might feel that the conversation was applicable to himself. We sometimes had the feeling that he was talking to a particular person through someone else; as if purposely not addressing one individual directly.

He came back to the theme of good and evil, active and passive, positive and negative, very frequently. I had been impressed with what he had said about Mme. Schernvall and himself in this regard when he had told me about the recovery of the earrings; it seemed to me to be a continuation of a theme on which he had spoken recurrently: the two-sided nature of man and the need to acquire or create a reconciling force. This force, in an exterior sense, had to be created in human relations between individuals; in an "interior" sense, it had to be acquired or created within an individual as part of his own development and growth.

One of the most important things about Gurdjieff's pronouncements, talks, lectures, or discursions (everyone had his own name for them), was the enormous sway he had over his listeners. His gestures, his manner of expressing himself, the incredible range of tone and dynamics in his voice, and his use of emotion, all seemed calculated to spell-bind his auditors; perhaps to mesmerize them to such an extent that they were unable to argue with him at the time. Unquestionably, however many questions might come to a listener's mind when Gurdjieff had finished speaking, a deep and lasting impression had always been made before such questions arose. Not only did we not forget what he said to us, it was usually impossible to forget what he had said, even if one wished to forget it.

Shortly after the earring episode with Mme. Schernvall, he brought up once again the question of men and women, their roles in life, and, as an additional element, the specific roles of the sexes in his work or, for that matter, in any religious or psychological work which had self-development and proper growth as an aim. I was surprised and puzzled then, and many times later when he spoke on the subject, by his reiteration of the fact that not only was his work "not for everyone" but that "women did not need it." He said that the nature of women was such that "self development" in his sense of the phrase was something that they could not achieve. Among other things, he said: "Nature of woman is very different from that of man. Woman is from ground, and only hope for her to arise to another stage of development— to go to Heaven as you say—is *with* man. Women already know everything, but such knowledge is of no use to her, in fact can almost be like poison to her, unless have man with her. Man have one thing that not exist in woman ever: what you call 'aspiration'. In life, man use this thing—this aspiration—for many things, all wrong for his life, but *must* use because have such need. Man—not woman—climb mountains, go under oceans, fly in air, because must do such thing. Impossible for him not to do; cannot resist this. Look at life around you: Man write music, man paint pictures, write books, all such things. Is way, he think, find Heaven for self."

When someone did object that the sciences and the arts were not, after all, exclusively confined to the world of the male, Gurdjieff laughed: "You ask question about woman artist, woman scientist. I tell you world all mixed up, and this true thing I say. True man and true woman not just one sex—not just male or female. Even you," he made a sweeping gesture covering all of us, "sometimes understand this because sometimes you surprised when you see man who feel thing like woman, or woman who act like man; or even when in self feel feelings proper to opposite sex.

"We all live in what we call universe, but this only very small solar system, smallest of many, many solar systems— even very unimportant place. For instance, in this solar system, people bi-sexual: necessary have two sexes for reproduction of kind—primitive method, which use part of a man's aspiration for creation of more people. Man who can learn how to achieve higher self—how go to proper Heaven —can use all this aspiration for development of self, for what you call immortality. In world as now exist, no man able do this: only possibility for immortality is reproduction. When man have children, then all of him not die when his body die.

"Not necessary for woman do work of man in world. If woman can find real man, then woman become real woman without necessity work. But, like I tell, world mixed up. Today in world real man not exist, so woman even try to become man, do man's work which is wrong for her nature."

XXVII

SHORTLY AFTER MADAME OSTROVKY'S death, the atmosphere at the Prieuré seemed to change; part of it was definitely due to her death (Gurdjieff, for example, was living with a woman who became pregnant a few months later); part of it was simply because I was, inevitably, growing up. Questions that had not occurred to me previously loomed in my mind. What was I doing in such a place, what was the purpose of the school, what sort of man, after all, was Gurdjieff?

I suppose that early adolescence is a "normal" time in which a child begins to evaluate his surroundings, his parents, the people around him. It was easy enough for me to answer my questions concerning why I was there: the aimless, haphazard series of events that had led me there was fresh in my mind. But, by this time, the question of whether or not I wanted to be there became a different one. Up to that time I had had no control over the course my life had taken; nor had it occurred to me that I could have had any influence in determining that course. At thirteen, I still had no voice and no power over my "destiny" or my future, but I did have questions about them.

In the course of the comings and goings of all types of people at the Prieuré—visitors, semi-permanent residents—there were always discussions about Gurdjieff, about the purpose and / or value of his work. There were a great many "students" who left the Prieuré under more or less violent emotional circumstances: sometimes because Gurdjieff did not want them there, sometimes because of their own attitudes and feelings about him as a man.

During the two years that I had been there, I had been aware of, and had certainly subscribed to, the feeling and the belief that Gurdjieff could do no wrong; that whatever he did was purposeful, necessary, important, "right". I had not, up to then, needed to make any decisions about him on my own. But a time came when I began to look at him against my own background, with my own unconsciously acquired values, and to make some attempt to evaluate the man, the students, the school. A great number of questions, mostly unanswerable, arose.

What was the power of this man whose word was law, who knew more than anyone else, who held absolute sway over his "disciples"? There was no question in my mind about my personal relationship to him. I loved him, he had taken the place of my parents and he had unquestioned authority over me and devoted loyalty and affection from me. Even so, it was obvious that much of his effect on me, and his power over me, was due to the feelings of others—generally feelings of reverence and respect—and to my natural desire to conform. On the other hand, my personal feelings of awe and respect were less important than my fear of him. The fear had become unquestionably genuine the more I came to know him.

It had been impressive, enlightening and even amusing to watch him, at close range, when he reduced people to a pulp, as he had done in the case of Mr. Orage, in my presence. But was it not also significant that Mr. Orage had left the Prieuré shortly after that and had not returned? I had been told that he was teaching the Gurdjieff "work" in New York since that time, and it may have been that whatever Gurdjieff had done to Mr. Orage had been necessary; but, finally, who was to determine that?

Gurdjieff himself was no help. One of the unforgettable things he had said, and he had repeated it many times, was that what he called the "good" and "evil" in man grew together, equally; that man's potentiality to become either an "angel" or a "devil" was always equal. While he had spoken, frequently, of the necessity to create or acquire a "reconciling force" within oneself in order to deal with the "positive" and "negative" or "good" and "evil" sides of one's nature, he had also stated that the struggle, or "war", was never-ending; that the more one learned, the more difficult life would, inevitably, become. The prospect seemed to be one of "the more you learn the harder it will get." When he was countered, occasionally, with protests against this rather grim outlook on the future, he seemed invariably to answer with the more or less irrefutable statement that we —individually, or as a group—were unable to think clearly,

were not sufficiently adult or grown-up to judge whether or
not this was a proper and realistic future for man; whereas,
he knew what he was talking about. I had no arguments
with which I could defend the charge of incompetency
against me; but I had no absolutely acceptable proof of his
competence, either. His force, magnetism, power, ability,
and even wisdom, were, perhaps, undeniable. But did the
combination of these attributes, or qualities, create, automatically, the quality of competent judgment?

It is a waste of time to argue or to do battle with people
who are convinced. The people who were interested in
Gurdjieff always ended up in one of two categories: they
were either for him or against him; they either stayed at the
Prieuré, or continued to attend his "groups" in Paris,
London, New York and elsewhere, because they were at
least reasonably convinced that he had some kind of an
answer; or else they left him and his "work" because they
were convinced that he was a charlatan, or a devil, or—more
simply—that he was wrong.

Given the goodwill of his auditors, he was incredibly
convincing. His presence and his physical magnetism were
undeniably and generally overwhelming. His logic — in
practical ways — was impossible to refute, and never
coloured or distorted by emotion; in that respect, in the
purely *ordinary* problems of life, there was no question but
that he played fair. He was a considerate and thoughtful
judge in dealing with questions or disputes which arose in
the course of running an establishment such as the Prieuré;
it would have been ridiculous, and illogical, to argue with
him or to call him unfair.

However, going back in my own mind at that age to such
things as my various experiences with Miss Madison, what
had he done to her? What was the effect on her when he
rewarded all those who had defied her orders? Why had he
put her in that position of authority? Of course, Miss
Madison was physically present as an answer to those
questions. She seemed to have become that much more a
follower, that much more a devoted disciple, and apparently
did not question what he had done to her. But was that, in

the long run, any answer? Was it, perhaps, merely proof
that Miss Madison was overpowered by his magnetism, his
positive force?

I had the feeling then—and I have no valid reason to
change that feeling or opinion almost forty years later—that
he was perhaps searching for some individual or some force
that could or would oppose him effectively. There were
certainly no such opponents at the Prieuré. Even at that
age, I began to have a certain contempt for the abject
devotion of his adherents or "disciples". They spoke of him
in hushed tones; when they did not understand a particular
statement he had made, or something he had done, they
blamed themselves, far too readily for my taste, for their
lack of insight; in short, they worshipped him. The atmosphere that is created, somehow, by a group of people who
"worship" an individual or a philosophy seemed then—and
still seems now—to carry the seed of its own destruction
with it; it certainly lends itself to ridicule. What was
perplexing to me was Gurdjieff's own ridicule of his more
convinced and devout followers (witness the case of the
ladies and the "famous old wine"). In my childlike, simple
way, I felt that he was likely to do anything at all—at the
expense of anyone—for "fun"; to see what, if anything, was
going to happen.

In my opinion he not only played games with his
students, but the games were always "loaded" in his favour;
he was playing against people he had called "sheep" to their
faces; people who, in addition, accepted the term without
protest. Among the devout there were a few who fenced with
him verbally, but, in the long run, they seemed to be the
ones who were the most "possessed" or "convinced"; daring
to joke with him became proof of a certain intimacy with
him—a privilege accorded to them because of their total
agreement with his ideas—and in no sense an indication of
rebellion. The rebellious did not stay at the Prieuré to
exchange banter, and they were not permitted to stay to
challenge or oppose him; the "philosophical dictatorship"
brooked no opposition.

What began to obsess me, at thirteen, was a serious and,

to me at least, a dangerous question. What was I dealing with? I did not mind the fact that he was perhaps making as much of a fool of me as he seemed to be making of others; I didn't know whether he was or not. But, if he was, I wanted to know why. I could not deny that it was amusing to me, as a child, to see Gurdjieff "expose" adults, to make fun of them, but did it serve any constructive purpose?

Even at that age I was somehow conscious that evil could, conceivably, produce good. When Gurdjieff would speak of "objective" morality and "subjective" morality, I was not left entirely in the dark. In the simplest sense it seemed to mean that custom governed subjective morality, whereas what Gurdjieff called "objective morality" was a matter of natural instinct and individual conscience. In discussing morality, he recommended living in accordance with the particular moral customs and habits of the society in which one lived—he was very fond of the phrase "When you live in Rome, live as the Romans do"—but he stressed the necessity of an individual, objective, personal "morality", based on conscience, rather than tradition, custom or law. Marriage was a good example of a subjective moral custom; objective-ly, neither nature nor individual morality required such a sacrament.

I did not feel especially confused when I learned that the title of Gurdjieff's first book was "Beelzebub's Tales to His Grandson" or "An Impartial, Objective Criticism of Man". The idea that the devil—or Beelzebub—was the critic did not appal me. When Gurdjieff stated that Christ, Buddha, Mohammed, and other such prophets, were "messengers from the gods" who had, finally, *failed,* I could accept the implicit theory that perhaps it was time to give the devil his chance. I did not, as an adolescent, have such a good opinion of the world that I found it difficult to accept Gurdjieff's verdict that it was "all mixed up" or "upside down" or, in my own translation of his terms, a general mess. But, if the mentioned prophets had, for some reason "failed", was there any assurance, then that Gurdjieff (or Beelzebub) was going to succeed?

Fail or succeed at what? I could accept the theory that

there was something "wrong" with humanity, but I resisted the statement, on the part of an individual, that he knew exactly what was "wrong". Also, acceptance is not conviction, and in order to discuss seriously a cure it seemed to me logical that one would have to be convinced that the illness existed. Was I, then, going to be forced to form an opinion about the "condition of man"—to make a diagnosis? I was not equipped to do so, but I was not averse to making an attempt in that direction. The only answer that I could find was, of course, no answer at all.

All these speculations led back, inevitably, to Gurdjieff, the man. When he prescribed an exercise, such as "self-observation", with the avowed aim of getting to "know oneself", I had no argument with him and he had the weight of all organized religion behind him as he had pointed out. Perhaps the difference lay in the particular method, and I was in no position to judge the merits of his methods. The aim, however, was not a new one.

If I was to accept the premise that man is inferior to nature—and I was in no position to deny it—then I was immediately forced to consider the possibility that Gurdjieff, being a man, did not necessarily have all the answers— assuming that there are any. His philosophy, as I understood it at that age, was unquestionably attractive. Was it anything more than that? All "mystical" ideas are attractive to the inquisitive for the perfectly simple reason that they are mystical or, in some way, mysterious.

Such questions are troubling; they can threaten the selfconfidence, the "raison-d'être", of a human being completely. My doubts and questions were like a nest of concentric circles—the very reason for life itself, for human existence, seemed to boil down to whether or not I could or would accept Gurdjieff as the man who held the key. The simple fact of living in his presence had made it impossible for me to retreat (which is not necessarily the proper word) into any "belief" or "faith" in any other existing religion or theory of life. I was attracted by his repudiation of organized activity—whether religious, philosophical, or even practical, I was further attracted by his seeming support of individual truth, or action. But what was terrifying was the inevitable concept of the uselessness of human life—individual or collective. The story of the acorns on the oak tree had impressed me as a child. The concept of human life as simply another form of organism—which might or might not develop — was new to me. But was Gurdjieff's work, actually, the proper means by which to grow into an "oak"? Was I, finally, dealing with the devil? Whoever he was, I liked him; I was certainly smitten with him. Even so, it remains significant that my only serious attempt at suicide occurred that year. I was tortured by the questions that did not cease to torment me—tortured to the point that I could not continue to ask them of myself, relentlessly, without finding some sort of answer. Obviously, to me, the only person who *might* have the answer was Gurdjieff himself, and since he was also, in all probability, the villain, I could not ask him directly. What I did was to drink a small bottle of wood alcohol. On the face of it, this was not a very determined effort, but I intended it seriously—the bottle was marked "Poison" and I believed it. The results of the attempt were not particularly dramatic. I became sick to my stomach, and did not even have to take an emetic.

The attempt was made at night, and when I saw Gurdjieff the following morning, when bringing him his customary coffee, he took one quick look at me and asked me what was wrong. I told him what I had done and also, rather shame-facedly, about my immediate physical reaction of sickness. At that moment I no longer cared whether he was the devil or not. His only comment was that in order to commit suicide successfully the effort had to be whole-hearted. He did not ask me why I had done it, and I remember having the curious sensation that as we faced each other that morning we were being completely, dispassionately honest with one another.

XXVIII

My questions and doubts about the Prieuré and Mr. Gurdjieff, obsessive as they had been for a short time, subsided rapidly. I was not concerned about this, but relieved to slip back into the day-to-day working routine, as if a great load had been removed from my shoulders.

The only obvious changes in the general life at the Prieuré after Madame Ostrovsky's death were that Gurdjieff began to take frequent trips for periods of several days or even as much as two weeks at a time; and that when he was in residence there were usually a great many more guests on weekends. When he would go on a trip, he would often take as many as five or six people with him, and almost everyone anticipated the possibility of being selected to accompany him. It became a kind of *cachet* to have been on a journey to Vichy or Évian or any of the popular resorts that he liked to visit. Gurdjieff's given reason for these trips was that he needed to travel and to see more people because of his writing, which he usually did now in cafés and restaurants, often sitting in the centre of a group of people, drinking coffee and writing interminably. Many of the people who went with him were actively engaged in the translation of his writings into various languages; in addition, he liked to travel with an entourage.

I saw less of him at this time, mostly because of his more frequent absences, but even when he was at the Prieuré I did not have as much private contact with him as I had had in the past. On the whole, I was glad of this, for although my questions had subsided in the sense that they were no longer at the forefront of my mind, my fear of him and a general lurking suspicion of his motives had at least partially replaced my personal and, up to then, rather complete devotion to him. I continued, however, to have either an accidental or perhaps in some way purposeful series of experiences with him.

One day when he was expected to return from one of his journeys, I was working in the kitchen, helping in the preparation of one of the usual, elaborate dinners which were always served on the days he returned. As I was moving a large kettle full of boiling water in order to stoke the fires, I somehow spilled it on me, mainly on my entire right arm. I dropped the kettle, howling with pain, and Madame Schernvall, the cook of the day, screamed for help and sent someone for the doctor. Instead of the doctor, Gurdjieff appeared, completely unexpectedly, in the kitchen. He had arrived much earlier than we had anticipated. Without a word, and not even seeming to listen to Madame Schernvall's almost hysterical explanation of what had happened, he strode over to me, pulled me over to the stove, removed the iron rings and exposed the red-hot fire. He then seized my burned arm and held it, with all his force, over the open fire—probably not for more than a few seconds, although it seemed an eternity to me. When he released me, he said very seriously and calmly that the proper way to fight fire was with fire. "This way," he said, "you not have scar on arm. Burn already gone."

I was amazed and very much impressed—not only with the painful treatment, but also because of his completely unexpected appearance at just that moment. Inevitably, it did seem to be one of those fateful occurrences which I could not simply charge off to coincidence. Madame Schernvall told me, after he had left, that she had had a similar experience with him several years before, and knew that what he had done to me was the proper treatment for a burn, but that she would never have had the force or the courage to do it. We both remained overawed for the rest of the day and Madame Schernvall certainly encouraged my temptation to feel that his appearance at that time had been in some way supernatural. We continued to talk about it for several days, mostly because, as he had predicted, there was not only no scar, there was no pain and no physical evidence of any burn at all.

Gurdjieff's treatment of me from then on took a different form, and, in spite of the lack of private, personal contact with him, it did seem to me that he often singled me out for no obvious reasons.

A few weeks after the "burn cure" we were again

preparing a large dinner as there were to be a great many guests that evening. The principal guest was the gendarme who had discovered Gurdjieff after his automobile accident a few summers before. When he arrived, he was installed in one of the sumptuous guest rooms on the same floor as Gurdjieff's room, and was then introduced to all of us. Gurdjieff praised him and told us how much he, and all of us, owed to this man. If it had not been for him, he, Gurdjieff, might easily be dead, and so on. The gendarme, in turn, told his version of the story; and he was greatly impressed with Gurdjieff as a person because of two specific things that had happened. The first was his discovery of Gurdjieff. He had been riding home at night, going off duty, when he had come upon the wrecked automobile, and had of course stopped to investigate the accident. The amazing thing about it was that, although seriously injured, Gurdjieff had somehow managed, apparently in a state of shock, to get out of the car, take a pillow and blanket from the car and lie down at the side of the road—the pillow under his head, and well covered with the blanket. Considering his injuries, the gendarme could not — to this day — bring himself to believe that Gurdjieff had done all this without assistance.

The second thing that had amazed him was that, although it had taken him almost two years after his recovery, Gurdjieff had managed to search him out, find him, and finally persuade him to come to the Prieuré as his guest for the weekend. There was, apparently, some reason for astonishment in this connection, although I never fully understood it; the records did not give the gendarme's name or something of the sort. Whatever it was, it had taken a great deal of effort and persistence in this case, and the gendarme was almost unable to accept the fact that someone had gone to that much trouble to thank him for what was, after all, only the normal performance of his duty.

The gendarme was seated at a place of honour at the table and Gurdjieff, as the meal began, poured the usual glasses of Armagnac for everyone (customarily, it was necessary—it was one of his rules—to drink a great number of toasts during a meal, and he always filled the glasses himself), including the gendarme. But the gendarme balked. His respect and friendship for Mr. Gurdjieff were boundless, as he said, but he was totally unable to drink strong liquor —the most he ever drank was an occasional glass of wine.

Gurdjieff was always persistent when people objected to drinking these strong toasts with him, but in this case he was adamant. He argued, pleaded, even begged the gendarme to drink with him, and the gendarme categorically, and as politely as possible, refused. Finally, Gurdjieff said that the dinner could not proceed without the participation of the gendarme in these toasts, and, as if trying another tack with him, said that any man worth his salt had not only to be able to drink such toasts, but must actually drink them. He waved away the man's protests and said that he would show him that the liquor would not have any bad effects. "This not usual place," he said, meaning the Prieuré, "here is such good-will that anyone can drink without bad effects. Even children can drink here." To prove this point, he called me over to him—I was serving at the table that night.

When I was standing next to him, he poured a water glass full of Armagnac, and told me in Russian to drink it down at one gulp. I did, although I had never tasted such strong liquor before. When I had swallowed it, the tears came to my eyes, and my throat was burning, but I managed to get to the kitchen where the horrified cook told me to eat bread rapidly to ease my throat. The cook was his sister-in-law and was often highly critical of him. She told me firmly that only a mad man would force a child to drink "that stuff" and then sent me back to my duties as waiter. The liquor had such an immediate effect on me that, while I did continue to pass various dishes to the assembled guests, I only did so by staggering around the table and shoving the platters at them, feeling giddy and completely unconcerned. I had never experienced such a sense of carefree well-being in my life. I thought it was particularly comical when Gurdjieff, each time I arrived near him, would direct the attention to me and my complete sobriety. I remember having a strange feeling of separateness as if I had actually departed from the confines of my own body and was able to watch myself, as if from a distance, tottering gaily around the table with the heavy platters in my hands. I was especially pleased when the gendarme, apparently thanks to me, gave in and drank several toasts with Mr. Gurdjieff and the other guests. I felt that it was all thanks to me and congratulated myself on some great, but not very well defined, accomplishment.

Even so, and in spite of my high spirits, the dinner seemed interminable, and I was greatly relieved when I was able to stagger off to my bed at a very late hour. It seemed to me that I had only been asleep for a few minutes when I heard the insistent ring of my buzzer. I was amazed to see that it was daylight, and managed to get into my clothes and answer the inevitable coffee summons. Gurdjieff laughed at me when I appeared in his room, and asked me how I felt. I said that I supposed that I was still drunk and described to him the way I had felt the night before. He nodded sagely, and told me that the liquor had produced a very interesting state in me, and that if I could achieve that kind of self-awareness when sober, it could be a very important accomplishment. Then he thanked me for my part in his experiment with the gendarme and added that he had picked me, especially, because it was very important that I should learn how to drink, and to learn at my age what the effects of liquor could be. "In future, when drunk," he said, "try to see self this same way as you saw last night. This can be very good exercise for you, will also help to not get drunk."

XXIX

Lᴀᴛᴇ ᴛʜᴀᴛ ꜱᴜᴍᴍᴇʀ, Tom and I were chosen to be members of the party of five or six who were to accompany Mr. Gurdjieff on his next trip away from the Prieuré. We were among the first children to be selected for this honour and I looked forward to the day of our departure with anticipation and enthusiasm.

It was not until we were actually on the road that Gurdjieff informed us that our destination was Vichy, where he planned to stay for several days and write. Within the first hour or two, I learned quickly enough that travelling with Gurdjieff was not an ordinary experience. Although we were not, as far as I knew, in any hurry to reach our destination, he drove his car as if possessed. We would tear along the roads at a high rate of speed for a few hours, then he would stop abruptly to spend two or three hours at a café in a small town, where he would write incessantly; or we might stop somewhere in the country, along the side of the road, and unload great hampers of food and drink, blankets and pillows, and have a leisurely picnic after which everyone would take a nap.

Short of any actual mechanical breakdown, we seemed to have an unusual number of unnecessary experiences on the road. Someone—it might be me, or any one of the party— would be delegated to sit next to Gurdjieff with an open map with which to guide him. He would start off, having told the map reader which road he wished to take, and would then rapidly accelerate to top speed. The map reader's job was to watch the road signs and tell him when to turn off and otherwise give him directions. Invariably, he would manage to speed up before reaching any intersection, and almost equally invariably would fail to make a proper turn. Since he refused to go back, it was then necessary to guide him on whatever road we had happened on in the general direction of our destination. Inevitably, there would be long arguments, usually beginning with his cursing of whomever happened to be reading the map at the time, and finally joined in by everyone. There seemed to be a purpose in this,

since it happened regularly no matter who was seated next
to him as guide, and I could only ascribe it to his desire to
keep everyone stirred up and alert.

Although we carried two spare wheels and tyres with us
—one on each running board—we could have used several
more. Even in those days, changing a wheel after a flat tyre
was not a very complicated operation. With Gurdjieff,
however, it seemed to become an engineering problem.
When a tyre did go flat, and this happened often, everyone
would descend from the car, different jobs would be assigned
to the various members of the group—one would be in
charge of the jack, another in charge of the removal of the
spare tyre, another to remove the wheel that had to be
changed. All of these jobs were then supervised by Gurdjieff
personally, usually in conference with everyone who was not
actually doing something. All work would stop from time to
time and we would have long conferences about whether the
jack would support the car at that particular angle on the
road, which was the best way to remove the lugs from the
wheel, and so on. Since Gurdjieff would never take time to
have a tyre repaired at a gas station, once the two good
spares had been used up, it became a question of not merely
changing a wheel, but actually removing the tyre, repairing
it, and replacing it on the wheel. On this particular trip, we
had enough men to do this, but what with the arguments
and conferences and a good deal of recrimination about why
the tyres had not been repaired, this process took hours, and
most of this time the entire group, with the women
appropriately dressed in long dresses, would stand around
the car in a huddle, advising and instructing. These groups
of people gave passing motorists the impression that some
great misfortune had overtaken us and they would frequently stop their cars to offer help, so that sometimes we would
be joined by another large group which would also contribute advice, consolation, and sometimes even physical help.

In addition to the hazards of tyre repairs and finding
ourselves almost constantly on the wrong road, there was no
way that Gurdjieff could be induced to stop for gasoline.
Whatever the gas gauge might read, he would insist that we

could not possibly be out of gas until the inevitable moment when the motor would begin to cough and splutter and, although he would curse it loudly, the car would stop. Since he was rarely on the proper side of the road, it would then be necessary for everyone to get out of the car and push it to one side of the road while some individual would be selected to either walk or hitch-hike to the nearest gas station and bring back a mechanic. Gurdjieff insisted on the mechanic because he was positive that there was something wrong with the car; he could not have done anything so simple as run out of gas. These delays were a great annoyance to everyone except Mr. Gurdjieff who, once someone had gone in search of help, would settle himself comfortably at the side of the road, or perhaps remain in the car, depending upon how he felt at the moment, and write furiously in his notebooks, muttering to himself and licking the point of one of his many pencils.

Gurdjieff also seemed to attract obstacles. If we were not out of gas or on the wrong road, we would manage to run into a herd of cows or a flock of sheep or goats. Gurdjieff would follow such animals along the road, sometimes nudging them with the bumper of the car, and always leaning out of the driver's side hurling imprecations at them. We ran into a herd of cattle during one of my tours of duty as map reader, and this time, to my surprise and great pleasure, as he cursed at and nudged one of the slower cows in the herd, the cow stopped dead in front of the car, stared at him balefully, raised her tail and showered the hood of the car with a stream of liquid manure. Gurdjieff also seemed to think of this as being especially hilarious and we promptly stopped to rest at the side of the road so that he could do some more writing while the rest of us did what we could to clean up the automobile.

Another habit of Gurdjieff's which complicated these voyages was that, having made numerous stops to eat, rest, write, and so forth, during the day, he would never stop driving at night until so late that most of the inns or hotels would be closed by the time he decided that he needed to eat or sleep. This always meant that one of the group—we all loathed this duty—would have to get out of the car, and beat on the door of some country inn until we could raise the proprietor, and, frequently, the entire town. Presumably for the sole purpose of creating additional confusion, once the owner of some inn or hotel had been awakened, Gurdjieff would lean out from the parked car, shouting instructions— usually in Russian—about the number of rooms and meals that would be necessary and any other instructions that might come to his mind. Then, while his companions unloaded mountains of luggage, he would usually engage in long, complicated excuses to whomever had been awakened, deploring in execrable French, the necessity of having awakened them and the inefficiency of his travelling companions, and so forth, with the result that the proprie- tress—it was nearly always a woman on such occasions— was completely charmed with him and would look at the rest of us with loathing as she served an excellent meal. The meal, of course, would go on interminably with long toasts to everyone present, especially the owners of the inn, plus additional toasts to the quality of the food, the magnificence of the location, or anything else that struck his fancy.

Although I thought the journey would never come to an end, we did manage to reach Vichy after a few days of this unusual manner of travelling. We did not arrive, of course, until very late at night, and again had to awaken a great many of the personnel at one of the big resort hotels, who, at first, informed us that they had no room. Gurdjieff inter- vened in these arrangements, however, and convinced the manager that his visit was of extreme importance. One of the reasons he gave was that he was the Headmaster of a very special school for wealthy Americans, and he produced Tom and me, both very sleepy, as proof. With a perfectly straight face, I was introduced as Mr. Ford, the son of the famous Henry Ford, and Tom was introduced as Mr. Rockefeller, the son of the equally famous John D. Rockefel- ler. As I looked at the manager, I did not feel that he was swallowing this tale completely, but he managed (he was obviously tired, too) to smile and look at the two of us with deference. The one problem that remained to be settled was that there were not, in spite of Mr. Gurdjieff's possible importance, enough rooms for all of us. Gurdjieff considered this information seriously and finally devised some way in which we could all be accommodated without any improper mingling of the sexes, into the rooms that were available. Mr. Ford, or not, I ended up sleeping in his bathroom, in the bathtub. I had only just climbed into the tub, exhausted, with a blanket, when someone appeared with a cot that was squeezed into a narrow space in the bathroom. I then moved into the cot, whereupon Mr. Gurdjieff, greatly exhilarated by all these complications, proceeded to take a very hot and long-lasting bath.

The stay at Vichy was very peaceful as compared to our trip. We did not see Gurdjieff except at meals, and our only duty during our stay there was that we were under orders to drink certain specific waters which were, according to him, very beneficial. He gave orders about this water-drinking in the dining-room, which was full, much to our embarrassment and to the great enjoyment of the other guests in the hotel. The particular water that I was to drink was from a spring called "Pour les Femmes" and was a water whose properties were considered extremely beneficial for women, especially if they desired to become pregnant. Fortunately for me at the time—I was in an extremely good humour and enjoying the general spectacle he was making in the hotel— I thought that it was an extremely funny idea for me to drink waters which might induce pregnancy and enjoyed regaling him at meals with an account of the large number of glasses I had managed to drink since I had last seen him. He was very pleased with this and would pat my stomach reassuringly and then tell me how proud he was of me. He continued to refer to Tom and me in a loud voice as Messrs. Rockefeller and Ford, and would explain to the maitre-d'hôtel, the waiters, or even the guests at nearby tables, about his school, and his remarkable pupils—indicating his young American millionaires-to-be—making learned remarks on the "real properties" of the waters of Vichy which were actually known only to himself.

To add to the general uproar of our stay at Vichy,

Gurdjieff met a family of three Russians: a husband and wife and their daughter who must have been in her early twenties. He persuaded the hotel staff to rearrange the dining-room in order that this Russian family should be able to take their meals with us, and we became even more the centre of attraction of the hotel, what with the enormous quantities of Armagnac consumed at each meal, usually complete with toasts to all of the guests individually as well as to everyone at our table. It seems to me now that I only had time to eat tremendous, never-ending meals (I was not required to drink toasts, however), leave the table and race to the "Pour les Femmes" spring and consume large quantities of spring water and then rush back to the hotel in time for another meal.

The Russian family were very much taken with, and impressed by, Gurdjieff and after a day or so he had completely revised their water-drinking schedule, insisting that their régimes were completely wrong, so that the daughter ended up drinking, regularly, a water known, naturally, as "Pour les Hommes". She did not, however, find this particularly odd or funny, and listened very seriously to Mr. Gurdjieff's long, scientific analysis of the properties of this particular water and why it was the proper water for her to drink. When I asked him about this one night while he was taking a bath next to my cot in the bathroom, he said that—as he would prove to me sometime in the near future —this particular girl was very suitable for experiments in hypnosis.

We did not stay in Vichy for more than a week, and when we reached the Prieuré, late at night, after an equally harrowing return trip, we were all exhausted. Mr. Gurdjieff's only comment to me after the trip was that it had been a fine trip for all of us, and that it was an excellent way to "changer les idées".

XXX

SOMEWHAT TO THE surprise of all of us at the Prieuré, the
Russian family that Gurdjieff had met in Vichy took him up
on his invitation to visit the school. After welcoming them
personally, he arranged for someone to entertain them
during the afternoon, and then closeted himself in his room
with his harmonium.

That evening, after another "feast", the guests were told
to come to the main salon at a certain hour, and they retired
to their rooms. During that time, he assembled all the rest
of us in the salon and said that he wanted to explain,
beforehand, an experiment which he was going to perform
on the daughter. He reminded us that he had told us before
that the daughter was "particularly hypnotizable" but he
now added that she was one of the few people he had ever
met who was susceptible to hypnotism of a special sort. He
described the more or less popular form of hypnotism which
usually consisted in requiring the subject to concentrate on
an object before hypnotism could be induced.

He then said that there was a method of hypnotism,
generally unknown in the western world, that was practised
in the Orient. It could not be practised in the western world
for a very good reason. It was hypnotism by the use of
certain combinations of musical tones or chords, and it was
almost impossible to find a subject that responded to the
western or "half-tone" scale on, for example, an ordinary
piano. The special susceptibility of the Russian girl who was
visiting the Prieuré with her parents was that she was
actually susceptible to combinations of half-tones, and it
was this factor that was unusual about her. Given an
instrument which could produce audible differentiations of,
say, sixteenth-tones, he would be able to hypnotize, in this
musical manner, any one of us.

He then had M. de Hartmann play, on the piano, a
composition which he had written that very afternoon,
especially for this occasion. The piece of music came to a
kind of climax on a particular chord, and Gurdjieff said that
when this chord was played in the presence of the Russian

girl, she would immediately go into deep hypnosis, completely involuntary and unexpected on her part.

Gurdjieff always sat on a large, red couch at one end of the main salon, facing the entrance to the room, and when he saw that the Russian family was approaching, he indicated to M. de Hartmann that he was to begin to play, and then motioned to the guests to come in and seat themselves as the music was playing. He indicated a chair in the centre of the room for the daughter. She sat down in it, facing him and in full view of everyone in the room, and listened to the music intently, as if very moved by it. Sure enough, at the given predicted moment when the particular chord was played, she seemed to go completely limp and her head fell against the back of the chair.

As soon as M. de Hartmann finished, the alarmed parents rushed to the girl's side and Gurdjieff, standing by them, explained what he had done and also the fact of her very unusual susceptibility. The parents calmed down soon enough, but it took more than an hour to bring the girl back to consciousness, after which she was for perhaps two additional hours in a highly emotional, completely hysterical state, during which someone—designated by Gurdjieff—had to walk up and down on the terrace with her. Even after that, it was necessary for Gurdjieff to spend a large part of the night with her and her parents in order to persuade them to stay on at the Prieuré for several more days, and to convince them that he had not done her any irreparable harm.

He was apparently completely successful because they did agree to stay on, and the daughter even obliged him by submitting to the same experiment two or three times again. The results were always the same, although the period of hysteria after she returned to consciousness did not last for quite so long.

There was, of course, a great deal of talk as a result of these experiments. A good many people seemed to feel that there had been connivance on the part of the girl, and that there was no proof that she was not working with him. Even so, and without any medical knowledge, it was unquestionably true that she had been hypnotized, with or without her cooperation. Her trance was always complete, and no one could have feigned the manifestations of absolutely uncontrolled hysteria which always resulted.

The purpose of the experiments was something else again. They may have been conducted to dramatize the existence of a form of "science" which was unknown to us, but they also seemed, to some of us, just another demonstration of the way Gurdjieff would often "play" with people; they certainly stirred up another series of questions about Gurdjieff's work, his aims, and his purposes. The fact that the experiments seemed to prove a certain amount of unusual power and knowledge on his part was not, finally, necessary to most of us. Those of us who were at the Prieuré of our own choosing hardly needed such demonstrations to prove to us that Gurdjieff was, at least, unusual.

The experiments reawakened some of my questions about Gurdjieff, but more than anything else they produced a certain resistance in me. What I began to find difficult and irritating about just such things was that they tended to lead me into a realm in which I was lost. Much as I might have liked, at that age, to believe in "miracles" or to find reasons and answers concerning man's existence, I wanted some sort of tangible proof. Gurdjieff's own personal magnetism was often enough proof of his superior knowledge. He was generally credible to me because he was sufficiently "different" from other people—from anyone I had ever known—to be a convincing "super" man. On the other hand, I was troubled because I would always come up against a seemingly obvious fact: anyone who sets himself up as a teacher in any mystical or other-worldly sense had to be some sort of fanatic—totally convinced, totally devoted to a particular course, and, therefore, automatically opposed to the socially accepted, generally recognized, philosophies or religions. It was not only difficult to argue with him, there was nothing to argue against. One could, of course, argue about questions of method or technique but before that it was necessary to have agreed on some aim or purpose. I had no objection to his aim of "harmonious development" for mankind. There was nothing in the words that anyone could oppose.

It seemed to me that the only possible answer would have to lie in some sort of results: tangible, visible results in people—not in Gurdjieff—he was, as I have said, convincing enough. But what about his students? If they had been practising his method of harmonious development for several years, most of them, wouldn't it be somehow visible?

Except for Madame Ostrovsky, his deceased wife, I could think of no one other than Gurdjieff himself who had "commanded" any sort of respect by the simple fact of their presence. One thing that a great many of the other, older students did have in common was what I thought of as a kind of "affected serenity". They managed to look composed and controlled or unruffled most of the time, but it was never quite believable. They gave an impression of being outwardly controlled that never rang quite true, particularly as it was easy enough for Gurdjieff to upset their equilibrium whenever he chose to do so, with the result that most of the senior students were always alternating between states of outward calm and hysteria. Their control seemed to me to be achieved by repression or suppression—I always felt that these words were synonyms—which I could not believe was desirable or worthwhile as an aim, other than socially. Gurdjieff frequently gave the impression of serenity, also, but it never seemed to be false in his case—generally speaking, he manifested whatever he happened to want to manifest at a particular time, and usually for a reason. One might well argue with the reason, and discuss his motives at length, but at least there was a reason—he appeared to know what he was doing and to have a direction; which was not so in the case of his students. Where his students seemed to attempt to rise above the ordinary tribulations of life by affecting a certain disregard for them, Gurdjieff at no time manifested calmness or "serenity" as if it were an aim in itself. He was far more likely to fly into a rage or to enjoy himself in an apparently uncontrolled fit of animal spirits than any of his students. On many occasions I heard him mock the seriousness of people, and remind them that it was essential for any well-rounded human being to "play". He used the word "play" and pointed out the example of nature—all animals knew, as humans did not, the value of "playing" every day. It seemed as simple as the trite "all work and no play makes Jack a dull boy"; no one could accuse Gurdjieff of not playing. By comparison his elder students were lugubrious and morose and were not very convincing examples of "harmonious development" which — if it was generally harmonious—would certainly include humour, laughter, etc., as at least aspects of well-rounded growth.

The women, particularly, were no help. The men, at least in the baths and at the swimming pool, did engage in earthy backyard human humour and seemed to enjoy themselves, but the women not only did not indulge in any humour, they even dressed the part of "disciples", wearing the kind of flowing clothing that is properly associated with people who become involved in "movements" of whatever kind. They gave the outer impression of being priestesses or novitiates in some religious order. None of it was either enlightening or convincing to a thirteen-year-old.

XXXI

THERE WERE TWO additions to the usual "winter" population of the Prieuré after the exodus of the summer students in the fall of 1927. One of them was a woman, whom I only remember as being named Grace, and a new arrival, a young man by the name of Serge. There was a certain amount of gossip about both of them. In the case of Grace, who was the American wife of one of the summer students—also American—she interested us because she was not a new arrival but had stayed on after her husband had gone back to America; also, because she was a rather "unusual" student. None of us knew what she was doing at the Prieuré, as she had never participated in any of the group work projects, and was also exempt from such duties as working in the kitchen or performing any household activities. And, while no one questioned her status or her privileges, there was a good deal of speculation about her.

Serge was a different matter. While I do not remember any specific announcement from Gurdjieff about his arrival at the Prieuré, we all knew, through the "student grapevine", that he was on parole from a French prison; in fact, the gossip was that his parole had been arranged by Gurdjieff personally as a favour to an old friend. None of us had any exact information about him; we did not know what his crime was (the children all hoped it was somthing at least as lurid as murder) and he, like Grace, was apparently also exempt from participation in any regular functions at the school. We only saw these two "students" (if that is what they were—we did not really know) at meals and in the salon in the evenings. Grace, in addition, used to make what we thought of as mysterious trips to Paris at frequent intervals—mysterious only because, in the case of most people, such trips were not only not frequent but their purpose was usually known to all of us.

They both turned out to be very unusual additions to our winter group. Late in the fall, when I was on concierge duty, Grace was brought back to the Prieuré in the custody of two gendarmes. She and the gendarmes had an interview with

Mr. Gurdjieff immediately after their arrival, and when the gendarmes left, Grace retired to her room and did not even appear for dinner that evening. We did not see her again until sometime the next day, when she appeared once more at the concierge with all her bags packed and departed. We did not learn until a few days later that she had been picked up in a department store in Paris for shop-lifting and, according to the gossip (Gurdjieff never so much as mentioned her name), it had been necessary for Gurdjieff to guarantee her immediate departure from France back to America as well as to pay some large sum to the department store. The mystery of her isolated work at the Prieuré was also cleared up at that time. She had spent her time sewing, mostly making clothes for herself, with the materials she had been "lifting" in Paris. She was a topic of general conversation for some time after her departure—it was the first contact that any of us had ever had with crime at the school.

Since Serge was known to be—or at least to have been—a criminal, our attention now focused on him. We had heard that he was the son of French-Russian parents, that he was in his early twenties, but other than that we knew nothing about him. He did not reward our interest by doing anything spectacular—for several weeks at least—until, just before Christmas, he simply disappeared.

His disappearance was first noticed when he failed to appear at the usual Saturday evening Turkish bath. That particular Saturday was somewhat unusual for winter-time because of the large number of guests that had come down from Paris for the weekend, among them several Americans who lived in Paris permanently. Although the fact of Serge's non-appearance at the bath was mentioned, no one was particularly concerned; we did not think of him as a full-fledged member of the group and he seemed to have a special status which had never been defined and which might, therefore, include such eccentricities.

As the next day was Sunday—the one day when we did not have to get up and go to work at six o'clock in the morning—it was not until quite late, sometime before the

customary "guest" lunch, that we learned that several of the
Americans had lost money or jewels, or both, and that Serge
had not reappeared. There was a great deal of talk about
this at lunch and many of the guests inevitably concluded
that the disappearance of their valuables and the disappearance of Serge were, of course, connected. Only Gurdjieff was
adamant, maintaining that there was no connection at all.
He insisted firmly, and, it seemed to most of us, unreasona-
bly, that they had simply "misplaced" their money or
jewellery, and that Serge would reappear in due course. In
spite of the arguments and talk about Serge and the
"robberies" everyone managed to eat a big lunch and there
was even more drinking than usual. By the time lunch was
over and Gurdjieff was ready to retire for the afternoon, the
Americans who had been, as they by this time insisted,
robbed, could not talk of anything else and were considering
taking such measures as calling the police in spite of
Gurdjieff's command that Serge was not to be implicated.

When Gurdjieff had retired to his room, it seemed natural
enough for this group of Americans to sit together in one of
the smaller salons and commiserate with one another as
well as discuss whatever action they might take, and to
drink during these discussions. Mostly because I spoke
English and was also well known to all of them, they sent
me to the kitchen for ice and glasses, having produced
several bottles of liquor—mostly Cognac—from their rooms
or their cars. For some reason or other, they began to insist
that I should drink with them, and since I felt, as they did,
that Gurdjieff was wrong about Serge, I was glad to join
their group and even felt honoured to be invited to share
their liquor. By mid-afternoon, I was drunk for the second
time in my life, and enjoying it very much. Also, by that
time, the liquor had fanned our feelings against Gurdjieff.

Our drinking bout was interrupted very late in the
afternoon when someone came to get me, announcing at the
same time that Gurdjieff was preparing to leave for Paris in
a few minutes and that he wanted to see me. At first I
refused to go with them, and did not go to the car to see him
until he had sent a second person to get me. When I got to

the car, followed this time by all my adult drinking companions, Gurdjieff looked at us all sternly, and then told me to go to his room and get a bottle of Nujol. He said that he had locked his door, and now could not find the key, and I had the only other existing key to his room.

I had my hands in my pockets at the time, and was feeling very courageous and also still angry with him. Although I was actually clenching the key in one hand I said, for no explicable reason, that I had also lost my key. Gurdjieff became very angry, began to shout at me, talking about my responsibilities and saying that losing his key was practically a crime, all of which only served to make me more determined. He ordered me to go and search my room and to find the key. Feeling very exuberant by then, and with the key still firmly in one hand in my pocket, I said I would gladly search my room but that I knew I would not find the key because I remembered losing it earlier in the day. Whereupon I went to my room, and actually made a search of the bureau drawers, and then returned to tell him that I could not find it anywhere.

Gurdjieff went into another tantrum, saying that the Nujol was very important—that Madame de Hartmann had to have it while she was in Paris. I said that she could buy some more at a drugstore. He said, furiously, that since there was already some in his room he was not going to buy any more and, further, that the drugstores were closed on Sundays. I said that even if there was some in his room, we could not get it without his key or my key, which were both lost, and that since even Fountainebleau had a "pharmacie de garde" open on Sundays, there must surely be a similar one in Paris.

All the spectators, particularly the Americans with whom I had been drinking all afternoon, seemed to find all this very amusing, particularly when Gurdjieff and Madame de Hartmann drove off, finally, in a rage without the Nujol.

I remember nothing further about that day except that I staggered to my own room and went to sleep. Sometime during the night I was very ill and the following morning I had my first experience with a real hangover, even though I didn't call it by that name at the time. When I appeared the next day, the Americans had departed and I was the centre of everyone's attention. I was warned that I would be severely punished and that I would most certainly lose my "status" as Gurdjieff's "caretaker". Sober, but with an aching head, I agreed and looked forward with horror to Gurdjieff's arrival that evening.

When he did arrive, I went to the car, like a lamb to slaughter. Gurdjieff did not say anything to me immediately and it was not until I had carried some of the luggage to his room and opened the door with my key and we were alone, that he held up his key, shook it at me, and said: "So, you find key?"

At first I said, simply, "Yes." But after a momentary silence I was unable to contain myself and added that I had never lost it. He asked me where it had been when he had wanted it the day before, and I told him that I had had it in my pocket all the time. He shook his head, looked at me incredulously, and then laughed. He said he would think about what he was going to do to me and would let me know later.

I did not have to wait for very long. It was just about dusk when he sent for me to come to see him on the terrace. I met him there and, without saying a word at first, he held out his hand. I looked at it and then looked up at his face inquiringly. "Give key," he said flatly.

I was holding the key in my hand in my pocket, as I had done the day before, and although I did not say anything, I did not hand it over, but simply looked at him, silent and imploring. He made a firm gesture with his hand, also without speaking, and I took the key out of my pocket, looked at it, and then handed it to him. He put it in his pocket, turned away from me and started to walk down one of the long paths, paralleling the lawns, in the direction of the Turkish bath. I stood in front of the terrace, watching his back fixedly, as if unable to move, for a very long time. I watched him until he had almost disappeared from sight and then I ran to the bicycle rack near the student's dining-room, jumped on my bicycle, and raced down the path after him. When I was within a few yards of him, he turned to look at me, I slowed down, got off my bicycle and went up to him.

We stared at each other silently for what seemed to me a very long time, and then he said, very quietly and seriously: "What you want?"

The tears came into my eyes and I held out my hand. "Please give me the key," I said.

He shook his head, very slowly, but very firmly. "No."

"I'll never do anything like that again," I pleaded. "Please."

He put his hand on my head, a very faint smile on his face. "Not important," he said. "I give you other work. But you now finished with key." He then took the two keys out of his pocket and held them up. "Have two keys now," he said, " you see, I also not lose key." Then he turned away from me to continue his walk.

XXXII

THE HABITS OF day to day living at the Prieuré occupied me
to such an extent that I was very little concerned with my
"family" life except for the letters I occasionally received
from my mother in America. Also, although Jane and
Margaret were permanently established in Paris, since Jane
and I had reached a point of no communication, I rarely
thought about them. I was brought back suddenly to the
reality of my mother when, in early December of 1927, she
wrote me that she was coming to Paris for Christmas. I was
very pleased with this news, and promptly answered her
letter.

To my amazement, only a few days later, Jane appeared
at the Prieuré for the special purpose of discussing my
mother's impending visit. I understood that, in view of her
legal rights, it was necessary for her to give us permission to
visit our mother in Paris and Jane had come to consider
giving us this permission and also to consult Gurdjieff about
it, and, doubtless, to find out how we felt about it.

Jane's argument that our serious work at the Prieuré
would be interrupted by my mother's visit not only seemed
to me absurd, but also brought all my questions to the fore
again. I had been willing enough to accept the obvious fact
that everyone connected with Gurdjieff and the Prieuré was
"unusual"; the very word also meant that they were possibly
special people—superior to or in some way better than
people who were not involved with Gurdjieff. However,
when I was confronted with this statement about serious
work, I felt forced to make another attempt at evaluation. I
had felt uncomfortable about my relationship with Jane for
a long time, and it was unquestionably unusual for a legal
guardian to visit a school and for her and her adopted son
not to speak to one another for almost two years, but this
did not, at first glance, seem superior. Since I had no
ammunition with which to argue against the statements
that I was either "impossible" or "difficult" or both, I had
accepted this verdict on Jane's part; but after hearing her
arguments about this impending visit I began to think

again.

Since Jane's arguments only increased my stubborn determination that I was going to spend Christmas in Paris with Lois, Jane now insisted that not only did I have to have her permission but that I had to have Gurdjieff's permission too. All of this naturally led to a conference with Gurdjieff, although I realized later that only my continued insistence made that conference necessary.

We met solemnly in Gurdjieff's room and he listened, rather like a judge in a tribunal, to Jane's long account of her, and our, relations with my mother, and the importance of Gurdjieff and the Prieuré in our lives—what she wanted for us in the future, and so forth. Gurdjieff listened attentively to all of this, thought it over with a very serious look on his face, and then asked us if we had heard everything that Jane had said. We both said we had.

Then he asked, and even at that moment I thought it very adroit of him, if we realized how important it was "for Jane" that we stay at the Prieuré. Once more, we both said that we did, and Tom added that he also thought that any absence would "interrupt" his work.

Gurdjieff gave me a questioning look, but did not say anything. I said that except for the fact that I would not be available to do work in the kitchen or at some other task I did not think that my presence would be missed, and that, in addition, I was not aware of the importance of whatever it was I was supposed to be doing at the Prieuré. As he said nothing immediately in answer to this, I continued, adding that he had reminded me on many occasions that it was necessary to honour one's parents, and that I felt that I would in no sense be "honouring" my mother if I refused to see her; and that, in any case, I must owe her a good deal if only because, without her, I would not be alive to be anywhere—including the Prieuré.

Having listened to all of this, Gurdjieff then said that there was only one problem that had to be solved: it would be difficult for my mother if only one of us went to see her. He said that he wanted us to make our decisions honestly and individually, but that it would be better for everyone if we came to the same decision—either not to see her at all, or for both of us to visit her over Christmas.

After considerable discussion, in his presence, we arrived at a compromise which he accepted. We would both go to Paris to spend Christmas with Lois, but I would go for two weeks—the entire time she would be in Paris—and Tom would only go for one week, which would include Christmas but not New Year's. He said that he liked the holidays at the Prieuré and did not want to miss all of them. I said, promptly, that the holidays meant nothing to me; what was important to me was seeing Lois. To my great delight, Gurdjieff gave the necessary permission—two weeks for me, one week for Tom.

Although I was very happy to see my mother again, I did not consider Christmas or her visit an overwhelming success for anyone. I was very conscious of the opposite positions of Tom and me—and inevitably reminded of the different decisions we had made some years before when it had been a question of spending Christmas with my father—and as long as Tom stayed in Paris, the fact that he was still determined to leave at the end of one week hung over all three of us like a cloud. And when he did return to the Prieuré after one week that cloud was replaced by the cloud of Lois' imminent departure. We talked a great deal about Jane and Gurdjieff, the fact of the adoption, and, perhaps for the first time since the year that we were adopted by Jane, the whole question became important again. For various reasons, most of which I no longer remember, it was evidently impossible for either of us to return to America at that time, but the very discussion of the question made me aware that, were it possible for me to leave France and return to America, I would certainly do so. My relationship with Jane—lack of relationship would have been more accurate, as I had not talked to her for almost two years except for the arguments about Christmas—was my main reason for wanting to leave. In every other way, and in spite of frequently being puzzled by Gurdjieff, I was content enough to be at the Prieuré. But at that time, with the entire question of why we were there, the emphasis upon the fact that Jane was our legal guardian, and the impossibility of being able to leave, all coming into strong focus at the same time, I began to resent everything and everyone, perhaps especially my own powerlessness. Lois was excluded from this resentment for the simple reason that she was, at that time, equally helpless and in no position to alter the situation.

Sad as I was when Lois left and I returned to the Prieuré, in another sense I was at least temporarily relieved of the pressure of all the questions that had come up. Nothing had changed, and I had to accept the situation, which turned out to be considerably less agonizing than worrying about it in futile attempts to find a way out of it. Even so, the resistances that had manifested themselves actively for the first time that Christmas did not vanish into thin air. I was determined that I would do everything I could to change the situation, even if I had to wait until I "grew up", which, quite unexpectedly then, no longer seemed to be in the distant, unforeseeable future.

XXXIII

My AWAKENING RESISTANCE to what I thought of as the "trap" I was in had little to do with Gurdjieff or the Prieuré itself. I was convinced that had I been a free agent (which, of course, at least implied adulthood) and had told Gurdjieff that I wanted to leave his school, he would have told me to leave at once. With the sole exception of Rachmilevitch, Gurdjieff had never asked—or tried to persuade—anyone to stay at the Prieuré. On the contrary, he sent a great many people away even when they would have given a great deal for the privilege of staying. Rachmilevitch's case was hardly in point, in any event, since he was paid to be there, according to Mr. Gurdjieff, and even he had only been "asked" to stay. For these reasons, I did not think of Mr. Gurdjieff as an obstacle.

The real obstacle, in my mind, was Jane; and since she was rarely at the Prieuré and then only for a day or two at a time, I tended to look upon Tom as her tangible representative. The experience of Christmas with my mother, and our different attitudes and feeling about it, had widened the existing gap of disagreement between Tom and me. Either Gurdjieff or Jane had arranged for the two of us to share a room at the Prieuré that winter, and this new arrangement, of course, was not conducive to increased harmony.

During the years in which we had grown up together, Tom and I had both become accustomed to the use of different weapons. We were both impulsive and impatient, but we expressed ourselves in different ways. When we would quarrel with one another, our disagreements would always take the same form: Tom would lose his temper and would begin fighting—he had a great admiration for boxing and wrestling—and I would scorn fighting and confine myself to sarcasm and invective. Now, confined in the same room, it was as if we suddenly found ourselves in the strange position of having had our weapons changed for us. One night when he persisted in his general defence of Jane and his criticism of me, I at last managed to goad him into hitting out at me—it was, I remember, important that he

should strike the first blow—I hit him with all my strength
and with the added force that seemed to have been building
up inside me for some time. The blow was not only a hard
one, it was completely unexpected, and Tom crashed to the
tile floor of our bedroom. I was terrified when I heard his
head hit the floor and then saw that he was bleeding—from
the back of his head. He did not move immediately, but
when he did get up and seemed to be, at least, alive, I took
advantage of my superior position of the moment and told
him that if he ever argued with me again I would kill him.
My anger was genuine, and I meant—emotionally—what I
was saying. The momentary fear I had experienced when he
hit the floor had disappeared as soon as he had moved and I
had felt immediately, self-confident and very strong—as if I
had liberated myself, once and for all, from physical fear.

We were separated a few days later and no longer lived in
the same room, which I found a great relief. But even this
was not the end of it. It had also, apparently, been brought
to Mr. Gurdjieff's attention, and he spoke to me about it. He
told me, seriously, that I was stronger than Tom—whether I
knew it or not—and the strong should not attack the weak;
also that I should "honour my brother" in the same sense
that I honoured my parents. Since I was, at that time, still
sensitive about my mother's visit, and about Tom's, Jane's,
and even Gurdjieff's attitudes about it, I answered angrily
that I was not the one who needed advice about honouring
anyone. He then said that the position was not the same—
Tom was my older brother, which made a difference. I said
that the fact of his being older did not make any difference
to me. Gurdjieff then told me, angrily, that I should listen,
for my own benefit, to what he was saying to me and that I
was "sinning against my God" when I refused to listen. His
anger only increased my own feeling of anger and I said that
even if I was at his school, I did not think of him as my
"God", and that whoever he was he was not necessarily
always right about everything.

He looked at me coldly, and finally said quite calmly that
I had misunderstood him if I thought that he was representing himself as a "God" of any sort—"you still sin against

your God when you not listen to what I say"—and that since I would not listen to him, there was no point in talking to me any further about it.

XXXIV

THE ONLY PERMANENT job that was assigned to me that
spring was the care of a small, enclosed garden known as
the Herb Garden. It was a small, shady triangular area near
the irrigation ditch that ran through the property, and
except for a certain amount of weeding, watering and hoeing
there was not very much work to do there. The rest of the
time I worked at the same old routine jobs and on various
projects.

My jobs, however, were of less interest to me that spring
than some of the events and new arrivals. The first
excitement of the year was the *dénouement* of the "Affaire
Serge". We learned about it through one of the Americans
who had suffered the greatest losses in what we had all
come to think of as the "robbery". After the Americans had
put the police on his trail, and several months after the
actual robbery, he had been caught in Belgium, and
although no valuables had been found on him, he had
confessed the robbery to the police and some of the jewels
had been found in the possession of an Arab "fence" in Paris.
Serge had been brought back to France and imprisoned.
Gurdjieff at no time made any comment on his failure to
"rehabilitate" Serge, and the Americans who had been
robbed generally thought that Gurdjieff was at fault for
having allowed him to stay at the Prieuré in the first place.
Gurdjieff did have some defenders among the older students, however, and their defence consisted in pointing out
that jewels and money were unimportant—particularly to
wealthy people—but that Serge's life did have value and
that his imprisonment would probably ruin him for life, and
that it was unfortunate that the police had been brought to
the case. To a great many of us, however, this reasoning
seemed to be nothing more than an attempt to maintain the
position of Gurdjieff as never being wrong in anything he
did — the common attitude of the "worshipful". Since
Gurdjieff took no interest in the entire question, and since
Serge was in prison, we lost our interest in the case soon
enough.

For a short period in the late spring I was again assigned to work on the lawns, not mowing them this time, but straightening and trimming the edges and borders. To my surprise, I was even given a helper, which made me feel like a dependable, experienced "old hand". I was even more surprised when I found that my helper was to be an American lady who, up to this time, had only made occasional weekend visits to the Prieuré. This time, as she told me, she was going to be there for two whole weeks, during which time she wanted to be a part of the "tremendously valuable experience" of working at what she called the "real thing".

She appeared the first day, looking very glamorous and colourful; she was wearing silk orange pants, with a green silk blouse, a string of pearls and high-heeled shoes. Although I was amused at the costume, I kept a perfectly straight face as I explained to her what she would have to do; I could not refrain from suggesting that her costume was not entirely appropriate, but still did not smile. She waved away my suggestions as unimportant. She set to work, trimming the border of one of the lawns, with ardour, explaining to me that it was necessary to do this work with one's entire being and, of course, to observe oneself—the famous exercise of "self-observation"—in the process. She was using an odd sort of tool or implement which did not work well: it was a kind of long-handled cutter, with a cutting wheel on one side and a small ordinary wheel on the other. The cutting wheel, of course, was supposed to actually cut the edge of the lawn in a straight line, while the other wheel helped to support and balance the apparatus and to give it power. The use of this implement required a good deal of strength to cut anything at all, since the blade was not very sharp; also, even when it was used by a strong man, it was then necessary to go over the edge that had been "trimmed" with this machine with a pair of long-handled garden shears and straighten up the border or edge.

I was so interested in her approach to this work and also in her manner of doing it that I did very little work myself, but watched her as she worked. She walked very gracefully, breathing in the country air, admiring the flowers, and, as she put it, "immersing herself in nature"; she also told me that she was "observing" her every movement as she worked and that she realized that one of the benefits of this exercise was that one could, through continuous practice, make every movement of one's body harmonious, functional, and therefore beautiful.

We worked together at this job for several days, and although I finally had to actually trim all the edges and borders after her on my hands and knees with the long-handled shears, I enjoyed it very much. I had long since discarded the idea that work at the Prieuré was intended to produce the expected results (except of course in the kitchen) but that the work was done for the benefit of one's inner being or self. I had often found it very hard to concentrate on these invisible benefits, and much easier to simply, and unimaginatively, try to accomplish the visible, obvious, physical task. It was a pleasure to achieve a handsome, straight edge at the side of the lawn or flower bed. Not so with the lady, who when she realized, inevitably, that I was following her and doing all her work over again, made it clear to me that as long as our "selves" or our "inner beings" were benefiting from what we were doing it would not matter if it took us all year to finish the work—that, in fact, if we never finished it it would not matter.

I liked the lady well enough; I certainly enjoyed being her temporary "boss" and I had to admit that she looked handsome on the lawns, that even though she did not seem to accomplish anything that was visible, she was persistent and reported regularly for work. Also, for all I knew, she might have been doing a great deal of good work on her "inner being". I had to admit that she obviously made a point when she said that the actual results—on the land, as it were—were not very important. The grounds were living evidence of this—littered as they were, with unfinished projects. All the work of uprooting trees and stumps, building new vegetable gardens, even the actual construction of buildings which remained unfinished, attested to the fact that physical results did not seem to matter.

I was sorry when our work on the lawns came to an end, and although I was dubious about the benefits she had, or had not, acquired in those few days, I had enjoyed my association with her. It gave me a somewhat different point of view about the school as a whole, and its purposes. While I had realized that none of the work was ever considered important from the simple point of view that it needed to be done; that there was, in short, another aim—the engendering of friction between people who worked together plus possible other, less tangible or visible results—I had also assumed that the actual accomplishment of the task itself had, at least, some value. Most of my jobs, up to that time, had supported this view: it surely mattered, for instance, that the chickens and the other animals were fed and cared for, that the dishes and pots and pans in the kitchen were washed, that Gurdjieff's room was actually cleaned every day—with or without benefit to my "inner self".

Whatever thoughts I may have had about all of this and about her, the lady left after about two weeks, and seemed to feel herself "immeasurably enriched". Was it possible, after all, that she was right? If it had done nothing else, her visit had served to increase my need to re-examine the Prieuré and the reasons for its existence.

XXXV

MY NEXT TEMPORARY job on a project was the repair of the study-house roof. The construction of the roof was a simple affair of beams placed in such a way that they formed a peaked roof, with about eight feet of air-space at the centre between the peak of the roof and the ceiling. The beams were at intervals of about one yard — lengthwise and crosswise—and were covered with tar-paper which had begun to leak in various places. The job turned out to be exciting and rather perilous. We mounted the roof on ladders and from then on it was necessary to walk only on the beams, of course. It was also necessary to bring rolls of tar paper and pails or buckets of hot tar with us up the ladders. After a few days of walking on four- or six-inch beams we became reasonably proficient at this work and even made a sort of test of skills out of racing along the beams carrying a bucket of hot tar, or balancing a roll of tar paper on our shoulders.

One young American who was making his first visit to the Prieuré, and who was not only aggressive and very competitive but who also thought that everything at the Prieuré was, as he put it, "a bunch of nonsense", was determined to be more daring, more skillful and more foolhardy than anyone else. After about one week he had manifested his superior agility to the point where none of us even attempted to compete with him. Even so, he seemed unable to stop showing off and continued to demonstrate his superiority over all the rest of us. His performance began to irritate all of us and to make us nervous; we did not go so far as to hope that he would have an accident—any accident could have been very serious as it was a high roof—but we did begin to long for something to happen that would bring an end to this exhibition of bravado.

The end did come, sooner than we had anticipated, and in a much more spectacular way. Later, it seemed inevitable that he would, of course, have been carrying a pail of boiling tar when he did make a false step on to the unsupported tar paper and fall through the roof. The only thing that saved him from very serious injury was that he had fallen just over the small balcony so that he did not actually fall more than about fifteen feet. However, what made the fall a brutal and painful one was that he did not let go of the bucket of tar and was not wearing a shirt at the time. One whole side of this body was very badly burned and covered with hot tar.

As the boiling tar had also flowed down inside his trousers, it was almost impossible for him to walk, so we moved him to a place in the shade while someone raced for Gurdjieff and the doctor. The only remedy—or, in any case, the remedy that was used—was to remove the tar from his body with gasoline, which took more than an hour, and which must have been almost unimaginably painful. The young man appeared to have tremendous endurance and courage, and submitted to this ordeal without flinching, but when it was over and he had been properly bandaged, Gurdjieff lashed into him in a great fury for his stupidity. He defended himself valiantly but without making much sense; the argument turned into a stream of invective against Gurdjieff and his ridiculous school, and ended with Gurdjieff ordering him to leave as soon as he was well enough.

While I could not help but feel great sympathy for the American, I did feel that Gurdjieff was completely right, although to revile the young man at that particular time had seemed unnecessarily cruel. I was very surprised when Gurdjieff, the following day, unexpectedly called to me when I was returning from work in the evening and, unpredictable as always, complimented me on my good work on the roof and gave me a large sum of money. I said that I had to admit, in all honesty, that since I was the only person working on the roof who was not a full-grown man, I had done considerably less work than anyone else and did not feel that I should be rewarded.

He gave me an odd smile, insisted that I take the money, and said that he was rewarding me for not having fallen through the roof or otherwise injured myself while I worked on it. He then said that he was giving me the money on the condition that I think of something to do with it for all the rest of the children—something that would be valuable for all of them. I left him, pleased with all the money I had in my pockets, but extremely puzzled as to what I could do with the money that would be valuable for all the other children.

After thinking about the problem for two days, I finally decided to share it with them, although not quite equally. I kept a larger share for myself since I was the one who had, for whatever odd reasons, "earned" it.

Gurdjieff did not wait for me to tell him about what I had done, but sent for me and asked me, as if he was especially interested. When I told him, he was furious with me. He shouted at me, told me that I had not used my imagination, that I had not thought about it, and that I had not done anything valuable for them; also why had I kept a larger share for myself?

I said, calmly enough, that I had come to realize that nothing at the Prieuré was predictable and that he had made it clear to me often enough that things were never "what they seemed" to be. I maintained firmly that I had only emulated him. By giving me this totally unexpected large sum of money, he had, along with it, given me a condition and a problem concerning its disposition. Since I had been unable to think of anything "valuable" to do with the money, all I could do was pass the problem along to the other children—my injunction to them being that they had to do something valuable with it for themselves. As to why I had kept a larger sum for myself, I said that I felt I deserved the larger sum because it was thanks to me that they had the opportunity to make this important decision about the value of money.

Although he had listened to me without interruption, his anger had not abated and he said that I was behaving like a "big-shot" and that he was extremely disappointed in me; that I had failed him.

To my own surprise, I stood my ground and said that if I was behaving like a "big-shot" it was because I had many examples of such behaviour to emulate, and that if he was disappointed in me he should remember that it was he who had told me, repeatedly, that one should learn never to be disappointed in anyone, and that, again, I was only following his advice and his example.

Although he told me then that I was, as usual. "sinning against my God" by talking to him in this way, he asked me what I was going to do with the money that I had kept for myself. I said that it was only possible either to spend money or to save it. That, for the time being, I was going to save it since I was clothed, fed and housed and did not need to spend it, but that I would spend it when I found something that I needed—or wanted—to buy.

He looked at me in disgust, remarking that what I had said indicated that I had typical middle-class morals and that I had not learned anything at all from him during the time that I had been at the Prieuré. I replied, rather hotly, that I was fully aware of those possibilities and that, as to learning, when I looked around me at his other students, I was not convinced that anyone else was learning anything either; that, in fact, I was not sure that there was anything to learn there.

Quite calm by this time, he said that I failed to realize that the value of the Prieuré was not necessarily obvious, and that time would tell whether anyone learned anything by being there. Then, for the second time, he said that it was useless to continue talking to me and added that I was not to continue my work on the roof of the study-house but that I would be assigned to other work.

XXXVI

My "other work" consisted of several things; clearing various areas of the property of stinging nettles, which had to be done without wearing gloves; working, with one other person, on the construction of a stone house which had been partly built—and never worked on—ever since I had first been at the Prieuré; and, to my amazement, helping in the translation of parts of Gurdjieff's book from a preliminary French translation into English.

After a few hours on the job of pulling out nettles, I soon learned that with care, by pulling them out by the roots and avoiding handling the stems or leaves, it was possible to uproot them without being painfully stung by them. I also learned, quite incidentally, that they could be used to make an excellent soup. In any case, as I was still pondering about the American lady's remarks about the value of work, the uprooting of nettles did seem to have practical value as well as whatever it might have been doing for my "inner being", since it eliminated weeds and also provided soup.

As to the building of the house, I was convinced that the lady was undoubtedly right—no visible progress was made on the building so I assumed that all the progress was "spiritual". I was the helper on this job, and my "boss" decided that the first thing we were to do was to move an enormous pile of stone, located about fifty feet from the house, to an area next to it. The only sensible way to do this, he informed me, was for me to stand by the rock pile, throw individual rocks to him, and he would then throw them into a new pile near the building. When this was done, we would use the stones which had been moved to construct partitions or walls inside the building; the outer wall had been erected three or four years previously. I was warned that there was a definite rhythm to this rock throwing which had to be observed as it would make the work much less tiresome; also that in order to keep the proper rhythm it was necessary for us to sing. We only managed to sing and throw rocks for about two hours when my companion and "boss", distracted by something, failed to catch a rock that I had heaved in his direction, and was felled by it as it struck him on the temple.

I helped him to his feet and then walked with him as he more or less staggered in the direction of the main building, presumably to consult the doctor about the effect of this blow. Gurdjieff saw us at once as he was sitting in front of the terrace in one of his usual writing places, and when he heard what had happened, examined the man, pronounced him in no danger, but said that we were to discontinue working on that particular construction. With a rather amiable smile in my direction he told me that it was apparently impossible for me to be involved in any kind of work without causing trouble, and that I was a born troublemaker. Given some of my past experiences at the Prieuré I took this to be, if not exactly a compliment, at least praise of a kind.

I was fascinated, however with the work on his book. An Englishman had been assigned to make a rough, preliminary translation from the French version of the book, and my job was to listen to it and read it and to make suggestions as to vernacular and Americanisms that would correspond as closely as possible to the French version which I was also to read. The particular chapter was on the subject of the continent of Africa and dealt mainly with Gurdjieff's explanation of the origin of monkeys.[1]

What began to interest me much more that summer than any of my daytime tasks were the nightly readings of the sections of Gurdjieff's books, usually in Russian or French but sometimes in English—depending upon the latest completed translations—and Gurdjieff's comments on his aims and purposes. In the simplest terms, he would usually reduce what had been written in the chapter that had been read that evening (his comments always followed the readings) to a kind of synopsis or simplification of what he was trying to convey in writing.

I was particularly impressed by his statement that his

---

[1] Gurdjieff, G.I., *All and Everything;* (Beelzebub's Tales to his Grandson; or an Impartial, Objective Criticism of Man). E. P. Dutton & Co., Inc., New York, N. Y.

purpose in writing this book was to destroy forever the habitual values and ideas of people, which prevented them from understanding reality or living according to "cosmic laws". He was then going to write additional books which would prepare the ground, as it were, for the acquisition of new understanding and new values. If, as I saw it, the existence of the Prieuré had the same aim: to destroy existing values, then it was more comprehensible. If, as Gurdjieff had so often said, the world was "upside down" then perhaps there was a definite value in what he was apparently attempting to do at this school. It might be quite true, as the American lady had suggested to me, that one should not work for the immediate, obvious result of the particular work one was doing, but for the development of one's being. Even though I was not convinced that Gurdjieff had all the answers to the dilemma of human life—as someone had called it—it was certainly possible that he, as well as anyone else, might have them. What he did do was at least provocative, unpredictable, irritating and, usually, interesting enough to arouse questions, doubts, and controversies.

In the course of his talks and comments on his writings, he frequently digressed from the subject of whatever had been read, to talk in general terms about almost anything that either came to his mind, or might be brought up by one of the students. When someone, through some association with the chapter that had been read that evening, brought up the question of the worlds of east and west, and the lack of understanding between the oriental and the occidental mentalities, Gurdjieff talked at some length on the misunderstandings that were created in the world by this lack of understanding, saying that it was due, at least in part, to lack of energy in the east and lack of wisdom in the west. He predicted that a day would come when the eastern world would again rise to a position of world importance and become a threat to the momentarily all-powerful, all-influential new culture of the western world, which was dominated, according to him, by America—a country that was very strong, to be sure, but also very young. He continued to say that one should look at the world in the same way that one looked at a man, or at oneself. Each individual was a world, of itself, and the globe—the big world in which we all lived—was, in a sense, only a reflection or an enlargement of the individual world in each one of us.

Among the purposes of all leaders, messiahs, messengers from the gods, and so forth, there was one fundamental and very important purpose: to find some means by which the two sides of man, and, therefore, the two sides of the earth, could live together in peace and harmony. He said that time was very short—it was necessary to achieve this harmony as soon as possible to avoid complete disaster. Philosophies, religions and other such movements had all failed to accomplish this aim, and the only possible way to accomplish it was through the individual development of man. As an individual developed his own, unknown potentialities, he would become strong and would, in turn, influence many more people. If enough individuals could develop themselves —even partially—into genuine, natural men, able to use the real potentialities that were proper to mankind, each such individual would then be able to convince and win over as many as a hundred other men, who would, each in his turn, upon achieving development, be able to influence another hundred, and so on.

He added, grimly, that he was in no sense joking when he had said that time was short. Further, he said that history had already proven to us that such tools as politics, religion, and any other organized movements which treated man "in the mass" and not as individual beings, were failures. That they would always be failures and that the separate, distinct growth of each individual in the world was the only possible solution.

Whether one believed him whole-heartedly or not, he made a convincing and passionate case for the importance of individual development and growth.

XXXVII

WHAT WITH ADOLESCENCE, lack of supervision, lack of interest, and just plain laziness, I managed to do as little work as possible in the Herb Garden. I avoided going there except when it was necessary for me to bring various herbs to the kitchen. When the quality of the herbs became noticeably poorer and when I was at times unable even to supply a small quantity of some particular herb, someone must have taken it upon themselves to investigate the garden and report their findings to Gurdjieff.

The result was that Gurdjieff made a personal inspection of the garden with me, walking up and down between all the small beds, examining every plant. When he had finished he told me that as far as he could see, I had done absolutely nothing at all there in the way of work. I had to admit that I had done very little work, but defended myself to the extent of pointing out that I had done some occasional weeding. He shook his head and said that in view of the state of the garden it would be better not to defend myself at all. He then assigned several of the children to work with me in the garden until it was in proper shape, and instructed me as to what had to be done to the various plants: hoeing between rows, trimming certain plants, dividing and replanting others.

Although the children were very annoyed with me for having shirked my own work and thereby caused them to have to work on "my" garden, they all pitched in and we carried out Gurdjieff's orders very easily and quickly. It was a very small plot of land and it could not have taken us more than a day or two. When we had finished the work, Gurdjieff pronounced it satisfactory, complimented all the other children on their work, and said that he wanted to have a talk with me, alone.

He first told me that I could see for myself that I had not performed a task that had been assigned to me, and that it had been necessary for him to intervene in my work and take measures to repair the damage that had been caused by my neglect. He said that this was a very good example of the way in which one person's failure to accomplish his duty could affect the general welfare of everyone else and that, while I might not think of herbs as important, they were important to him and were needed in the kitchen; also that I had caused him an unnecessary, if minor, expense because various plants had had to be purchased, which would not have been necessary if I had done my job properly.

He went on to say that it was true, in one sense, that the herb garden was not important; what was important, however, was to be responsible and to do one's work, particularly when that work could affect the welfare of others. However, there was another, still more important reason for accomplishing any assigned task, which was for one's own sake.

He spoke again about the exercise of "self-observation" and said that since man was a three-centred or three-brained being, it was necessary to do exercises and perform tasks that were valuable for all three centres, not just the physical or "motor" centre; that "self-observation" as I knew it was a purely physical exercise in that it consisted in the observation of one's physical body and its movements, gestures and manifestations.

He said that there were various important exercises having to do with "self-remembering" which was a very important aspect of his work. One of them was to conscientiously and with all one's concentration, try to remember, as on a movie film, everything that one had done during each entire day. This was to be done every night before going to sleep. The most important thing in the exercise was not to let the attention wander—by association. If one's attention did wander from the focus upon the image of oneself, then it was absolutely necessary to begin all over again at the beginning each time this happened—and it would, he warned, happen.

He talked to me for a very long time that morning, and emphasized the fact that everyone had, usually, a particular, recurring problem in life. He said that these particular problems were usually a form of laziness, and that I was to think about my laziness, which took a fairly obvious physical form, as in the case of the garden: I had simply put off doing anything in the garden until someone had taken notice of that fact. He said that he wanted me to think seriously about my laziness—not the outward form, which was not important, but to find out what it was. "When you see that you are lazy, necessary find out what this laziness *is*. Because in some ways you already lazy for many years, can take even many years for you to find out what it is. Must ask yourself, whenever you see your own laziness: 'What is this laziness in me?' If you ask this question seriously, and with concentration, is possible someday you will find answer. This important and very difficult work I give you now."

I thanked him for what he had said and added that I was sorry that I had not done my work in the garden and that I would do it properly in the future.

He brushed aside my thanks and said that it was useless to be sorry. "Is too late for that now, and is also too late to do good work in the garden. In life never have second chance, only have one chance. You had one time to do good work in garden, for self; you not do, so now even if you work all your life, in this garden, cannot be same thing for you. But also important not be 'sorry' about this; can waste all life feeling sorry. There is valuable thing sometimes, thing you call remorse. If man have real remorse for something he do that is not good, this can be valuable; but if only sorry and say will do same thing better in future is waste of time. This time is already gone forever, this part of your life is finished, you cannot live over again. Not important if you do good work in garden now, because will do for wrong reasons—to try to repair damage which cannot be repaired ever. This serious thing. But also very serious not to waste time feeling sorry or feeling regret, this only waste even more time. Must learn in life, not to make such mistakes, and must understand that once make mistake is made forever."

XXXVIII

In the course of the readings of Gurdjieff's book, and particularly in his comments or talks which always followed them, he frequently discussed the subject of love. He pointed out that, in any attempt or effort to get to know oneself, it was always necessary to start with the physical body for the simple reason that it was the most highly developed of man's three centres; it was for this reason that "self-observation" always started by the observation of the body alone. While the body grew automatically and mechanically, practically without supervision, nevertheless it was a more properly developed centre than either the emotional or mental "brains" (or centres) because it did, even if only automatically, perform its proper functions. Most bodily functions were not only more or less compulsive, they were also reasonably comprehensible and therefore not too difficult to satisfy.

In relating the observation of the body to love, he again used the example of the two hands or arms, saying that love could be defined as "one hand washes the other". He also said that the body could achieve harmony within itself when it was used properly, when both hands worked together, and that this was a good place to start on the consciousness or awareness of what love really should be. In order for people to be able to work together, it was necessary for them to love each other, and to love the same aim. In this sense, in order for a human being to function properly and in accordance with his proper humanity, it was necessary for all of the component parts of a human being to love each other and to work together for the same aim—self-development and self-perfection; the difficulty was, of course, that given our abnormal habits and education we had no genuine conception of what proper development or "perfection" could be. He warned us against any misinterpretation of the word "perfection", stating that our associations with this word— our ideas of a "perfect" state—were improper, and that it was generally better to use the term "development".

The main indication or clue about love that we could learn

from the physical body was the physical form of love, in other words, sex. In the primary sense, the purpose of sex was reproduction, which was actually only a synonym for creation. Love, therefore, in any sense—whether physical or not—had to be creative. He also said that there was a proper form of what might be called "sublimation" of sexual energy; that sex was the source of all energy and when not used reproductively could still be used in an equally creative sense when sublimated and used as energy for other types of creativity. One of the misuses of sex that had arisen through bad training, the wrong type of education, and improper habits, was that it had become almost the only vital form of human communication. It was possible for people to "join actively" in other ways than physically; to, as he put it, "touch each other's essences", but human beings had lost this faculty many, many years—many centuries—ago. If one was observant, however, it was possible to realize that this "touching of essences" still occasionally took place between two individual human beings, but only by accident, and that it was then almost immediately misunderstood and misinterpreted and descended into a purely physical form which became valueless once it had been expended.

In talking further about the relations between individuals, he said that sex, again, was the "highest expression of the physical body" and the only "holy" expression of self that was left to us. In order to achieve any other forms of "holiness" within ourselves, it was profitable to try—in other areas of our lives—to emulate this "essence-touching" process; and the completely open "sharing of common truth" between two individuals was almost "visible" in a compulsive sexual relationship. He warned, however, that even sex —compulsive as it might be to most individuals—often dwindled into a simple process which only involved the particular satisfaction, gratification or release of a single individual, instead of both of them, and that in such cases there would not have been any openness or honesty between them.

When asked to define a proper, objectively moral love between people—one for another—he said that it would be necessary to develop oneself to such an extent that it would be possible to "know and understand enough to be able to aid someone else in doing something necessary for himself, even when that person was not conscious of the need, and might work against you"; that only in this sense was love properly responsible and worthy of the name of real love. He added that, even with the best of intentions, most people would be too afraid to love another person in an active sense, or even to attempt to do anything for them; and that one of the terrifying aspects of love was that while it was possible to help another person to a certain degree, it was not possible to actually "do" anything for them. "If see another man fall down, when he must walk, you can pick him up. But, although to take one more step is more necessary for him even than air, he must take this step alone; impossible for another person to take it for him."

XXXIX

IN SPEAKING OF his methods of self-development and proper growth, Gurdjieff would often emphasize the fact that there were many dangers that would inevitably be encountered in the process. One of the most frequent obstacles was that, at times, the performance of a particular exercise (he was referring to individual exercises prescribed by him for particular individuals) would produce a state of exhilaration or well-being. He said that while such a state of exhilaration was proper to the correct and serious performance of such exercises, one danger lay in our misconception of "results" or "progress"; it was necessary to remember that we should not expect results at all. If we did an exercise expecting a certain result, it was valueless. But, if we achieved a recognizable result, such as a feeling of genuine well-being, even though this was a proper, temporary, result, it did not in any sense mean that one had "achieved" anything permanent. It could mean that some progress was being made but it was then necessary to work that much harder in order to make such "results" a permanent part of oneself.

He referred, frequently, to a sort of riddle: a man, accompanied by three mutually hostile organisms, a lamb, a wolf, and a cabbage, arrives at the edge of a river which has to be crossed in a boat which can only carry two—the man and one other—"passenger" at a time. It is necessary to transport himself and his "companions" across the river without the possibility of one of them being able to attack or destroy the other. The important element in the story was that the general human tendency was to try to find a "short-cut", and the moral of the story was that there is no short-cut: that it is essential, always, to make the necessary number of trips to ensure the safety and well-being of all the passengers. He said that in the beginning, even though it would seem a waste of valuable time, it would frequently be necessary to make extra trips rather than to risk any possible danger. However, as one became accustomed to his exercises and methods, one should eventually be able to make only the exact number of trips required and still not endanger any passenger. It was also necessary to recognize the fact that in the case of the man, the lamb, the wolf and the cabbage it would be necessary to take some of the passengers on a return trip which would also seem a waste of time.

He used the same "riddle" as an example of the "centres" or "brains" of man; the man representing the "I" or the consciousness and the other three the physical, emotional, and mental centres. In addition to stressing the fact that the physical centre was the most developed of the three, he said that the mental centre was practically undeveloped, and that the emotional centre, which was partly developed—but in all the wrong ways—was completely "savage". He said that we responded to the needs of the body compulsively, which was proper as long as our bodily habits were good ones, since it was necessary to satisfy the needs of the body, or "machine", in the same sense that one would take proper care of a motor car since it was our only means of "transportation". With the emotional centre, since we knew almost nothing about it, the problem was much more difficult. Most of the errors of violence that were committed in the course of life were emotional, since we did not know how to use emotion properly in the course of our lives, and had only learned to form improper emotional habits from the moment we were born. He said that emotional "needs" existed that were just as compulsive as our physical needs such as hunger, sleep, sex, etc., but that we did not understand what they were and knew nothing at all about how to satisfy such emotional "cravings". One of the first steps was to understand that emotion was a kind of force within us. He frequently compared it to a balloon or to the reservoir of air that served to make a pipe-organ function. The pipes of the organ could be considered examples of various types of emotion, each pipe labelled differently: i.e., one pipe would be anger, another hate, another greed, another vanity, another jealousy, another pity, and so forth. One step towards the proper use of emotions was to be able to use the force or "air" in the reservoir in whichever of the pipes was proper or appropriate in a given situation, in

much the same way as one consciously struck a certain note
on an organ in order to produce a particular tone. If, for
example, one felt—for whatever reason—anger, when anger
was not appropriate to a particular circumstance or situation, instead of expressing anger, it should become possible
for us to consciously divert that energy into whatever
emotion was necessary or proper at the time. All existing
emotions, all feelings, had purpose; there was a reason for
their existence and a proper use for each of them. But
without consciousness or knowledge we used them blindly,
compulsively and ignorantly, without any sort of control,
producing the same effect in our emotional life as would
have been produced, musically, by playing a pipe-organ as
an animal might play it, without any knowledge, and
without music—simply at random. The great danger of
uncontrolled emotions was that "shock" generally produced
effects in oneself and in others, and the force of shock was
emotional. If from lack of consciousness or knowledge, one
felt — mechanically — anger, instead of, for instance,
compassion, at a time when compassion was the proper
emotion, only havoc and chaos could be produced.

Most of the problems in communcation and understanding between individuals resulted from just such emotional
shocks which were inappropriate, unexpected, and therefore
usually harmful and destructive. One of the subtler dangers
involved in this was that people frequently tried to use a
"shortcut" to the use of proper emotions. While feeling
anger, they would attempt to control this feeling and
express a different emotion—such as happiness, or love, or
anything except anger. Since, whether we knew it or not,
the simulated emotion did not convince other people emotionally, the result was that, in spite of the outward
expression, the actual emotion or feeling would have been
"recognized" as anger in any case, and having been sensed
or felt in this way by another individual, in spite of not
having been expressed honestly, it could be even more
dangerous as it could only serve to arouse, although perhaps
unconsciously, suspicion and hostility.

XL

IN SPITE OF my first beginning interest in the "theoretical"
aspect of the Gurdjieff work at the Prieuré, this interest was
cut short by two letters which I received shortly before
Christmas in the year 1928. One was from Jane, who had
arranged that Tom and I would spend Christmas with her
in Paris, and I gathered that it was to be in the nature of a
reconciliation between Jane and me.

The second letter was from my mother in Chicago, who
had been able to convince my stepfather that it was time for
me to come back to the United States; there was even an
enclosure from my stepfather asking me to come back and
assuring me that I would be supported, educated, and
welcome. My decision was instantaneous, and did not
involve any inner conflicts. I wanted to return to America.
Because my mother's letter indicated that Jane would not be
either consulted or notified until they had heard from me, I
decided not to mention the possibility of my leaving France
until after Christmas.

We did go to Paris for Christmas, and Jane and I were
reconciled. Since our relationship had always been charac-
terized by its explosive quality, once we had, very emotionally, buried the past, I could not keep to my resolve, since I did
not feel that I should disguise my intentions and wishes
once we were on good terms again. I told Jane, honestly, and
because of my new found goodwill towards her, that I
wanted to return to the United States.

But I had forgotten that, as a minor, I could not leave
Jane's custody, and that I should have to stay at the
Prieuré, at least until I was of age.

It would be uninteresting and boring to even attempt to
describe the nine months that followed. As far as any willing
participation on my part was concerned, I might as well
have left the Prieuré that very day. Although I continued to
perform, in a desultory way, whatever work was assigned to
me, my memory of that entire time is nothing more than a
blur, punctuated only by letters from America and from
Paris, visits by Jane to the Prieuré for the purpose of further

argument, plus lectures and advice from many of the older students who had been brought into the argument by Jane, all of which, as was usual with me, only served to increase my determination to leave at any cost. I was particularly surprised, during the summer of that year, that Gurdjieff had not been brought actively into the question of my departure. He was finally brought into it in the early fall, presumably because of the influence and persistence of my mother and stepfather who had by this time even bought me a ticket, and had probably even gone so far—although I have no personal knowledge of this—as to threaten some sort of legal action. In any event, something had happened to cause Jane to consider agreeing to my departure. Her arguments now took the form of appeals to my good sense, rather than simple, straightforward threats.

Instead of seeing Gurdjieff at the Prieuré, I was taken to Paris to see him, in the company of Jane, at the Café de la Paix, which was his usual "writing café" when he was in Paris. We went there in the evening and Jane proceeded to talk for a very long time, advancing all of her arguments, deploring my resistance and the fact that I did not understand or realize that I was probably giving up the greatest opportunity for knowledge, and education, that I would ever have; she also went into the legal position at some length.

As always, Gurdjieff listened carefully and thoughtfully, but when she had finished he did not have very much to say. He asked me if I had listened to everything that she had said and if I had considered the whole situation. I said that I had and that my decision remained unchanged. He then told Jane that while he did not feel that there was much use for her to continue to argue with me about my decision, he would consider the whole situation and would talk to me, personally, in the near future.

When we had left him, Jane told me that, for me to leave at all, it would be necessary to break the adoption in so far as I was concerned—none of this related to Tom in any way —and that this could only be done through the American Consul in Paris; that it was very difficult and might even be impossible, and also that I was causing nothing but a great deal of trouble for everyone else in addition to giving up the opportunity of a lifetime. All I could do was listen and wonder if she would ever stop raging at me, and I took recourse in total silence.

Gurdjieff did talk to me, but only very briefly, when we were both back at the Prieuré. He said that he wanted to know if I had considered and evaluated my relationships to my mother, to Jane, and to himself and the school conscientiously and if, having done so, I still wanted to go back to America. I said that I thought I had to the best of my ability, that I had been unhappy with Jane for several years now; as to himself and the Prieuré, I had no particular desire to leave the school or to part from him, but that I did want to be with my own family; that I was an American and would not, in any case, stay in France for the rest of my life. I felt that I belonged in America.

Gurdjieff did not object to any of this, and said that he would not oppose my leaving and that when Jane consulted him about it, he would tell her so.

The effect of Gurdjieff's decision not to oppose me was remarkable. Not only did Jane capitulate, but came to the Prieuré and announced that all the details — tickets, passport, legal papers, etc.—had been arranged. I was to leave in a few days and she, accompanied by Tom and a friend of hers, would drive me to Cherbourg to take the boat. I felt, instinctively, that this was an unnecessary journey and protested that I could just as well go on the train, but she was insistent about making the trip with me and putting me on the boat.

I said goodbye to Gurdjieff early in the afternoon of the same day that I was to leave. He was going to Paris and would not be there when we departed. The usual crowd was assembled at the entrance to the main building around his car, and he said goodbye to everyone. I hung back, feeling depressed and uncertain now that the moment was upon me, I went over to him, and first he shook my hand, looked at me with a smile on his face, and said, rather sadly I thought: "So you decide to go?"

I was only able to nod my head at him. Then he put his arm around me, leaned over and kissed my cheek, and said: "Must not be sad. Sometime maybe you will come back; remember that in life anything can happen."

At that moment, for the only time in many months, I regretted my decision. Whatever had taken place at the Prieuré, whatever I had or had not experienced or learned, my affection for Gurdjieff had remained essentially undiminished. I realized, although not immediately, that if he had at any time put the question of my departure on a personal, emotional level—the end of my personal association with him—I probably would not have left. He did not; as I have said, he always seemed to me to play fair.

XLI

WHAT WAS THE effect upon me of my years with Gurdjieff as a child, and what did I learn at the Prieuré?

I am tempted to answer that question with another question: How is it possible to evaluate such an experience? There was no training or education available at the Prieuré which would serve to prepare any individual for success in the ordinary sense of the word; I had not learned enough to enter a college, I could not even pass a final high school examination. I did not become a benevolent, wise, or even a more competent individual in any visible sense. I did not become a happier, more peaceful. or less troubled person. A few things I did learn—that life is lived today—right now— and that the fact of death is inevitable; that man is a perplexing, confusing and inexplicable, unimportant cog in the universe—are perhaps things that I might have learned anywhere.

However, I might well go back to the year 1924, and repeat that whatever else existence is or may seem to be, it is a gift. And like all gifts . . . anything is possible . . . there might be a miracle inside the box.

Book Two

GURDJIEFF   REMEMBERED

I

I HAD SPENT ABOUT FOUR and one-half years of my early adolescence as a resident student, in Fountainebleau, France, at Georges Gurdjieff's "Institute for the Harmonious Development of Man", also known as the "Gurdjieff Institute", or, more familiarly, "Le Prieuré", during the years 1924 to 1929. I left there at the age of fifteen to return to Chicago and my family which, at that time, consisted of my mother, Lois, my stepfather, Bill, and a half-sister, Linda, then about seven years old.

My departure had been a difficult one in many ways. For various reasons, mostly because of my mother's long illness, I had been legally adopted by Jane Heap and Margaret Anderson (my mother's sister) and it was through them that I had gone to live at the Gurdjieff school. When I decided to return to America, it became necessary to "break" that adoption, a process which involved considerable legal and personal unpleasantness. My arrival in America was further complicated by the fact that while I was on the ocean the now-famous stock market crash of 1929 came to a head.

Although I had expected that my mother would meet me in New York upon arrival, it did not turn out that way. There was no one at the dock, and I was in the odd position of being a recently "unadopted" minor who was not permitted to leave the ship unless I could be placed in someone's custody. The authorities put me firmly into the hands of an organization known as "The Traveller's Aid Society" whose only solution was to keep me on the ship while they made some attempt to get in touch with my family in Chicago. It was not an auspicious homecoming.

I watched as the ship—the *Leviathan,* at that time the world's largest ocean liner—emptied, and I remained, staring over the railing, like some piece of unclaimed excess baggage. The dilemma was finally solved by the arrival of a man, whose name I no longer remember, who was a business associate of my stepfather and who claimed me in my family's name. He was a pleasant, sympathetic man, but with very little helpful information. He did not know why my mother was not there, but he did know that I was to be given money, put on a train and dispatched to Chicago, all of which he accomplished efficiently so that I found myself on the "Broadway Limited" rattling through the night in the direction of Chicago. I had been, and still was, alarmed at my mother's non-appearance at the ship, but assumed that this would be cleared up upon my arrival in Chicago. It did not turn out to be quite so simple.

There was no famililar face at the Chicago station. Bewildered, I had visions of once more finding myself in the hands of the "Traveller's Aid" and hesitated to ask questions for fear of the resulting "aid". After searching the platform nervously, I was approached by a rather formidable-looking middle-aged woman who asked me my name, and upon learning it, told me that she was there in place of my mother, who was ill. I had, apparently, known this woman as a child but it was some time before my memory was jogged into any recognition of her. When I questioned her about my mother's illness she was merely nervous and vague, and told me that my stepfather, Bill, would explain it all to me when I saw him that evening.

Arriving at our apartment on the south side of the city, I found that there were two people I did remember: my half-sister, Linda, and the coloured woman, Clara, who had been our nurse and housekeeper when I was a very young boy. Even Clara, however, was mysterious about my mother, so I spent the afternoon waiting impatiently for Bill's return from his office and the moment when my questions would be answered.

When he did arrive, about six that evening, the mystery continued. He merely greeted me, with some reserve, and told me that he would "talk to me" later that evening. Then, to my surprise, he mixed a cocktail and asked me if I smoked and drank. I replied, honestly, that while I did not make a habit of either, I had been known to do both. He smiled and offered me a drink and a cigarette, both of which I accepted. He asked me a great many unimportant questions—about my trip across the ocean, etc., but kept the conversation rigorously general. By this time, I had accepted the fact that I would get no information until he chose to give it to me, so I did not press him. However, it did seem a long time before we had finally finished dinner and my sister had been put to bed. I had already understood that she had to be disposed of before he would talk to me.

When we were, at last, alone in the large livingroom of the luxurious apartment overlooking Lake Michigan, Bill's nervousness seemed to increase, and he offered me another drink and cigarette, which I again accepted. After a great deal of fumbling, hemming and hawing, he finally sat down facing me, and with a stern expression on his face, produced the document that had been prepared in Paris to dissolve the adoption, a copy of which had been handed to me as I boarded the ship at Cherbourg. I had read it, of course. Not only had I read it and been shocked by it, but I also remembered Jane's words when she had given it to me—on the gangplank of the tender: "You may be shocked when you read this," she had said, "but try to realize my position and remember that it was very difficult to break the adoption without some reason that would be legally valid."

The essence of the document was that I was being "expelled" from the Gurdjieff school because I was "morally unfit". The phrase had no specific meaning for me, at fifteen, and while I had been genuinely shocked and hurt by it, I had taken some meagre comfort from Jane's explanation and, in the course of the trip, had finally assumed that the document had had to be worded that way for, as she had said, "legal reasons" which were beyond my capacity to understand at that age.

How easily do the young place their trust in adults! In addition to that document, I had with me the last letters I had received from Lois and Bill—letters of welcome and glowing descriptions of their preparations for my future. I would be sent to college, I had nothing to worry about now, I had been away too long, it was time I had a good home, and so on . . . *ad infinitum*. I had already accepted, and believed, these welcoming missives, and my reading of the legal papers had not discouraged me. True, it had worried me, but I counted on the love and trust of my welcoming family, and completely discounted the possible effect of the, to me, meaningless legal phraseology.

Bill, document in hand, corrected my mistaken assumptions in very short order. He began by acknowledging his and Lois' letters, reminding me, however, that they had been written before the document had been received. I said, in all my fifteen-year-old innocence, that I did not see why the "meaningless legal phrases" should alter anything and also quoted to him what Jane had said about it. He thought this over briefly and then said, to my astonishment, that he had thought over the whole question and had come to the conclusion that, since Jane was, as he knew, a difficult person, there was some possibility that she had distorted or exaggerated the facts.

Exaggerated! I asked him what he meant by that and he replied quickly that there must obviously be some truth in the document but that he would like to hear my version of what I had done in order to be expelled. When I said that I did not know what he meant and that, in any case, I had not been expelled, he said that nothing could now be gained by lying.

For his sake, perhaps I had better point out that he was a lawyer and had great respect for legal documents. In any event, after the preliminary conversation, during which we had arrived at some kind of dead-end, he took another tack and asked me if I understood the meaning of the words "morally unfit"? I said that I knew, roughly, that they signified something unpleasant but that they had no precise meaning for me.

He then produced a long letter from Jane which, as he pointed out quite unnecessarily, amplified the meaning of these words. I sat in a kind of frozen horror as he read excerpts from the letter, which, according to him, had been the cause of my mother's hospitalization a few days before, because of a complete nervous collapse. According to the letter, there was very little question but that I was some sort of sexually depraved delinquent given, principally, to the practice of corrupting other, smaller, children. When he had finished reading, I remained silent, and he then poured me another drink and asked me if I realized the problem which now faced him. I shook my head dumbly and said I did not know what he meant, so he amplified his position by pointing out to me that if the allegations in Jane's letter were true, he could not, of course, safely allow me to inhabit this apartment in company with his seven-year-old daughter, my half-sister. With a glance at the drink in my hand, he also mentioned that he did not know of any other fifteen-year-old boys who "smoked and drank".

I then took a deep breath, and a drink, and asked him if he believed that the "allegations" (his word) were true. He said that he was "reserving his opinion" until he had heard my side of the story.

I had been told that the Gurdjieff school was a "preparation for life" of a different, and better, sort than could ever be found in ordinary schools or under ordinary "life conditions". While this may have been true, I did not, at that moment, feel prepared for the problem facing me. After some deliberation (perhaps the preparation had been better than I realized) I said that it seemed to me, in general, that people believed what they wished to believe. I added that, obviously, if I admitted to the "crimes" suggested by the letter, he would believe me. On the other hand, if I denied them, since the charges had been made, he would always wonder if I were telling the truth or not. I said further that since I had no way of proving my "innocence" the only course left to me was to say nothing. That I would leave up to him —not to decide which one of us, Jane or me, had been telling the truth—but simply to decide whether or not Jane had been honest. Thwarted and frustrated by this attitude, Bill pressed me for three hours for an affirmation or a denial, but I remained resolutely firm and told him that I was leaving the decision squarely in his hands and on his conscience without any further comments. By midnight, he had decided to continue to "reserve his decision" and told me that, temporarily, I would be allowed to stay in the apartment. He added that he had arranged for someone to take me to visit my mother the following day.

I slept that night, in the library, with a great many

misgivings. The world, that night, seemed very large indeed, and equally hostile.

* * *

The by now (to me) famous legal document was only the beginning. I did see my mother the next day and, while she greeted me with the kind of affection that was natural to a mother who has not seen her son for a long time, the seed of suspicion had been sown in fertile soil. She was not in the hospital for very long and I was very happy when she came back to live with us, but it also came to mean that I was under double surveillance. I don't know exactly what was expected of me but, looking back, it might have resolved the whole problem had I, as it were obediently, either raped my sister or at least initiated her into some strange and reprehensible sexual practices. The fact that I did not, instead of clearing my name, only prolonged the suspense.

To add to this, I received—in the course of three or four weeks after my arrival in Chicago—several letters from people who had been mutual friends of Jane and of my family and, therefore, of mine. Jane's "coverage" of the events leading up to my return to America had been as complete as possible—as if she had been a one-woman "Associated Press". The content of all these letters was more or less identical. The writer, having heard from Jane, was sorry to hear of my progress in delinquency and felt that it would be better, for all concerned, if I would not make any attempt to get in touch with them.

Having, by this time, resigned myself to the obvious "hostility" of the adult world, I did not express very much feeling when I received these letters. I sensed, somehow, that any sort of protest would be useless and that my only ally—if I had one—was time.

In the meantime, certain definite decisions and arrangements had to be made that related to my future. Largely because of the stock market crash (although we seemed to me affluent enough), it was decided that the idea of my going to college was out of the question. However, I would at least have to have a respectable high school diploma. I was enrolled in high school as a senior, in spite of my previous lack of any acceptable or accredited high school training; apparently certain tests were enough to accomplish this. However, after completing less than one semester (with straight "A's" except in Zoology which I loathed and did not pass) it was decided that I could get along without any further formal education — or any diploma — and Bill's solution was to offer me a job in his law office—I was to be paid $12.00 per week and would have to pay for my own transportation and my laundry; food would be "thrown in" without further expense to me.

After I had been working, presumably satisfactorily, for a few months, my mother told me that she had to talk to me about an important decision she would have to make. She found that she could no longer bear life with Bill and had decided to either divorce him or, at least, separate from him legally. I was sixteen at that time and the recent events of my life seemed to have come full circle, to a total stop. By the fall of that year, 1930, events had followed events rigorously. After a separation and the beginning of a suit for divorce, I found myself living alone on $15.00 a week (I had been given a $3.00 a week raise), still working in my stepfather's office. My mother and my half-sister had fled to Europe and when Bill, who had also made a separate trip to Europe, on business, returned and found them absent, I found myself out of a job.

So, by September of 1930, all the threads had been cut. I was then living alone, without a job, on the accumulated savings from my small weekly salary.

What does all this have to do with Georges Gurdjieff any reader may well ask. In a sense, nothing; except that, having trusted and perhaps worshipped him for about five years, my feelings for and about him were now strongly reinforced. No one else in the world, or in my experience of the world, seemed willing to give me "house-room" and while the knowledge of his existence was a distant comfort to me, he was somewhere in France, about four thousand miles from Chicago.

II

DURING THE PERIOD 1930 to 1932, I lived a rather solitary existence. I had found a job as a combination file-clerk and French translator, and was able to live on my small weekly salary.

It was in the fall of 1931 that I came into contact with a group of about twenty-five people who constituted the so-called "Chicago Gurdjieff Group". Although I came to know most of them personally and attended their "group meetings", I found it difficult to understand their interest in Gurdjieff. They seemed to me to have been attracted to his teaching for a variety of not very good reasons—because of loneliness, or perhaps because they considered themselves misfits or outcasts. Most of them had dabbled in the arts, theosophy, the occult, or something of the sort, and had come to Gurdjieff as if in search of another "cure" for their life problems of whatever nature. Gurdjieffian theory—whatever it might be—seemed acceptable to them precisely because it was difficult to define. While Gurdjieff himself had always made sense to me as an individual, I had not had much contact with his "theories" when I had been at the Prieuré. These theories, as presented and discussed by this Chicago group were a total mystery to me. I began to sense a certain danger in his teaching when it was carried on without his personal supervision.

My more or less unconscious exposure to Gurdjieff's ideas while I was at the Prieuré had given me some ideas of my own. I thought of his teaching as something that was intended to stimulate interest in personal self-development, but certainly not as a philosophy that had any bearing on—or interest in—the everyday problems of people. It did not pretend to answer questions or offer solutions to existing difficulties, but (or so it seemed to me) suggested the possibility of a new way of life; a way of acquiring new values and a new morality. How this was accomplished was another question—and I had learned not to ask about that.

The meetings in Chicago, generally, consisted of readings of Gurdjieff's first book which purported to be, in his own

words, "an objective, impartial criticism of the life of man",
and these readings were usually followed by a discussion
period during which these followers seemed to me to
attempt to relate his writings to their own individuality.
Since the writings were obviously critical of ordinary values,
standards and social morality, the group members usually
interpreted these criticisms as meaning that any values
which ran counter to the prevailing morality were worthwhile. With this view of life, such things as free love,
adultery, or any radical social behavior became almost
automatically justified. In other words, while Gurdjieff
seemed to me to offer a means of acquiring a new point of
view towards life, through work and personal struggles, the
prevailing attitude of this particular group of followers was
that of substituting new values for old by rote, without any
consideration of the means; no attempt was made to acquire
— through conscious effort — a new perspective. They
behaved as if it were possible simply to decide that they had,
overnight, acquired them in their sleep much as if they had,
without any effort whatsoever, suddenly ceased to need to
smoke cigarettes.

One of the major differences—for me—between this group
and the adults who had, presumably, been involved in the
same sort of "work" at the Prieuré, was that these people
were all Americans and most of them had never been to the
Prieuré. The strictly "American" nature of the group was
impressed upon me through the question of morality.
Europeans—at least the Europeans I had known in France
and at the Prieuré—appeared to think of "morality" as a
code of behaviour covering general human activity including, among a great many other things, sexual activity. To
these Americans—or for that matter most other Americans
with whom I had any contact—"morality" was confined to
sexual codes, and extended perhaps as far as table manners.
But no further. Having had, up to that point in my life, no
sexual experience, I was both surprised by, and unprepared
for, this kind of morality. It came as a distinct surprise to
me, therefore, to learn that a good deal of the interest in
Gurdjieff himself seemed to be based on the assumption

that life at the Prieuré must have been indiscriminately "free", meaning "licentious". I knew, of couse, that Gurdjieff was the father of some illegitimate children. I also know, however, that Gurdjieff (contrary to the opinions of these, and other, people) quite frankly imposed restrictions upon his "disciples" that he did not impose upon himself. He would have been the first person to tell you that he was "extraordinary"—in the sense that he was not bound by average behavioural rules. Once I had begun to comprehend this "American morality" I understood why much of the discussion, following the book readings, was concerned with such questions as free love, etc. The book itself did not, in my opinion, even go into such subjects, but it did lend itself to interpretation of all kinds.

Although these readings left me almost completely in the dark—for the simple reason that it was a difficult book to read and required complete attention and concentration on the part of the reader or listener—there was enough comprehensible material in it to hold my interest and to make me begin to think about the man and his work in a different way than I had before. When the book is read as a straight forward criticism of man's history on the planet Earth, it can have a stimulating, thought-provoking effect and I doubt that this first book was intended as anything more than a critique. In general, although it suggests that there are solutions to the "human dilemma" it does not actually do much more in that direction than to further suggest that there are means which lead to solutions—no actual solutions or answers are given. So much of the criticism in the book is new or radical that it was difficult, if not impossible, to argue against it. In order to retain an interest in the Gurdjieff work one had to accept his view of life, in the same sense that it would, I assume, be necessary to have faith in order to become a genuine, honest follower of, say, the Catholic religion.

The group members, generally, managed to avoid the dilemma of this "faith" or "commitment" by the rather simple expedient of deciding that the Gurdjieff writings were primarily allegorical and, therefore, subject to whatever interpretation they chose to give them. It was rather like getting married without benefit of a licence or a ceremony. I was still young enough to read such a simple statement as the fact that "constipation was the universal disease, particularly of Americans, because their toilet seats were too comfortable", and accept it as meaning nothing more than what it said. I could understand someone arguing that constipation was not a universal disease, but I could not understand it when some group member asserted that Gurdjieff did not mean constipation in the usual sense, but, rather, something emotional or mental. In fact, while the style in which the book is written seems enormously complicated — at least on first reading — the complexity seems to me to be an attempt at absolute precision and calculated to avoid the possibility of any interpretation or "double meaning". When the book states that man, as such, does not have a soul but only has the rather faint possibility of acquiring one, I think the statement is literal, and I further assume that Gurdjieff, towards this aim, means quite simply what it says. I do not, of course, mean that any reader was compelled to *agree* with such a statement, but I do not feel that it means anything else. I, personally, find the statement acceptable, and am not concerned with whether any other person believes it. My only argument would be with those who assume that it contains a separate, or allegorical, meaning.

Among other things, Gurdjieff, along with accepted religions, seemed to say that one should "love one's enemies", i.e., not have any enemies, and it did not seem to me that such a statement was open to question. The problem, if there was a problem, might lie in the interpretation of the word "love". Gurdjieff's own definition of it—to know enough to be able to help others even when they could not help themselves—was good enough for me and had only one meaning.

By and large, the Chicago "group" fitted in with other Gurdjieff "disciples" I had known—people who were content to take on certain ritualistic, physical attitudes which lacked any inner content. After a short period of association

with Gurdjieff and exposure to his writings, people frequently changed the outer expression of themselves and were
given to affectations in speech and dress, usually intended
to express reverence. One element that was conspicuously
lacking in most of Gurdjieff's followers was the one element
which he, himself, expressed abundantly — humour. In
consequence, the meetings were charged with an atmosphere of grim, humourless, devotion—and a consequent lack
of perspective. It seemed to me that if we were as idiotic and
un-formed as Gurdjieff depicts us to be, it is practically
impossible to see ourselves objectively without a sense of the
ridiculous. The very posturing and attitudinizing of the
group members was evidence of a certain misplaced seriousness. While it was obvious that any solution to the human
predicament would involve serious, hard work, the contem-
plation of ordinary human behaviour was not without its
ridiculous aspects. The spectacle of a group of adult, human
beings, discussing—in hushed tones—their weaknesses,
sins, and general fallibility certainly had its humorous side
to me, perhaps particularly because I was one of the group.

III

It was with some misgivings that I learned that Mr. Gurdjieff was going to make a visit to Chicago during the winter of 1932. Even now, some thirty years later and with the aid of hindsight, I find it difficult to understand why I did not want to see him. Part of my feeling was unquestionably due to the fact that I had come to believe that I had probably made a mistake when I left the Prieuré in 1929. I felt that I was not, because of my departure, a loyal or faithful follower. In addition, while I had some genuine interest in his writing, and real affection for Gurdjieff as a man, my association with the Chicago group had made me question the validity of his work in all its aspects. I was still looking for some proof—some quality in the behaviour of his followers—that would convince me that he was something more than a powerful human being who was able to mesmerize a good many individuals at will. My interest in his writing was—at that time—nothing more than curiosity concerning his particular speculations and criticisms of mankind. It was not a whole-hearted agreement with his point of view.

I did see him, but not without a good deal of resistance on my part. In fact, if I had not received a message from him asking me to come to see him, I would not have seen him at all. As it was, the meeting was not very satisfactory to me. I went, with a small group of his followers, to meet him at a restaurant in downtown Chicago. It was a noisy place, with music and dancing, and after he had greeted me affectionately, we proceeded to sit in this din without any further exchange. The other people talked to him incessantly, mostly about uninteresting and, to me, unimportant personal problems, and for a long time my only participation in the proceedings was that he sent me on several errands—to buy cigarettes for him, to buy some special kind of cheese, to telephone some particular group member to come to meet him, etc. Finally, when there was a lull in the general conversation, Gurdjieff turned to me, indicating the couples dancing on the crowded dance floor and asked me if I realized that dancing was a very interesting and almost perfect example of what he called "titillation". I felt that I understood what he meant, i.e., "waste", and said so. He then asked me if I knew that titillation was "social masturbation" which, mostly because of my age, embarrassed me. I managed to say that I agreed with this and he then said that it was time for me to look objectively at the life of people—to observe human manifestations, and to try to understand the difference between genuine, essential, normal human behaviour and "titillation" or "masturbation". He added that while he had used this example of dancing, I should learn to recognize this "masturbation" in other spheres of human activity. As an example, he said that people frequently learned very quickly to turn anything —even their religion and their so-called serious beliefs—into some meaningless form of titillation. I made some reference to his statement of many years before that much of mankind was inevitably destined to become nothing more than fertilizer and he was very pleased that I had remembered that conversation. He said, however, that he had been studying the American language recently and had learned many new and useful terms; that he now wanted to change the term "fertililzer" to "shit" because the latter word was a "real" word . . . an honestly expressive word that gave the proper flavour of that particular human condition. He went on to say that I, like most young people—particularly Americans—always looked at the world upside down. For example, I assumed that anyone I met was good, honest, upright, etc., etc., and only learned the truth about people through disillusion. This attitude was a long, slow and improper process. "You must learn to look right side up," he said. "Every person you see, including yourself, is shit. You learn this and then when you find something good in such shit people—some possibility not to be shit—you will have two things: you will feel good inside when you learn this person better than you think, and you will also have made proper observation. Just so, when you can observe self, if you already think self is all shit then when see something good in self will be able to recognize at once and will also feel joy. Important that you think about this."

The immediate association in my mind was with the Chicago group members and it did have the effect of changing my attitude about and towards them. Instead of feeling disappointment with them for not manifesting some sort of worthiness because of their association with Gurdjieff's work, I began to look for something else. It did seem a great deal more honest and realistic to look at people, including myself, as worthless—or shit, as he put it—and then discern some small, valid element in them. And, to my surprise, it amounted to a more compassionate view of humanity as well. Instead of watching with a critical eye for signs of failure, I began to watch for signs of success—as one might be delighted when a dog learned a trick—rather than berating it whenever it failed to learn something.

Whether or not this change in my attitude was what Gurdjieff intended is open to question. That was the effect it had on me, and it seems to me that the effectiveness of the Gurdjieff work—or for that matter of any work of that kind —is necessarily determined by the receptivity of the person towards whom it is directed. Be that as it may, the conversation made my future association with the Chicago group, and with people in general, a much less disturbing and much more acceptable process. There was a short period during which the paradox of considering people "shit" and thereby finding myself more in harmony with them, was confusing to me, but I did not puzzle over that for long. I was glad of the change, and that was sufficient.

Our conversation ended that evening with a rather cryptic anaylsis—by Gurdjieff—of my association with him. Humorously, and apparently relishing some private joke, he said that the other people present were learning his work in a very different way than I had, and that because of my childhood association with him I had certain problems and struggles which they would never experience. "You not wish to come to see me tonight," he said, "so necessary for me— very busy man—to take time to send for you. This because you now have struggle between real self and personality. You not learn my work from talk and book—you learn in skin, and you cannot escape. These people," and he indicated the other group members, "must make effort, go to meetings, read book. If you never go to meeting, never read book, you still cannot forget what I put inside you when you child. These others, if not go to meeting, will forget even existence of Mr. Gurdjieff. But not you. I already in your blood—make your life miserable for ever—but such misery can be good thing for your soul, so even when miserable you must thank your God for suffering I give you."

Before Mr. Gurdjieff left Chicago, I had a private interview with him. I had been puzzled by his remarks about my special problems in relation to his work and had not had any particular desire to pursue the subject further; I was tired of confusion, and his words had only added to my already perplexed state. But, when he asked me to help him cook a meal in his apartment, I did not feel that I could refuse. As it turned out, there was very little work for me to do, and he spent most of our time alone together asking me rather ordinary questions about my family, the work I did, and so on. It was reminiscent of being visited by some old relative who had deigned to take an unexpected interest in some younger member of a family.

When we began to talk about the Chicago group, however, I made a rather impertinent remark about what I called their "phony" attitude towards his work, and particularly towards their so-called morality.

Gurdjieff, who did not usually—in my experience—have any particular taste for opinions or "gossip" about his groups or his disciples, seemed very much interested in my remark and pressed me for details. I went on to say, with a good deal of self-righteousness, that I was leery of his group in Chicago on at least two counts: their phony reverence, as I called it, and their tendency to use his work as an excuse for sexual promiscuity or at least a good deal of talk about sexual promiscuity. Being further prodded by him, I went on about their conception of morality seeming to me to be based almost entirely on sex and not on other customs.

He smiled at this and then said, to my surprise, that he found this completely understandable. "In fact, this is perhaps even good thing you tell me about group people. America is still very young, strong country. Like young people everywhere, all Americans very interested, very preoccupied with sex things. So very natural for them talk and act this way. And not bad thing they do. I tell many times that all work must start with body; like I tell many times that if wish observe self must start from outside, by observing movements of body. Only much later can learn how observe emotional and mental centres. Young people not have very much inside, so not much to observe yet. And this is also good thing, one of reason I come to America and have many American students. Europeans already blasé, know everything, or think know about philosophy, religion, other such things. This not true. They only have already formed inner self that makes them rotten inside because formed with unconsciousness. Americans more receptive because not closed up inside yet; they naïve, stupid, perhaps, but still real. Americans, particularly, have more chance grow properly as men because have not yet become— like you say—'phony' men. For yourself, I tell always remember look for reasons that eye cannot see. You already notice difference between American and European morality, but when make judgment must observe deeper if wish understand."

I then asked him why it was that I felt so many of his students to be insincere in their interpretations of him and of his work. He asked me to give him an example and I said that they never seemed to me to listen to what he said—that is, the actual words — but that they almost always immediately placed an interpretation on such words which was, to me, manifestly untrue.

"What you say is true," he said, "but if you see this then you must already begin to see how difficult this work. Other evening when I tell that you learn differently from others, I tell truth. When you come Prieuré first time you not yet spoiled, have not learn to lie to self. Already even then you can maybe lie to mother or father, but not to self. So you fortunate. But these people very unfortunate. Like you, when child, they learn lie to parents, but as they grow up also learn lie to self and once learn this is very difficult to change. Lying, like all other things, become habit for them. So when I say even ordinary thing, because they wish have reverence for their teacher—this reverence can be very bad thing, but is necessary for their good feeling—and because also wish not disturb their inside sleep, they find other meaning for what I say."

"In that case," I asked, "how can they ever learn anything from you—or from anyone else?"

"Maybe they not learn anything ever."

"Then why bother to try and teach them?"

He smiled, indulgently. "Because is possibility, even if very small, may learn."

It seemed logical enough, as he put it, but I doubted that there was much in store for most of the people who worked with him.

After leaving his apartment, as I reviewed the conversation, I wondered whether I was making an exception of myself in the sense that I felt I was learning more (or at least *something*) from him than his other students. And I wondered if I was not feeling a little "self-proud" of myself. After turning the questions over in my mind, I could not honestly tell myself that I was in any way particularly vain about my learning. I was proud, in a comparative way, that I had known him personally so much more intimately and for so much longer a time than many of his other students, but as to any actual learning, I could not evaluate it for the simple reason that if I was learning anything at all from him I didn't know what it was. That did give me a slight clue, but not a very satisfactory one. The clue was simply that if one did acquire knowledge, or learned something from him, it might not necessarily be visible or obvious.

IV

AFTER SEEING MR. GURDJIEFF in Chicago in 1932, there was
an interval of about two years during which I did not see
him again. I had moved to New York in the fall of 1933, and
one Saturday afternoon when I came home from work my
landlord told me that a very strange man, with a heavy,
foreign accent had come to see me and wanted me to get in
touch with him. The landlord, however, had not been able to
understand him, did not know his name, and only knew that
whoever he was, he was living at the Henry Hudson Hotel
in New York. I thought of Gurdjieff at once, although it was
difficult for me to believe that he had gone to the trouble of
finding my address and then coming to search for me in
person. I went to the hotel immediately and, as I had
expected, found him there.

When I got to his apartment in the hotel, he told me that
he had tried to find me earlier in the day, but that now it
was too late and that he had no further need of—or use for
—me. There was no affection in his greeting and he merely
looked bored and very tired. In spite of this, and because I
was glad to see him and worried about his great weariness, I
did not leave but reminded him that he had once told me
that "it was never too late to make reparations in life", and
that while I was sorry not to have been home earlier, there
was surely something I could do now that I had arrived.

He looked at me with a tired smile and said that perhaps
there was something I could do. He led me into the kitchen,
indicated an enourmous pile of dirty dishes and said they
needed to be washed; he then pointed to another equally
enormous pile of vegetables and said they needed to be
prepared for a dinner he was going to give that evening.
After showing these to me, he asked me if I had the time to
help him. When I had assured him that I did, he told me to
wash the dishes first and then prepare the vegetables.
Before leaving the kitchen, to rest, he said that he hoped he
would be able to count on me to finish both jobs—otherwise
he would not be able to rest properly. I told him not to worry
and went to work on the dishes. He watched me for a few

minutes and then said that several people had promised to help him that day but that there were no members of the New York group who were able to keep their promises. I told him that he had better rest while he had the opportunity and not waste his time talking to me, and he laughed and left the kitchen.

I was finished with my work when he returned and he was very pleased. He then began to cook the evening meal and told me to set the table for fifteen people, adding that some very important people—important for his work—were coming to dinner and that when the food was in the oven he would need me to help him by giving him an English lesson as it was essential that he talk to these people in a certain way—in a language that they would understand correctly.

When we had finished our work, he sat down at the table, told me to sit next to him and then began asking me questions about the English language. It turned out that he wanted to learn, before the guests arrived, all the words for the various parts and functions of the body "that were not in the dictionary". We spent perhaps two hours repeating every four-letter word that I knew, plus every obscene phrase I could think of. By about seven o'clock he felt that he was reasonanly proficient with our "slang" vocabulary which he, apparently, needed for his dinner. Inevitably, I began to wonder what sort of people would be coming to dinner. At the conclusion of this "lesson" he told me that it was for that lesson that he had been trying to find me, because I was the first person who, some years before Chicago, had given him the real flavour and meaning of the words "phony" and "leery"; it seems that these words, in the interim, had become very useful in his conversations with his American students. "These very good words," he said, "raw . . . like your America."

When the guests did arrive, they turned out to be a group of well-dressed, well-mannered New Yorkers, and, since Gurdjieff had gone to "prepare" himself for dinner, I greeted them and, according to his precise instructions, served them drinks.

He did not appear until most of them had been there for

about half an hour, and when he greeted them, he was very apologetic for the delay and extremely effusive about how beautiful the ladies looked and how much they were all honouring him by consenting to be the guests of a poor, humble man like himself. I was actually embarrassed by what seemed to be a very crude form of flattery and by his presentation of himself as an unworthy and very obsequious host. But, to my surprise, it seemed to work. By the time they were seated at the dinner table, all the guests were in a very mellow mood (they had had only one drink so it was not due to liquor) and they began in a somewhat jocular and superior way, to ask him questions about his work and his reasons for coming to America. The general tone of the questions was bored—many of the people present were reporters or journalists— and they behaved as if they were carrying out an assignment to interview some crank. I could already see them making mental notes and could imagine the sort of "funny" interview or feature story they might write. After some questioning by this group, I noticed that Gurdjieff's voice changed in tone, and as I watched him he gave me a sudden, sly wink.

He then proceeded to tell them that since they were all very superior people that they of course knew—since a simple person like himself knew it, then obviously they did —that humanity in general was in a very sad state and could only be considered as having degenerated into real waste matter, or to use a term that was familiar to all of them, pure "shit". That this transformation of humankind into something worthless was especially apparent in America—which was why he had come there to observe it. He went on to say that the main cause of this sad state of affairs was that people—especially Americans—were never motivated by intelligence or good feelings, but only by the needs—usually dirty—of their genital organs, using, of course (as he talked) only the four-letter words which he had practised with me earlier. He indicated one very well-dressed, handsome woman, complimented her on her coiffure, her dress, her perfume, etc., and then said that while she, of course, might not want everyone to know her motives or her desires, he and she could be honest with each other—that her reasons for turning herself out so elaborately were because she had a strong sexual urge (as he put it "wish to fuck") for some particular person and was so tormented by it that she was using every means and every wile she could think of in order to get that person into bed with her. He said that her urge was particularly, especially strong because she had a very fertile imagination and could already picture herself performing various sexual acts with this man—"such as, how you say in English? 'Sixty-nine'?"—so that, aided by her imagination, she was now at the point where she would do *anything* to achieve her aim. While the company was somewhat startled with this dissertation (not to say "titillated"), before anyone had time to react, he began a description of his own sexual abilities and of his highly imaginative mind, and described himself as capable of sustained sexual acts of incredible variety—such as even the lady in question would not be able to imagine.

He then launched into a detailed description of the sexual habits of various races and nations, during the course of which he pointed out that while the French had a world-wide reputation for amorous prowess, it would be well for the people present to make a note of the fact that those highly civilized French used such words as "Mama" and "Mimi" to describe some of their unnatural and perverted sexual practices. He added, however, that in all justice to the French they were, in reality, very moral people and sexually misunderstood and misrepresented.

The guests had all been drinking heavily during dinner—good old Armagnac as always—and after about two hours of unadulterated four-letter word conversation, their behaviour became completely uninhibited. Whether they had all come to believe and accept that they had been invited to an orgy, or for whatever reasons, an orgy—or the beginning of one—was the result. Gurdjieff egged them on by giving them elaborate descriptions of the male and female organs, and of some imaginative uses for them, and finally most of the guests were physically entangled in groups in various rooms of the apartment, and in various states of undress.

The handsome lady had manœuvred herself into a small bar
with Gurdjieff and was busily making "passes" of a rather
inventive nature, at him.

As for me, I was cornered in the kitchen by an overblown,
attractive lady who told me that she was outraged that
Gurdjieff should use such words in my presence—I did not
look more than about seventeen. I explained, quite honestly,
that I had taught them all to him—or at least most of them,
and she found this suddenly hilarious and promptly made a
pass at me. I backed away and told her that, unfortunately,
I had to do the dishes. Rebuffed, she glared at me, called me
various dirty names and said that the only reason I had
turned her down was because I was "that dirty old man's
little faggot", and only wanted him to "screw" me. I was
somewhat startled at this, but remembered Gurdjieff's
reputation for sexual depravity and made no response.

While the other guests were still hard at it, Gurdjieff
suddenly disentangled himself from the lady and told them
all, in loud, stentorian tones, that they had already con-
firmed his observations of the decadence of the Americans
and that they need no longer demonstrate for him. He
pointed at various individuals, mocked their behaviour and
then told them that if they were, thanks to him, now partly
conscious of what sort of people they really were, it was an
important lesson for them. He said that he deserved to be
paid for this lesson and that he would gladly accept cheques
and cash from them as they left the apartment. I was not
particularly surprised, knowing him and having watched
the performance of the evening, to find that he had collected
several thousand dollars. I was even less surprised when one
man told me—as it were, "man to man"—that Gurdjieff,
posing as a philosopher, had the best ideas about sex, and
the safest "cover" for his orgies, of anyone he had ever
known.

When everyone had left, I finished washing the dishes,
and to my surprise Gurdjieff came into the kitchen to dry
them and put them away. He asked me how I had enjoyed
the evening and I said, youthfully and righteously, that I
was disgusted. I also told him about my encounter with the

lady in the kitchen and her description of my relationship with him. He shrugged his shoulders and said that in such cases the facts were what constituted the truth and that I should never consider or worry about opinions. Then he laughed and gave me a piercing look. "Is fine feeling you have—this disgust," he said. "But now is necessary ask yourself one question. With who you disgusted?"

When I was ready to leave the apartment, he stopped me and referred again to my experience with the lady. "Such lady have in self many homosexual tendencies, one reason she pick on you—young-looking boy, seem almost like girl to her. Not worry about this thing she say to you. Gossip about sex only give reputation for sexiness in your country, so not important, maybe even feather in hat, as you say. Some day you will learn much more about sex, but this you can learn by self, not from me."

V

Mr. Gurdjieff stayed in New York for several months, through the winter and spring of 1934, and I saw him regularly. My relationship with him, more or less of its own accord, fell back into a pattern that resembled our earlier years at the Prieuré. Once again, I became a sort of functionary of the household, helping to cook, wash dishes, run errands, etc. I also attended meetings, lectures, and readings but without much active interest. I was far more involved with the man himself—as I had been as a child—than with his teaching.

I had planned to go to Chicago during my two weeks' vacation in the summer of 1934, and when Mr. Gurdjieff learned of this he decided that he would make a visit to Chicago at the same time as it would be convenient for him to have me as a travelling companion. I was very proud to be "selected" to act as his companion and secretary when he went to Chicago and I looked forward to the trip. For some reason, I think because he felt it would be a suitable time for him, we were to leave on a train at midnight. I was packed and ready for the trip early in the evening and went to his apartment in what I thought was plenty of time. What with his packing—piles of clothing, books, food, medicine, etc.,—he was not ready to leave the apartment until well after eleven p.m., and when we arrived at the station with only about ten minutes to spare we were met by a large delegation of the New York followers. It seemed that each one of them had some urgent last-minute business to take up with him, and about two minutes before train time I interrupted him impatiently, and told him we had to board the train. He said that we had to have a few more minutes—that the extra time was absolutely essential—and for me to talk to someone and arrange to delay the train. I looked at him dumbfounded, but realized that there was no arguing with him. I managed to find some official and made up some story about the improtance of Mr. Gurdjieff which, to my great surprise, was effective, and the official agreed to hold the train for ten minutes. Even so, Mr. Gurdjieff did not manage to complete his urgent farewells until the train was actually moving and I had to push him through the door of the last car with his six or seven pieces of luggage. As soon as he was in the moving train, he began to complain in a loud voice about having been interrupted and demanded that a bed be prepared for him immediately. The conductor, with my help, explained to him that our berths were thirteen cars ahead and that we would have to walk to them —very quietly, as most of the other passengers had boarded the train early and were already asleep—through the entire train. Gurdjieff looked appalled, sat down on one of his suitcases, and lighted a cigarette. The conductor or porter told him that smoking was forbidden except in the men's room and he groaned loudly about this hardship, but did consent to put out his cigarette.

It must have taken us—Gurdjieff, conductor, porter, and me—at least forty-five minutes to get to our assigned berths. Our progress — with all the luggage and with Gurdjieff's lamentations about the rude treatment he was receiving—was so noisy that we awakened almost everyone on the train. In every car, heads would appear through the curtains to hiss at us and curse us. I was furious with him, as well as exhausted, and greatly relieved when we found our berths. Then, to my horror, he decided that he had to eat, drink, and smoke, and began unpacking his bags in search of food and liquor. I was finally able to force him into the men's room. Once in there he settled down to eat and drink and to discourse in loud tones about the terrible service on American trains and the fact that he—a very important man—was being treated in this shoddy fashion. When we were finallly threatened—in no uncertain terms— by both the conductor and the porter, with expulsion from the train at the next stop, I lost my temper completely and said that I would be glad to get off the train in order to get away from him. At this, he looked at me in wide-eyed innocence and wanted to know if I was angry with him— and, if so, why. I said that I was furious and that he was making a spectacle of both of us, so he put his food and drink away sadly and then, lighting another cigarette, said that he had never inagined that I, his only friend, would talk to him in this way, and quite literally, desert him. This attitude only increased my anger and I said that once we arrived in Chicago I hoped never to see him again.

He then went to bed in his lower berth, still very sorrowful and still muttering about my unkindness and lack of loyalty, and I climbed into the upper berth hoping for some much-needed sleep. After about five minutes, punctuated by moans and groans from Gurdjieff as he tossed and turned in the lower berth, and by renewed hissing and cursing from the other passengers, he began to talk in a loud voice, complaining that he needed a drink of water, had to have a cigarette, and so forth. There were more threats from the porter and finally, at about four a.m., he settled down and did go to sleep.

We were the last passengers to awaken the next morning and while he dressed and made several trips to the men's room in whatever state of undress he happened to be at the moment, we were stared at by a car full of hostile travelling companions who had, of course, identified us as the troublemakers of the night before. After about one hour, I managed to get him to the dining car, hoping for a peaceful breakfast, but once again my hopes were dashed. There was nothing on the menu that he could eat, and we had long, irritating conversations with the waiter and the head steward about the possibility of procuring yoghurt and similar—at that time—exotic foods, accompanied by vivid descriptions of his particular digestive process and its highly specialized needs. After several long discussions, he suddenly gave in and ate, without any visible discomfort but with a great many complaints, a large American breakfast.

As the train did not arrive in Chicago until late that afternoon, I was not looking forward to spending the day in the Pullman car, but once again I hoped for the best. My fears, however, were well-grounded. I have never, in my life, spent such a day with anyone. He smoked incessantly, in spite of complaints from the passengers and threats from the porter; drank heavily, and produced, at intervals when we seemed momentarily threatened with peace, all kinds of foods, mostly different varieties of strong-smelling cheeses. Although he apologized profusely every time the other passengers complained about his behaviour, he also constantly found new ways to annoy, irritate and offend them— not to mention me.

When we did actually arrive in Chicago it seemed to me nothing less than a miracle. Whatever my opinion of the "Chicago group", when I saw a large number of them on the platform waiting to greet him, I was delighted. I helped him off the train with all his luggage and told him that I was leaving then and there and that he need not expect to see me again. When he heard this, he raised such an outcry on the platform that, for the sake of peace, I consented to go with him and the group members to the apartment they had rented for him. Although I was already furious and outraged, the sight of the fawning disciples made me even more angry. They had prepared, with obvious effort, a "Gurdjieff-type" dinner and they did everything they could think to please him. To my further disgust, he began to praise each one of them individually, telling them what a ghastly trip he had had on the train, how horribly I had treated him, and how different it would have been had only some of them— loyal, devoted, respectful followers—been along to take care of him properly and with the respect that was due to him. I was then promptly assailed by the more ardent members of the group, and attacked for treating their leader with such disrespect, and so on.

After about an hour of this, I reached some sort of breaking-point, and told him and the group I was leaving. Gurdjieff looked at me in amazement and said that he would not be able to stay in Chicago, all alone in such a large apartment, unless I was there with him; that I could not leave him alone under any circumstances. To the horror of the group, I told him that since he was now safely surrounded by a large bunch of the faithful, he could very safely dispense with my services and that I was sure he would find them able and willing to perform any of the services he might require. In the course of this outburst I described some of their possible services in a few of the well-chosen four-letter words that he and I had worked over in New York—and the group members regarded me with disgust as well as with increased horror.

I did not see him again in Chicago, in spite of several messages begging me to take him back to New York, and on my return to New York I carefully avoided him and the New York group until I knew that he had sailed back to France.

VI

THE NEXT TIME I SAW Mr. Gurdjieff—in New York a year or two later—I found that our relationship had changed in many ways. It had taken me several months to calm down after that nightmare journey to Chicago and I came to feel that he had—by his behaviour on that trip—forced me out of the pattern of hero-worship which had unconsciously formed in me in relation to him. I no longer "loved" him in that unquestioning, idealistic way, and I no longer looked back on my early years as I had—filled with pride because of my close relationship to the "master". I saw myself as having been useful in many very ordinary ways to a man who could always put people to use if they happened to be around him. At the next encounter with him I greeted him more as a kind of equal, although not without a feeling of genuine respect, and I left the work of serving, dishwashing and running errands, to other, more abject, members of the group. He made no objection to my new attitude and seemed content to treat me as a companion rather than a body-slave.

I must admit, however, that when we first met again—this time he was staying at the Great Northern Hotel—I came very close to falling back into the old pattern almost at once. Not only did he look weary and much older, but the atmosphere of the room—with milk cartons on the window-sill, and general disorder in the two small rooms—was shoddy. He sighed and groaned, complaining about the lack of interest and enthusiasm on the part of his so-called followers, and the fact that he had no money and was forced to earn it, in addition to attending lectures, readings, dance groups, etc. My immediate, natural response was to want to help him out in some way, but I managed to resist it this time. I did, however, go to see him (he had complained among other things, of being lonely) and in the course of some of these visits, I learned at first hand about some of the ways in which he "earned money" when it was not forthcoming in the nature of contributions from the disciples. I became acquainted with a stream of "patients"—at least they were not the usual "followers"—who came to him regularly for "treatments" of various kinds. Most of them were afflicted with something: they were alcoholics, dope-addicts, just plain neurotics, homosexuals, and what could be called "adult delinquents" of one kind or another. I gathered that they paid him well to "cure" them of whatever disease or manifestation happened to be afflicting them. I do not know in what the cures consisted, except that all of them required long and frequent visits with him at all hours of the day or night—in fact, whenever he could spare the time. Whatever means were used, the effect on the individuals was the usual one: they worshipped him, at least temporarily. The difference between them and the "group" members, was that in their case the worship was, if possible, even more personal and had nothing to do with his ideas or his "method". And this was combined, in most cases, with gratitude for the "cures".

This period of having to earn money did not last very long, and it was a relief to me when it was over. I had not enjoyed my visits to Gurdjieff at that time, and I was glad when he emerged from this rather woebegone characterization of a kind of quack-doctor living in shoddy circumstances. I can only assume that he was able to earn enough money—and perhaps cure enough people—to give up what had never seemed much more than an impersonation to me. The derelicts also vanished from the scene.

From that time on, when I did go to see him, I went to the Childs' restaurants, which he referred to as his "office", and where he liked to sit and do his writing, and I also made a few short boat trips with him—usually to New Jersey.

On one of those trips, when he was once more accompanied by several of "the faithful" (as I had now come to call the disciples) he introduced me to a man and a woman who were not, as he pointed out carefully, married. He said that the man liked to marry women and had been married and divorced several times, but that he had not yet married this woman—that he was, as it were, trying her out—and that, therefore, she was his "handkerchief". He went on to give a long dissertation on the relations between the sexes. He said that there was something—a kind of relationship that rarely existed in modern times—that was worthy of the term "real marriage"; that marriage as we knew it was more than legal sexual intercourse, and that since most people, men and women, were sexually motivated and therefore needed variety, such relationships rarely lasted and usually ended in divorce. He said that there were occasional exceptions to this rule—when a deeper, more valid relationship developed out of something that was purely sexual in the beginning, but that this was rare. Most relationships, whether legal or not, were merely that of man and "handkerchief", as witness this particular couple. "For him," he said, "this very convenient; he suddenly feel need or wish to blow nose—and always he have this handkerchief with him. And after blow nose, not necesary carry such excretion in pocket. This 'woman-handkerchief' can walk all by self. Very, very convenient for modern man. Especially convenient for this man because for him necessary blow nose very often; is his favourite diversion."

He smiled at the two of them after this description and they smiled back at him. Once again, I was astonished at the way in which people accepted these pronouncements. Not that I expected protests of outrage, but this meek agreement always surprised me. And agreement alone was not enough—usually they would manage to make some interpretation of just such a description of themselves that would turn out to be flattering to them, and would even go so far as to repeat their version of his comments—with, of course, their flattering interpretation — to other group members.

This conversation occupied us for most of the trip and when we arrived at the house of some friends of his in New Jersey, he insisted that they take us to a local market where he bought several pounds of garlic which he said he required for the preparation of some special dish that he wanted to make. When we had made the purchase, we returned to our hosts' house and he instructed everyone—seven or eight of us had come with him—to start peeling and otherwise preparing this mass of garlic. While I did not refuse outright to help with this chore, I simply did not participate, but sat with him on the terrace of the house and drank a good deal of Applejack, which he had only recently discovered. After some time had passed he suddenly asked me, pointedly, how it happened that I was not helping to clean garlic. I answered that I had not made the trip in order to clean garlic—that I simply did not want to help. He then asked me if I thought that I was in some way privileged, and I said, baiting him, that I did not really consider myself worthy of such important work. He poured us each another glass of Applejack and said that I would never be able to realize what trouble he had with his students. No matter how hard he worked with them, just when they reached a stage where he thought he could rely on them, they turned out to be unreliable, etc. He added that I was a good example, a case in point. He had spent years, involving an amount of effort that I could not even imagine, training me to be a worthy, reliable follower, and that now, just when it was important for me to help with the cleaning of the garlic, I was failing him. I said that if I had learned anything from him it was that one could not rely on others—particularly for such important tasks as garlic-cleaning.

He berated me for my irreverent manner of talking to him and then suddenly switched the conversation. He told me that it was a great satisfaction—personally—to him to watch a group of his devoted followers faithfully performing a task which he had assigned to them. We paused to look at the six or seven industrious followers working with the garlic, and I said, pouring another glass of Applejack for each of us, that I could easily understand his pleasure and that, for the time being, I was content to sit with him and share that particular joy. He then cursed me again for my lack of seriousness, but even so he laughed and we continued to drink together. After a fairly long silence, he suddenly asked me why I had not been coming regularly to the group meetings, readings, etc., and I said that I did not feel that I qualified, by my attitude—or in my heart—as a proper follower; that I disagreed with the general feeling of worship that was accorded to him by most of the New York group—or any group—and was uncomfortable in their atmosphere.

When I had said this, he looked at me quite seriously, and said: "You remember I tell you that what I teach is in your blood; that you cannot forget, no matter how you try?"

I said I did, and he said: "What you just tell me is proof of just this teaching. Group work is important, when people work together they can help each other, can make work easier; but since you have not right feeling with group you now make, unconsciously, difficulties and suffering for yourself. Just because of what I teach you in past you now make extra struggles for yourself. This can be good for your future, but also very difficult. You poisoned for life."

He did not say any more and we continued to drink in silence until all the garlic was ready. He then told them to soak it in some sort of solution—in a barrel—and that he would return at some future date to finish the concoction. I, at least, never heard of the garlic again.

VII

AFTER MANY VISITS TO the United States, over a period of more than ten years, Gurdjieff had become known to a rather large group of people, particularly in New York City. Perhaps inevitably, as some knowledge of his work filtered down by word of mouth to a larger public, he began to acquire a series of reputations. In addition to being known as a serious philosopher and mystic, he also became "famous" or "infamous" for being a charlatan, a quack, a faith healer, etc. As a result of these reputations, also because of certain misconceptions about him and his work, he began to be sought out and visited by people from all walks of life for a variety of reasons that had little to do with his primary aim. As has been pointed out, he brought a good deal of this upon himself during certain periods, such as the times when—for money—he performed "cures" for some people, or at least gave them some kind of treatments.

While I have often thought that some of these encounters or meetings could have been—and might better have been—avoided, it is difficult and perhaps unfair to attempt to assess his reasons for allowing himself to become involved with so many different people. At the time it seemed simple enough to speculate on the subject and I remember having felt that he was, in a sense, trapped by his own unquestionably genuine interest in people and his equally genuine desire to help anyone who was in any sort of trouble. He was, on the one hand, an easy target. But, given his complex nature, he unquestionably also amused himself with a good many of the "games" he played with people.

Most of those who came to him were, undoubtedly, in some sort of trouble and they were frequently sent to him by well-wishing members of any one of the American "groups". In almost all cases, the "trouble" was of a psycho-somatic nature, and the results of his advice were not always salutary, due, largely, to the lack of complete co-operation on the part of the suppliants.

In one instance, a group of well-wishers petitioned him to come to the aid of a woman in her early fifties who, after

having been—at least supposedly—a semi-alcoholic for
several years, had sought the advice of a medical doctor for
some ailment that did not pertain directly to her "alcoholism", and part of her doctor's treatment had been to forbid
her to drink alcohol in any form. Gurdjieff said that it would
be necessary for him to see the woman before he could
possibly consider doing anything for her, and after he had
seen her and questioned her he said that there was nothing
basically wrong with her except that she was going through
a period of chemical imbalance which was perfectly normal
for a woman of her age. He added, however, that her intake
of alcohol over a period of years was in no sense alcoholism
and that, in fact, she had an endemic need for a certain
amount of alcohol and that to discontinue drinking entirely
could be very serious—even fatal; he even prescribed the
amount she was to take daily and said that except for
certain perfectly normal symptoms that had to do with
change-of-life and would not last for a very long time, she
was — as long as she continued to drink the amount
prescribed — perfectly healthy. He added that it was
important for several reasons that his advice be followed
and that it should not be disclosed to the doctor. He also
said that he wanted to see her from time to time and that,
eventually, her need for alcohol would gradually diminish of
itself but that he would want to supervise the process. As to
his reasons for not telling the doctor about his advice, he
said that doctors, in general, did not like to have their
patients consult other doctors "behind their back" and to
have them consult someone like himself, who was not a
legally recognized physician, would make it inevitable that
any doctor would immediately repudiate his advice and his
prescriptions.

The woman in question was, of course, delighted with his
advice and showed immediate improvement, which, as
Gurdjieff pointed out, was largely due to the fact that he
had, essentially, agreed with her own diagnosis of herself.
He added that this was not always the case, of course, but
that this particular woman was, generally, "very much in
tune with her own system" and he urged her to follow her

own instincts when she manifested any form of illness and not to consult physicians except in emergencies or because of accidents which had nothing to do with her fundamental physical condition.

The woman remained in good health for many months, until a misguided well-wishing friend of hers, anxious to interest the doctor in Gurdjieff and to prove that Gurdjieff was, in most respects, a better doctor than the physician in question, told him that the woman's improvement was due entirely to following Gurdjieff's advice which had been the exact opposite of his. The doctor, reacting as Gurdjieff had predicted, convinced the woman that she was slowly poisoning herself with alcohol and promptly had her hospitalized—having managed to convince her somehow that Gurdjieff was, in reality, a quack—with strict instructions against the consumption of any form of alcohol and, in a very sharp period of time, the woman was dead.

Gurdjieff was very distressed in learning of her death and said that while it was true that the woman had been "very much in tune" with her physical self, she had not been a very intelligent or courageous person and that she had not had the basic moral strength to resist trusting — and continuing to consult—a recognized "physician-doctor". He also said that this was a very good example of what would inevitably happen when people consulted him and followed his advice—frequently radical—but did not, at the same time, manage to trust him completely.

A similar case involved a woman who was slowly dying in a hospital, to the great distress of her friends. Gurdjieff was persuaded to visit her and after seeing her said, although not to the woman herself, that her illness was not physical but that she had a strong desire to die—a death-wish as we would undoubtedly phrase it—and that she needed to have something to believe in and live for, as well as some immediate physical treatment. He managed, apparently, to convince her that there were reasons to continue her existence, and his treatment was to prescribe daily olive-oil enemas which were to be taken without the knowledge of her doctors. (She was able to do this by using a small baby-size syringe and having small amounts of olive oil brought to her.) He said that the reason for this prescription was that she had a condition which he described as a kind of long-term constipation due to her nervous and emotional state and that her intestines were coated with hard, dried waste matter which the olive oil would gradually break down, dissolve and eliminate.

The woman was enthusiastic, mainly because of Gurdjieff's interest in her, and the treatment worked and her condition improved rapidly. When, because of the woman's boasting about Gurdjieff's medical abilities, the doctors learned of his advice, the treatment was immediately discontinued. This time, however, the woman lived. But, when she was out of the hospital she was vituperative against Gurdjieff because he had "caused trouble for her with her doctors". Gurdjieff was amused by this and stated that she had achieved what he knew she needed—she now had a good reason to live—active hatred, with himself as the temporary target.

While there was a good deal of discussion—pro and con— among the group members, and others who knew about Gurdjieff, concerning these two cases, neither of them caused him any trouble with either the doctors or the authorities.

There was, however, one case that did cause him considerable trouble and which, eventually, made it difficult for him to stay in the United States or to reenter once he had left. This case, like the others, involved a woman. As I remember it, the woman—quite young—met him in Chicago and, in addition to her interest in his ideas, became greatly attracted to him physically. He discussed her case at one time in my presence and said that she was an unfortunate victim of modern society in that she was not generally accepted by other people because she was physically unattractive, found difficulty in communicating with others, and had certain unpleasant manifestions which, although due primarily to her innate shyness, were displeasing to other people. He said that it was natural enough that she should "fall in love" with a man like himself who had treated her

with kindness and consideration. He also said that while it
would be difficult, if he were able to work with her
personally for a few months, he would be able to do a great
deal for her and that she would automatically grow out of
her infatuation with him.

One major difficulty in this suggested programme was
that the young woman's family considered her a semi-
invalid and was very much opposed to her having any sort of
association with Gurdjieff. In spite of this, the young woman
managed to break away from her parents and follow
Gurdjieff to New York where she began to see him regularly
and to follow him about like a lost lamb.

For a time, she was an object of ridicule to many members
of the New York group and there was considerable loose
speculation about the nature of her association with Gurdjieff; many people, even among his so-called followers,
seeming only too glad to seize on any exceptional association
of Gurdjieff's as a proper topic for gossip and speculation.
He once spoke of this to me and said that it was the rather
sad, but usually unavoidable, reaction of people against
anyone they professed to admire.

While I know nothing about the nature of this woman's
association with Gurdjieff, I do know that it was suddenly
and rudely interrupted by the appearance of some members
of the young woman's family who proceeded to accuse
Gurdjieff of having "immoral sexual relations" with her and
followed up the accusation by having her locked up in a
mental institution.

Up to this point, particularly since there was no proof to
substantiate the accusations, things were not too serious,
although a good many of us were worried about possible
difficulties for Gurdjieff for "practising medicine without a
licence" and because of his status as a visiting alien in the
United States.

When the despondent young woman took her own life
after a week of incarceration, however, the picture became
very black. Because of renewed charges against Gurdjieff—
fanned, oddly enough, by the ardent feelings of some of his
supposed followers—he was put in custody on, I believe,

Ellis Island for a period of about ten days. During that time, I heard every known charge against him as well as a great storm of gossip and speculation, and also all the arguments of an opposing faction who had dedicated themselves to the cause of clearing his name. This latter group did, finally, prevail by using various kinds of pressure but his name was never, as far as I know, completely cleared and the incident remained a black mark against him. As a result, his stay in America was curtailed and he left a divided group behind him in New York.

Many years later, he referred to this episode and said that it had had one extremely meritorious result in that it had served as a shock which had separated "the wheat from the chaff" of his American adherents.

VIII

DURING ONE OF Mr. Gurdjieff's many visits to America, I
remember that he spent a great deal of time going to the
movies. He said that one great difficulty for him in the
western world was, that being of a basically oriental
temperament and nature, it was often hard for him to
comprehend the underlying western mentality. He said that
while most westerners would assert that the movies were an
exaggerated conception of American life and did not present
a true picture of America, he disagreed. He did agree that
the active physical behaviour represented in the movies was
exaggerated; however, he claimed that the underlying
motives—and the hopes, dreams, and desires of Americans
in general—were very accurately portrayed in films. In fact,
he said that only in the movies was the prevalent American
attitude towards sex, for example, revealed for what it really
was. He went on to say that his statements could not, in any
case, be challenged because the mentality of movie produc-
ers was obviously such that they could not invent anything
but could only copy—and occasionally distort—life, which is,
according to him, exactly what they did.

When he expanded on the subject of sex, in or out of the
movies, he said that it was perfectly obvious that while the
function of sex had originally only been to ensure the
reproduction and continuation of the human race, it had
become something very different since it had been "civilized"
in America and elsewhere in the western world. He said
that sex, being basically the source of all energy and
therefore, potentially, the well-spring, for example, of art,
had also become for most people nothing more than the most
titillating diversion of the many forms of amusement known
to modern man. Because of this, energy that could be used—
and was destined to be used—for a serious, and high
purpose, was simply wasted; thrown away in a frantic chase
after pleasure. While he did not specifically condemn other
ordinary, civilized habits, he criticized it from the point of
view that any waste is improper to man.

He suggested that human needs, generally, had not been

subject to the same kind of "perversion" as in the case of sex. The drives to eat, to eliminate waste matter from the body, to sleep, etc., were, in their own ways, equally strong. In fact, if a given individual had a sufficiently strong need to go to the bathroom—or was dying of thirst or hunger—no amount of sexual provocation could possibly come before any one of these needs. The pleasure involved in drinking water when really thirsty was, of course, different from the gratification of a sexual need, but equally compelling. He pointed out that this perversion of sex was a question that could be profitably studied and examined by everyone and that any diversion of the sexual impulse into more creative channels than sheer satisfaction could be a worthwhile task for anyone.

When people questioned him, as they often did, about specific sexual "perversion" he waved away their questions as hair-splitting. Perversion was perversion, no matter what particular form it might take—there was no question of "good perversions" or "bad perversions"—sex, generally, was perverted when it served to perform anything other than the basic intentions of nature: to produce children and to produce energy which was to be used for higher aims, certainly, than mere physical or emotional gratification. When improperly used such energy was always harmful.

Gurdjieff frequently used sex as a kind of shock-factor in dealing with individuals, I remember the case of one young woman, a dancer, whose principal attraction to Gurdjieff's work was that she was allowed to teach his dances to newcomers because she was a good dancer and a reasonably good teacher. Her interest in his work did not, however, seem to go beyond this pleasure in having a position of some authority. When she once challenged some statement he had made during the course of a lecture, he told her that he would have to give her a personal answer to the questions she was raising and would arrange for someone to give her a definite appointment to see him alone.

That night, after the lecture, he told me to go to her and invite her to come to his room at three o'clock in the morning—alone. He also told me to tell her that he would show her some wonderful things—things that she could not even imagine. When I gave her the message, she listened scornfully and with a show of a good deal of righteous shock and anger told me to tell him that she recognized a "proposition" when she heard one and that not only would she not come to his room but that she would no longer have anything to do with his work.

He was very amused when I relayed this reply to him and said that she had made an unfortunate, for her, but good, for him, choice. He said that her preoccupation with sex was such that she was no longer a good teacher of his dances and that he had chosen this means—face-saving for her—of dismissing her as a teacher. He added, however, that there were times when he was not above "diverting" himself in the current American fashion and that they might both have been rewarded had she agreed to visit him. Then he went on to say that it was just as well since he did not really have the time to deal with the reverberations that would undoubtedly have followed had she accepted his "proposition". He also said that her refusal would serve her as a topic of conversation and imaginative thought for the rest of her life. On the one hand, she could say that she had "rejected" the great Gurdjieff's advances, and on the other hand she could spend her life wondering what it would have been like had she accepted. I remember the reaction of one female group member on learning—from the dancer herself, of course, who lost no time in spreading the story—of the incident. With a pained look on her face, she said to me: "If it had only been me! What an opportunity! Can't you get me an appointment?" I suggested that she might approach him directly and let him know of her availability but, again sadly, she had to admit that she "didn't have the nerve".

It also seemed to amuse Gurdjieff to describe, always in accurate detail, the sex lives or the sexual history of some of the people who came to him for advice. He said that since sex, by its nature, only permitted of a rather limited repertory, it was simple to deduce the particular forms of satisfaction which were attractive to certain natures or temperaments. The descriptions were invariably vulgar and often amusing.

I have heard a great many stories and a great deal of gossip about Gurdjieff's own reputed sexual practices, most of which were obviously untrue and seemed to stem from the fact that anyone who has set himself up as a leader, or who has a "school" of an unusual nature, must also, more or less automatically, have an unusual and varied sex life. The only somewhat unusual truth about this aspect of his life that I know to be a fact is that he did have children by a few different women to whom he was not married; a normal, if not legal, performance, and a far cry from the practices, rites, and orgies which I have heard ascribed to him.

Even now, many years after his death, I find that it is not uncommon for people who know of him by reputation to inquire about his sexual practices, often suggesting that they must have been not only very interesting and unusual (and, incidentally, that I had certainly either participated in them or at least knew all about them), but even a part of his teaching; they are always disappointed—one might say even disillusioned—to learn the opposite, particularly to learn that he was married, reacting almost as if that was the final sin for anyone of his "peculiar" stature.

IX

IN SPEAKING OF CONTEMPORARY America, Gurdjieff sometimes made reference to the "new American Gods", the
scientists, and more particularly the personal gods—doctors
and psychiatrists. He seemed to feel that doctors were a
dangerous breed for, even though they were often motivated
by high-sounding principles such as a dedication to saving
the lives of people, they knew little about humanity, almost
nothing about the inter-relation of the mind, the emotions,
and the body, and that their aim was not, generally, to aid
or save people, but simply to eradicate disease. He said that
man was not only the chief, but perhaps the only, organism
that interfered constantly and radically with the balance of
nature, a very dangerous activity under any circumstances,
and particularly dangerous when men did not know what
they were doing and did not even take nature into
consideration. He said that nature was infinitely patient,
constantly adapting herself to the strains imposed on her by
these machinations of mankind, especially scientists, but he
warned that nature would, in the long run, be forced to "get
even", as it were, and impose a proper balance and harmony
on man.

As to doctors and disease, it would not be correct to say
that he was an advocate of euthanasia or that he thought
that the prevention of disease was a bad aim; but there is no
question but that the prolongation of human life, under any
and all circumstances and at any cost, was, in his opinion,
useless and, objectively, immoral. Each life had, according to
him, a purpose and rhythm of its own, and it was only our
abnormal fear of death and the fact that we seemed to
regard it as not only fearful but even evil, that forced us to
attempt to prolong physical life at any cost. It was especially
valueless since life, as we knew it, had little value or
conscious purpose even for those who were completely
healthy, physically, and in no way threatened by disease or
death. He was interested in the statistics concerning major
diseases—the primary killers—and said that the prevalence
of heart disease and cancer, for example, was proper to the

kind of civilization we had produced and in which we had to live. These two "diseases" along with lesser, non-fatal ailments, such as ulcers, were almost always the inevitable results of living in an unharmonious atmosphere under constant strain and pressure.

Many of Gurdjieff's adherents were depressed by his often-repeated, flat statement that human beings could really learn and could still "change" only until they reached the age—usually in their early twenties—of a certain kind of maturity: the moment when they ceased to grow automatically. Once that point had been reached, life was nothing more than a kind of running - down process, like the unwinding of a spring, and nothing new could be absorbed or learned. As many people had come to him long after reaching this "maturity", they were not only depressed by this theory but, usually, managed to interpret it to mean something entirely different—anything that would make it possible for them to have continued hope and feelings of encouragement.

At one time, I commented on the fact that I had seen people at the Prieuré, in various groups, and now again in New York, who seemed to me to interpret his ideas in such a way as to give themselves hope and a "good feeling" and often managed, by such interpretations, to avoid the simple truth or fact that he was stating. He said that it was important not to be hard on people, that one could not begrudge them hope and that if by this means they were able to continue with his teaching they might, somehow, absorb something of value—if not for this life—then for the next. He also said that this tendency to "interpret"—to make his theories more "digestible"—was an indication of how greatly people felt a need for reassurance, direction, or learning of some kind, and that it was a need that should not be despised. He also said that while one individual might be able to influence, in small ways, a great many other individuals, in the final sense one man could only pass on the knowledge he had acquired to one other man, which was one of the great trials of teachers throughout history. He also said that as one grew and learned in life one came to know that one's own suffering was as nothing when compared with the necessity of having to watch the seemingly unnecessary suffering of others. In a sense, he said that the hardest trial of life was the inability to alleviate the suffering of others—and what made it worse was that most human suffering was valueless in that it never served a useful purpose—was never experienced consciously, for a proper aim. Instead of "using" their suffering for the development of their higher consciousness, people spent all their time using every means they could find in an attempt to alleviate suffering that, in any case, could not be alleviated. He further said—and repeated it in his writings—that if individual men could ever learn to live with the constant knowledge and consciousness of the inevitability of their own, personal death, they would already have achieved a great deal in the way of growth and of preparing themselves for real learning. But the sad fact, according to him, was that the state of our consciousness, generally, was such that this realization was actually impossible. In certain states, to which men are subject, it was possible for them to long for death, and an end to human life struggles, but this was a very different thing from the conscious acceptance of the implacable, undeniable, inevitability of death for *oneself*. It was possible to envision the death of others, even those to whom one was greatly attached, but never our own.

During that period in New York, I remember feeling strongly that while Gurdjieff, in an outer sense, seemed to me a prophet of doom and disaster and hopelessness, he nevertheless gave an effect of great encouragement and hope. When I spoke of this paradox to him, he reminded me that he had often told me to look at things "upside down" or "from the other side of the coin" and that this very paradox, this "stick with two ends", while a potentially dangerous thing was also a very useful tool—in that it could give stimulus of such an order that one sometimes found energy and strength to work against odds that seemed impossible. He also said that any efforts of less than "super-human" strength were of no value anyway, once more pointing out that, in a sense, man's only hope was to fight to attain the "impossible". The only thing worth doing being something that "could not be done".

X

Perhaps because of the nature of his work and the problems of his students, Gurdjieff often discoursed on the question of good and evil. Basically, as he frequently pointed out, there are no such things as good and evil except as they exist in the form of moral concepts in the mind of man. But since his work dealt with mankind and since mankind, individually, was preoccupied with both good and evil they did, therefore, exist as problems in the sense that if one believes that something exists, it does exist—in this sense, mind is reality.

In an objective sense, Gurdjieff preferred what he called "objective morality" — a morality based on individual conscience and not on any social definitions of good and evil. In this sense, evil could be considered a term for whatever was improper to man as a function or a manifestation—anything that harmed an individual or his fellow men. In this limited sense, i.e., that good and evil exist if you think they do, Gurdjieff insisted that man's potentiality to manifest either good or evil was always equally strong and that it, in fact, grew as man learned more and developed more. While I had often heard arguments against this theory, it seemed simple and logical enough to me. As man learns and grows, his general potential, and his power, increases. It seems natural, therefore, that if one subscribes to moral concepts defined by the words "good" and "evil", man's potentiality to act in either sense is automatically increased. Surely Hitler and Stalin, together with millions of their followers, were convinced that their aims, and therefore their means of achieving them, were "good".

A good deal of misunderstanding entered into any discussions on this subject, largely because it is difficult for any large group of individuals to define what is good and what is evil, and then to agree on such definitions. It seems to me that when Gurdjieff used the terms he was using them in a special and rather narrow sense: referring to the constructive and destructive forces in man as related to his own growth and development. For example, he frequently warned that his work could only become more difficult as one learned more; in other words, as one grew one did not achieve any greater peace or any visible, or tangible reward —one did not become obviously "good"—but the struggle between any individual's capacity for "good" or "evil" for himself became that much more intensified. Mr. Gurdjieff himself, was an interesting example of this particular theory and I often thought that his personal power was such that he could very easily do as much harm as he could do good. When he advised a woman to give up her very well-paid position and incur debts in order to rid herself, finally, of her preoccupation with financial security, there were many people who thought this was "evil" advice, as there were those, also, who thought it "good". It depended, finally, upon the interpretaion given to the advice by the woman in question and the effect it had on her. (Incidentally, she followed his advice, and had to struggle for years to get out of debt; she thought it was an experience that contributed to her growth and understanding of life and of people, as well as something that did free her from her unconscious involvement with security.)

Because of the effect of Gurdjieff—the impact of his presence—on people, it was necessary for him to exercise a great deal of judgement in his dealing with them, particularly since most people came to him with a preconceived idea of his abilities and his teachings. Such preconceptions were usually not founded on any truth or fact and were only likely to be increased once the person concerned had actually met him. Because of his reputation, people rarely met an individual named Gurdjieff—they met a picture of him that had previously formed in their minds. A person who was convinced that Gurdjieff was dealing in "evil" black magic, on meeting him, would interpret anything he might say or do as proof that he was a "black magician".

Many years ago, Alistair Crowley, who had made a name for himself in England as a "magician" and who boasted, among other things, of having suspended his pregnant wife by her thumbs in an effort to produce a monster-child, made an unsolicited visit to Gurdjieff in Fontainebleau. Crowley was apparently convinced that Gurdjieff was a "black magician" and the ostensible purpose of his visit was to challenge Gurdjieff to some sort of duel in magic. The visit turned out to be anti-climactical as Gurdjieff, although he would not deny his knowledge of certain powers that might be called "magic" refused to demonstrate any of them. In his turn, Mr. Crowley also refused to "reveal" any of his powers so, to the great disappointment of the onlookers, we did not witness any supernatural feats. Also, Mr. Crowley departed with the impression that Gurdjieff was either (a) a fake, or (b) an inferior black magician.

Gurdjieff did use the terms "good" and "evil" in a rather simple, direct sense when he said that it was evil for a man not to honour his parents; that a "good" man, of necessity, did honour them. I think, also, that he would have classified murder as "evil", but beyond such obvious examples he made no pronouncements one way or the other. Certainly, a good part of his teaching was an attempt to help his students rid themselves of the ordinary concepts (moral) of both good and evil, and to replace their ordinary morality with an objective morality based upon the needs and dictates of conscience and that which was proper and natural to individual men. He insisted, however, that it was necessary to live one's life fully—within the framework of society—and that in order to do this and not be conspicuous, one had to subscribe, in public at least, to the prevailing social morality—in other words, it was necessary to "act" out one's role in the stage of life, but always to be able to differentiate between the outer "acting" man and the inner "real" man. He said that it was extremely difficult for anyone to do this properly, since the differentiation was often difficult to make—most people "acted" out their lives under the impression that they were living, when they were in fact, only reacting to life as it happened to them. He stated that, contrary to the principles expressed in the "Sermon on the Mount", as it was frequently interpreted, it was necessary to "hide one's light" from the ignorant and the uninitiated as they would only, quite automatically, attempt to destroy any such "light" or "knowledge"; however, it was equally important not to hide that same knowledge or "light" from oneself and from others who were working seriously and honestly towards the same goals of self-development and proper growth.

XI

MR. GURDJIEFF RETURNED to Europe in the late thirties and, while I did not know it at the time, I was not to see him again for many years. I had been seeing him regularly in New York while he had been there but I had not had much serious, personal contact with him. Before he left, however, I had a long talk with him during which he reiterated the fact that it was proper for me to go out and "experience" the world; that whether I was aware of it or not, I had "absorbed" enough material—at least for the time being— and that the important thing for me was to live life and put that material to use in whatever situations I might find myself. He did not, specifically recommend that I disassociate myself from his work or from the American groups, but when I questioned him about that he said that it was a question that would determine itself—that it was entirely up to me to do whatever I felt I should do about it.

During the ensuing years I did participte from time to time in group meetings and attended occasional readings of his books, but not for any long, sustained periods. In spite of this, there was no question of the influence which he still had over me. Rather like a child who considers a parent *the* final authority, I found that I never made any important decisions without at least attempting to consider them from the point of view of his teaching and I found, somewhat to my own surprise, that I tended to judge myself and others from a strongly moral and rather "puritanical" point of view. I was still young and relatively inexperienced and my judgments were likely to be harsh and very stern. Whether this was a result of my association with Gurdjieff (who was more "puritanical" or "righteous" in many ways than one would imagine) or simply an outcropping of my puritanical, middle-western American backgound, I am not sure, but as time passed I began to feel that a great deal of it stemmed from an unconscious reaction against his authority and an equally unconscious attempt on my part to free myself from his powerful influence. In any case, it was a genuine struggle, complicated by my strong feelings about Gurdjieff as a man and, as it were, a parent, and my equally strong "disapproval" of the behaviour of a great many of his followers.

An example of the conflict in me was that while I rejected most of the followers and would not attend their meetings, I continued, almost without knowing it, to revere him personally. There could have been no better illustration of this than when I met P. D. Ouspensky, his one-time student, who was conducting lectures and meetings in New York. I was told that he had announced a special series of lectures for persons who had, at any time, been associated with Mr. Gurdjieff, and, much against my better judgment, I was persuaded to attend the preliminary lecture which was to be a sort of introduction to the series.

A large group of Gurdjieff followers met Ouspensky at an apartment in New York where we listened to an interminable reading—quite incomprehensible to me—after which Mr. Ouspensky announced that he would answer any questions that any one of us might have before we "enrolled" (or did not enrol) for the ensuing lecture series. Various questions were asked and answered, but the only question that was of any interest to me was: "Why had Ouspensky 'broken' with Gurdjieff and publicly disassociated himself from the Gurdjieff work?" (In order to clear up any possible confusion, I would like to point out that one rumour had it that Gurdjieff had "dismissed" Ouspensky; but at the beginning of this "preliminary lecture" Ouspensky had stated that, whatever we might have heard to the contrary, it was he who had left Gurdjieff. Gurdjieff, characteristically, had never said anything about the break, one way or the other.) Ouspensky smiled at the question and said that the answer was very simple: When he had found out that "Gurdjieff was wrong" he had had to leave him—adding that the details of this discovery would be covered in the lectures to follow. I replied, with much greater feeling than I would have expected of myself, that I did not need to hear any more. It was a revelation to me to find that I was so fiercely loyal to Gurdjieff and to find that I was so positive that he could not have been "wrong" about anything. I did not attend any of

Ouspensky's future lectures and those who did were only able to tell me that they had been very interesting and that I should not have missed them.

Some years later there was a reconciliation between the Gurdjieff and Ouspensky "factions" and I believe that Ouspensky's books—especially *In Search of the Miraculous* —are recommended as reading for prospective Gurdjieff students. I have no personal information about this reconciliation as I was not present when it happened and have had no contact with any Gurdjieff—or other—group for about fifteen years. Ouspensky's books especially *In Search of the Miraculous* and *The Fourth Way* are unquestionably almost required reading for anyone interested in Gurdjieff; but it is perhaps needless to add that Gurdjieff's own published books—assuming that one has sufficient interest and stick-to-it-iveness to actually read them—are the only ones that give a real and undiluted flavour of the man and his teaching.

Although I had championed Gurdjieff in the face of Mr. Ouspensky, my subsequent reaction to my own outburst took me somewhat by surprise, although it only came over me very gradually: I was sick and tired of all would-be Messiahs, prophets, mystics — from Kahlil Gibran and William Blake (always associated in my mind because of their drawings) up to and including Ouspensky, Gurdjieff, Buddha, and Jesus Christ himself. It was a good, healthy, and angry reaction, and it was—at least momentarily—liberating. However wise, all-seeing, and powerful these individuals might be, it was finally necessary—or so it seemed to me—to judge them by the more obvious, and more hard-boiled truisms that they themselves sometimes quoted. "Birds of a feather . . . ", " . . . the company they keep", etc., as well as what now seemed to me to be an increasingly honest viewpoint: their accomplishments in terms that were comprehensible to me. I was not unaware of the fact that it was possible, if not quite likely, that I simply was not equipped to judge them—in other words, I was not a proper student for *any* philosophy—but the judgment had to be made, *for me*. Since I was not making it for anyone else, it was not likely to have any far - reaching harmful, or beneficial, influence.

I did not attempt to make any judgments about the dead. The main targets were the "seers" I had known myself; Ouspensky (I had known him at the Prieuré as well as during that brief encounter in New York) and Gurdjieff. I found that I did not know enough about Ouspensky to arrive at any conclusions of importance. I found, and find, *Tertium Organum,* and *A New Model of the Universe* and other writings of his wordy, over-intellectual, and generally incomprehensible—which is to say personally uninteresting. All of which is no judgment about their possible value.

As to Gurdjieff I found that I did not criticize him from the usual point of view. By that I simply mean that I was not at all disturbed about his lack of morals in the usual sense; it did not matter to me that he had illegitimate children, that he drank a great deal, or that he might have been a "magician" or a "charlatan", or as he called himself— a "devil". But if, in the final analysis, growth depended upon individual effort, if it was all "up to you" anyway, then why be a Messiah? Who, besides Gurdjieff himself, thought or knew that he was *chosen* or that he was unable to be anything other than a teacher. As an individual man, I knew him well enough to have very great, genuine affection for him. As a teacher . . . well, that was a completely different question. I could accept him in that role as I would accept the "teaching" which a parent gives to his child—it is a proper responsibility and an obvious one: the child is his. But as a leader of mankind? He must be, I concluded, just as fanatic and just as star-struck (although by something other than himself) as his pupils. Maybe. Maybe not. My "conclusions" did not get me anywhere, except to conclude that I did not have the proper "faith" or that I had not—in relation to Gurdjieff—"seen the light". But it was a relief to have wrestled with the problem. In a curious sense, I ended up liking him, as a person, even more. He began to seem to me in a very literal, paradoxical sense, the embodiment of that excellent phrase: " real, genuine phony". That *he,* but not necessarily everyone else, grew in such a way that the evil and the good within him progressed equally—I accepted whole-heartedly. But not for myself. I was on the side of something—even if I didn't know what it was. I wanted to believe in "good", and I wanted to fight for it. I suppose it was something like suddenly finding out that you believe in God.

This "state of being" of mine did not last for very long. The simple fact of World War II put an end to most of my feelings, in fact to almost any "religious" feelings in me—but even so, it was near the end of the war that I had my most shattering and important contact with Gurdjieff.

XII

Even now, I find it difficult to describe my next meeting with Mr. Gurdjieff, in the late summer of 1945, a few weeks before the first atom bomb fell on Japan. Any description of that meeting must necessarily be preceded by an account of, and explanation for, my personal state at that time.

I had been employed from 1940 to 1942 in New York and Washington—working mostly for the British government— and had become very much involved, emotionally, with the "war effort". At the time of my draft call, there was some consideration of the possibility of my being deferred, but on the whole I felt that it would be somehow "wrong" for me to avoid the experience of actual war and I made no effort to obtain any deferment.

I was absorbed into army life rapidly enough, although I was completely appalled by it and by the people with whom I came into contact. I was certainly aware of the truth that one tends to lead one's life within a small social circle of one's own kind and class—I felt that I had never even known of the existence of many of the types and classes of people I met in the course of my first few weeks in the service.

Once overseas, and quite without any awareness of my own, I began to be unconsciously filled with horror at the effects of war. My American upbringing—in spite of several years in France as a child — had certainly been no preparation for mass bombings and other such horrors. However, as I have said, I was not aware of these reactions at all at the time. I had a good behind-the-lines secretarial job (or so I thought) and contented myself by simply doing a reasonably efficient piece of work as my part in the war. Since the army, day by day, is primarily boring, I was happy to be busy enough not to have time to do any active thinking. But any strong, even if buried, feelings must somehow and sometime find expression, and after several months I gradually slid into a long-term depression. Along with this depression I began to over-eat and to gain weight. This was followed by something that was grimmer than any depression. I had a series of what seemed to me to be miraculous escapes that began to take on an air that was, to me, almost sinister. I will describe two of them, as examples: On one occasion, while on manœuvres in England, I was working at my desk in the "command" tent, in the company of several officers—nine or ten, at least. There was, as usual, an air raid going on at the time but no one was paying much attention to it. I got up and left the tent to go to the field latrine and during that short absence, a bomb hit the tent and everyone in it was blown to bits. To make it eerier, my typewriter landed within a few feet of me, in excellent condition.

Another time, while on a weekend pass at Torquay on the southern coast of England, I was standing, with another enlisted man, against a building overlooking the park below us. Without any air raid warning we were suddenly being strafed by six German fighter planes which had come in "below" the radar, almost at sea level. It had happened so quickly that neither my friend nor I did anything at all . . . we simply stood there, dazed. A great many people in the park were killed and when one of the planes strafed the building where we were standing, my friend was cut in two by the bullets, which missed me by a few inches although we were not more than three feet apart.

As I have said these were only two of the incidents—and there were many more—that began to have a curiously sinister effect upon me. At first, my reaction was one of wonder—why was it that I was the one who had not been killed? And there was a period when I almost believed that I was leading a "charmed" life, that I had been in a sense selected, or chosen, not to be killed. But as time wore on and there were more and more such escapes I began to resent them actively. I watched so many of my fellow-men die during that period that I began to wish that I could die in their stead. The enormity of war—the very fact of it—was more than I could comprehend, and as it continued to proceed senselessly and endlessly, life itself seemed to me to lose whatever meaning it had had—and I was not at all sure that it had any. There were no feelings of righteousness, patriotism or loyalty that could conceivably justify such wholesale murder and I had very grave doubts about the meaning of human existence. I thought of Gurdjieff frequently during those days, trying to imagine how he would explain, if he could, the act of war, but I was unable to imagine any answers or explanations that he might have had.

Finally, on the continent after D-day, the problem became of such importance to me that I could not think about anything else and I came very close to the edge of a complete nervous collapse. When I was faced with hospitalization, I somehow managed, in my highly nervous state, to convince my commanding officer, a general, to give me a pass to go to Paris where I would be able, I hoped, to see Mr. Gurdjieff. I don't know, even now, quite how I was able to convince the general. We were stationed in Luxembourg at the time and there was a standing order that no one from that area was to be given any liberty in Paris, except for the most important reasons. Also, I do not know what reasons were given in my case, but I had apparently made an impression on the general for he did obtain special permission for me.

When I left for Paris, I had not slept for several days, I had lost a great deal of weight, had no appetite and was in a state very close to what I would have to call a form of madness. Even now, while I can remember the long train trip vividly (all the railway lines had been bombed and we were shunted backwards and forwards over a large part of Belgium and France in order to reach Paris) I remember, especially, my conviction that unless I managed to see Gurdjieff I would not be able to go on living. After an interminable ride, and thanks to a sergeant in the carriage with me who managed to force coffee and brandy down me and keep me wrapped in blankets during the night, we finally reached Paris. In one way, Paris itself—which I had learned to love as a child—was a kind of tonic and gave me a spurt of energy, at least enough to help the sergeant find a hotel room and to start me on my search for Mr. Gurdjieff, as I had no idea where he lived. The telephone book and the "Bottin" were of no help to me and, in my peculiar

psychological state, I began to despair. I managed, somehow, not to lose my head, and did eat a good dinner. After
that, I set out methodically to try and remember the names
of some of his students whom I had known in the past and
who might be in Paris then.

I had arrived in Paris at about four o'clock in the
afternoon and it was not until after nine that evening that I
finally located an older woman who had been at the Prieuré
when I had been there as a child. She not only assured me
that Mr. Gurdjieff was in Paris and that I would certainly be
able to see him the following day, but also offered me a room
for the night. I accepted gratefully and talked with her until
very late, which relieved my nervousness to some extent.
Even so, I was still convinced that I had to see him before I
could relax and did not sleep very well that night.

I had to spend most of the morning—fidgety and anxious
—in the company of my benefactress, as she assured me
that I would not be able to locate him—I no longer
remember why—until about noon. At eleven o'clock, she
gave me two addresses: one of a café where he habitually
had coffee in the late morning, and the other of his
apartment. I went to the apartment first, but he was not
there. I then went to the café and he was not there, either. I
became very irrationally upset and began to think that I
had lost my way in Paris (if not my mind), so I telephoned
the lady, telling her where I was and that I had been unable
to locate Mr. Gurdjieff. She did her best to reassure me and
suggested that I go back to his apartment—I had not, she
was able to assure me, lost my way—and wait for him there.
I followed this suggestion and went back. I could not get in
to the apartment, but the aged concierge, who seemed
alarmed at my desperate appearance and manner, brought
an armchair into the hall and placed it so that it faced the
entrance, and told me to try and rest—that he was sure to
arrive very shortly.

I waited for what seemed to me an interminable length of
time, forcing myself to remain seated in the armchair,
staring at the entrance. It was probably not more than
about one hour later when I heard the sound of a cane

tapping on the sidewalk. I stood up, rigid, and Gurdjieff—I had known it must be he, although I had never known him to use a cane—appeared in the doorway. He walked up to me without the faintest sign of recognition, and I simply stated my name. He stared at me again for a second, dropped his cane, and cried out in a loud voice, "My son!". The impact of our meeting was such that we threw our arms around each other, his hat fell from his head, and the concierge, who had been watching, screamed. I helped him retrieve his hat and cane, he put one arm around my shoulders and started to lead me up the stairs, saying: "Don't talk, you are sick."

When we reached his apartment, he led me down a long hall to a dark bedroom, indicated the bed, told me to lie down, and said: "This your room, for as long as you need it." I laid down on the bed and he left the room but did not close the door. I felt such enormous relief and such excitement at seeing him that I began to cry uncontrollably and then my head began to pound. I could not rest and got up and walked to the kitchen where I found him sitting at the table. He looked alarmed when he saw me, and asked me what was wrong. I said I needed some aspirin or something for my headache, but he shook his head, stood up and pointed to the other chair by the kitchen table. "No medicine," he said firmly. "I give you coffee. Drink as hot as you can." I sat at the table while he heated the coffee and then served it to me. He then walked across the small room to stand in front of the refrigerator and watch me. I could not take my eyes off him and realized that he looked incredibly weary—I have never seen anyone look so tired. I remember being slumped over the table, sipping at my coffee, when I began to feel a strange uprising of energy within myself—I stared at him, automatically straightened up, and it was as if a violent, electric blue light emanated from him and entered into me. As this happened, I could feel the tiredness drain out of me, but at the same moment his body slumped and his face turned grey as if it was being drained of life. I looked at him, amazed, and when he saw me sitting erect, smiling and full of energy, he said quickly: "You all right now—watch food on stove—I must go." There was something very urgent in his voice and I leaped to my feet to help him but he waved me away and limped slowly out of the room.

He was gone for perhaps fifteen minutes while I watched the food, feeling blank and amazed because I had never felt any better in my life. I was convinced then—and am now—that he knew how to transmit energy from himself to others; I was also convinced that it could only be done at great cost to himself.

It also became obvious within the next few minutes that he knew how to renew his own energy quickly, for I was equally amazed when he returned to the kitchen to see the change in him; he looked like a young man again, alert, smiling, sly and full of good spirits. He said that this was a very fortunate meeting, and that while I had forced him to make an almost impossible effort, it had been—as I had witnessed—a very good thing for both of us. He then announced that we would have lunch together—alone—and that I would have to drink a "real man's share" of fine old Armagnac.

As we ate an enormous lunch, drinking glass after glass of Armagnac, he told me to talk, just to talk about whatever had been troubling me. I found it difficult to begin for at that moment I had no troubles at all. I felt wonderful. But once I had begun, I was able to describe my entire history since I had last seen him, summarizing easily and using a form of "shorthand" which seemed completely natural to us both. He listened without comment, then said finally that what I had told him was of no real importance—nothing to worry about—and asked me how long I would be able to stay in Paris. I told him I had three days and he said that I was to come to his apartment for lunch and for dinner every day during that time, but that the rest of the time I was to go out and "play". "One thing you never learn," he said quietly and affectionately, "is how to play, even though I try to teach you this when you child. Now, you go out and do *anything* that will amuse you, any kind of play then come back here at ten o'clock." I asked him what was going on before ten o'clock and he said there was going to be a meeting. When I suggested that I should come to that, he said, laughing: "No, do not come to meeting with disciples. This not play and you already too serious." He said that I could, of course, have the room he had offered me but that if I could stay elsewhere it would be better for me as there were too many people coming and going at all hours in the apartment, and to see what I could arrange about some other place to stay.

I left him, made arrangements with my hostess of the previous evening to stay with her, and, following his advice, played for the rest of the day.

XIII

THE RETURN OF MY energy was not a momentary thing. I was still feeling wonderful when I returned to Mr. Gurdjieff's apartment at ten o'clock that evening, and after introducing me to a large group of his students as his *"real* son", who had been at his "real school", he immediately put me to work in the kitchen. Once again, he seemed very tired, and he left me in charge of the food while he went off to "rest". For the second time that day he was gone for fifteen minutes and when he reappeared I was struck once more by his renewed strength and energy.

We had a very lively—and for me—very amusing supper. We still communicated with one another in a kind of "shorthand" which was both amusing and irritating to the other guests; irritating largely because, to his apparent delight, I found most of his conversation extremely funny and could not refrain from laughing which only served to increase his amusement. The other guests were confounded largely because his remarks did not seem, on the surface, funny to them. There was one woman present who seemed especially irritated with our laughter because she spent most of the time asking his advice about various serious problems. As he listened to her questions he would wink at me and—the first time—told me in Russian, that if I listened carefully I would learn how funny the "truth" could be. She said, among other things, that being rich she was at a disadvantage in her understanding of his work and that she often assumed that her so-called friends would not really like her if she did not have any money.

Gurdjieff said that the solution to these problems was simple enough: (1) She could give her money to him, knowing that he would make good use of it; (2) She could then live among the poor and would quickly learn—since she would have no money—whether or not she had real friends. As to "understanding" his work, he said that she would have to learn first, to understand. His replies were so obvious and so typical of him when people insisted upon questioning him at meals which were, always, a period of diversion for him, that I could not help laughing which, again, amused him a great deal. When she objected to our laughter, he said that she should learn as I had recently learned, that laughter was, in *truth,* a very good medicine.

When we had finished our supper, he dismissed everyone but told me to stay and help him with the dishes. We did the dishes together and then retired to a small room—a sort of pantry with various foods and herbs hanging from the ceiling and stored on the shelves—where we drank coffee and he played on his harmonium. He played much of the music I had known at the Prieuré, and although we did not talk very much at first, it was a rather sentimental, emotional reunion. When he finished the playing, he broke our mood suddenly by asking me if I didn't need some American cigarettes. Once more, I began to laugh, since cigarettes were not only plentiful at that time in the army, but also very cheap. He laughed with me and said that it was a great pleasure to enjoy laughter with someone again —that one of the saddest aspects of his life was that his students were so impressed with him that they could never condescend to anything so low as laughter. I told him that I agreed with this but that I felt, as I had told him once before, that it was his own fault—that he put "the stars in their eyes". He agreed readily, and seemed pleased that I would "kid" him, as he put it. I said then that while I had refused the cigarettes, I would like to give him something and offered him several thousand francs which I had "made" on the black market—by trading in various currencies; an art which I had only learned recently. He looked at the money for a moment and then asked, seriously: "Why you give me this?"

I said that it was a sum which I had "made out of the blue" and illegally, and that I thought he could have more fun with it than I could. He smiled at my reply and then said, thoughtfully, that he had thought that I had intended the money as "payment" for something. I said quickly that I thought that money could only pay for "things" and this money because of its origins, the way I had acquired it, was really "play" money, and that while I had certainly needed to play—he did, also. He was satisfied with this and agreed to take it on that basis, but only if I would accept a carton of cigarettes. I laughed and said I would and he then said that it was important to exchange "useless presents" from time to time.

He then referred to his conversation with the woman at the supper table and said: "you see what trouble I have with students? She ask stupid questions and I give stupid answers, but even though stupid, they honest. But same is true even when someone—very rare—ask genuine question. When I give true answer, her unconscious already know answer is true because unless already know answer, unconscious cannot ask question. But, even so, she think I make joke, so will not listen. In teaching is necessary to remember that no one really asks questions. Impossible to ask question about something you not already know, already have good idea. So I only give answers which she already know. Answer to such question everybody already know. Is usual, when person ask me question, to already know two answers: one pleasant, one unpleasant. Not really ask question, only want confirmation; want pleasant answer from other person than self, because already know pleasant answer not right. But . . . if other person, like myself, give pleasant answer then can say to self that I tell this answer, and so not have to worry with conscience because is my fault. But for serious man is not necessary find new answers, but new questions. Once you ask question, this mean you already have a very good idea about answer. For teacher is important make student ask new questions. This reason why education in your country and in modern times upside-down. Teacher in school never make new student ask new question or try to discover new thing. Only answer old questions to which everyone already have answer or can find answer in self without effort."

He poured coffee and Armagnac for us again and then went on: "This woman not take me seriously and so will not discover anything. What I tell her is truth. If she could give up money and have to live like poor person she would create possibility for two things. First, would find out what other people like, how they live, and also find out much about herself, that she stupid, shit-person, only have value of her money. Cannot be understanding between rich and poor, because rich and poor, both, only understand money. One understand life with money and despise people without money. Other understand life without money and hate people who have money. This woman now hate self because guilty about being rich. Poor man hate self—or sometimes just life—because feel guilty about not having money or feel cheated by world. With such unreal, false attitude, impossible understand any serious thing like my work. For instance, this woman tell that I most important influence in her life—but would be impossible for her to give me her money—so, very simple, she not tell truth. I not important for her life, but only her money important. With poor man can be the same thing. Can believe in me and what I teach only if I first teach how to make money—this what poor man think. Not so. If I teach him how make money, then he will have only other problem—he will not be able to live without this money. But such people can learn important thing if can make effort in self to give up money—or, if poor, to give up desire for money. Impossible to do my work with all energy if also concerned with money. But all these things very difficult for your contemporaries. Not only cannot do. Cannot even understand why this question of money important. Such people will never understand real teaching of real possibility of learning anything."

He smiled at me, reminiscently, and then went on: "You remember Prieuré and how many times I have struggle with money. I not make money like others make money, and when I have too much money, I spend. But I never need money for self, and I not *make* or earn money, I *ask* for money and people always give, and for this I give opportunity study my teaching, but even when they give money still almost always impossible for them learn anything. Already they think of reward . . . now I owe them something because they give me money. When think of reward in this way, impossible learn anything from me."

XIV

Except for the fact that there were no grounds and gardens in which Mr. Gurdjieff's students could labour, the "teaching" of his method did not seem to me to have changed very much. There were still readings, lectures, dance groups, and interviews with particular students. The only thing missing in the general ambience was "The Prieuré" itself. On the other hand, there was a change—at least it was new to me—in at least a part of Gurdjieff's own activity.

I noticed almost immediately that there were a number of daily visits at his apartment by older people, most of whom did not appear to have much, if anything, to do with his "work". Not only were they old, but they all appeared to be poor. Gurdjieff's attitude towards these people bore little resemblance to his treatment of those persons who were, quite obviously, his students. He treated them with courtesy, kindness and, I gathered, generosity. During the course of one of our own private sessions in the "coffee room" I spoke, somewhat hastily, about this "retinue" and the fact that he appeared to me to be helping, if not actually supporting, a great many people who did not seem to be in any way involved in his work. I do not remember my own exact words, but I remember that the implication was that he was helping in the perpetuation of persons who, unless I had misunderstood him in the past, were—to use his phrase —nothing more than "fertilizer" and without any particular "possibilities".

Gurdjieff was not amused; on the other hand, he was not angry. Patiently, although I detected a note of irritation in his voice, he explained that I was confusing an issue and that I had not understood him completely in the past. In the first place, fertilizer *per se* was not a *bad* thing to be if there was—in this life—no other possibility, and, more to the point, if the given individual was not striving for some other destiny. "Not only you not understand this about my work," he said, " you also not understand about what kind of person I am."

After more coffee had been poured, and he had looked at me reflectively, he said: "I play many roles in life . . . this part of my destiny. You think of me as teacher, but in reality, I also your father . . . father in many ways you not understand. I also 'teacher of dancing', and have many businesses: you not know that I own company which make false eyelashes and also have very good business selling rugs. This way I make money for self and for family. Money I 'shear' from disciples is for work. But other money I make for my family. My family very big, as you see—because this kind old people who come every day to my house, are, also, family. They my family because have no other family.

"I give you good example why I *must* be family for such people. You not know, even though you hear about this, what life is like in Paris during war, while Germans here. For such people—people who come to see me every day now —was impossible even find any way to eat. But for me, not so. I not interested in who win war. Not have patriotism or big ideals about peace. Americans, with ideals, kill millions of Germans, Germans kill — with own ideals — English, French, Russian, Belgian . . . all have ideals, all have peaceful purpose, all kill. I have only one purpose: existence for self, for students, and for family, even this big family. So, I do what they cannot do, I make deal with Germans, with policemen, with all kinds idealistic people who make 'black market'. Result: I eat well and continue to have tobacco, liquor, and what is necessary for me and for many others. While I do this—very difficult thing for most people—I also can help many people."

I persisted: "But *why* did you do it? Why for *them?* "

He smiled: "You stupid still. If can do for self and students, can also do for others who *cannot* do such thing." He paused and then added, smiling enigmatically now: "Ask self why old lady, with very little money, every day feed birds in park. These people—this family—my birds. But I honest: I say I do this *for* people, and also for self. This give me good feeling. Lady who feed birds in park not tell truth. She tell only do for birds, because love birds. She not tell what pleasure she get."

My question now seemed to me somewhat silly, and I apologized for having asked about the "old" people.

He shook his head. "Not necessary be sorry. Is not bad question you ask me. But one more thing about this question. You notice all such people who come here are already old. Without me not have possibility die properly. Except me, such people not have family, and for future can only look towards death. If I help such people die in right way, this can be very important and very good thing. Someday you understand this better, but you still young."

XV

ALTHOUGH I WAS WITH Mr. Gurdjieff constantly during my three-day leave in Paris, he did not refer to my condition or "illness" at the time of my arrival. He kept me with him, alone, after the dinners and suppers at which there were always many guests, and when he did talk to me privately it was about the problems of his students, or about his difficulties with them. He told me that it would have been interesting for me to have been in Paris at the time that he had suggested to a number of his students that the war and its aftermath had provided a proper climate in which to learn the importance of living in the present. He said that, mostly because of our habits and preconceptions, it was very difficult for people to understand what was meant by "living in the present". Too many people would interpret this as an excuse for casting caution aside and would live "dangerously" without thought for the future. What he meant by "living now" was to expend all one's energy on living completely at the moment—experiencing life as fully as possible in the consciousness that this moment—this *now*—will never exist again. To many people this seemed to mean living fully in the sense of staying awake too long, drinking too much, or adopting an attitude of "eat, drink and be merry, for tomorrow we shall die", which was not what he intended.

It was true, he said, that in order to live completely in the moment it was necessary to be aware of the inevitability of one's own — possibly imminent — death. However, such awareness was not to be taken as an injunction to experience as much as possible or to overdo as much as possible while one was alive, but rather to be conscious of what one was doing and to try to occupy oneself "properly"—in such a way that one's experience would contribute to one's growth.

While he would not define "proper" activities clearly—one had to discover "proper" and "profitable" experience and activity for oneself—he did advise exercises that would help any individual to concentrate on conscious activity. Almost all such exercises were—in one way or another—a form of learning something more about oneself. For example, a

common exercise was to make a daily programme of activity
for oneself, and to be able to foresee and allow time for
inevitable interruptions or distractions and, especially, to
plan a proper amount of "work and play" for a given period
of time. He said that there was often value in over-reaching
—doing more that one "could"—but that one could not over-
extend one's energies and capacities consciously until one
had learned, through such an exercise, just how much
available energy, how large a capacity, and how much
available concentration one had that was "ready for use". He
said that any man, in a sense, had limitless energy, but that
such energy was not available to him if regular habits,
acquired from infancy, did not permit its expenditure—
habits of sleep, need for food, etc. Almost everyone was
unconsciously trained not to use all his energy; given such
training it was impossible, suddenly, to begin to use it. In
performing an exercise such as "programming one's activities" it was possible to find out a great deal about *self*.
Usually, an individual would try to do too much, but this
was not always a bad result because sometimes one could do
"too much" without bad results and could learn: (a) that the
planning was not accurate, and (b) that they did have more
energy than they had realized. In the beginning, however,
the purpose of the exercise was to be accurate and to plan
exactly—failing to do exactly what was planned, or doing too
much, were both incorrect and either under-doing or over-
doing was to be *punished*. I asked him what kind of
punishment and he said that the punishment "should fit the
crime" and that the very selection of a fitting punishment
was, in itself, an exercise. It was important, particularly,
not to over-punish oneself.

As to living in the present, or "living now", Gurdjieff said
that if I could tell myself honestly that during a given period
of time—whatever I happened to be doing—I at no time
thought of anything other than what I was doing, I would at
least have experienced the feeling of concentration and total
involvement in the moment. He said that, for young people
before they were contaminated, a sexual experience could be
used as a good example of "living in the moment", being

"totally involved", but he added that as one grew up in the ordinary way even sex ceased to be as compulsive and totally absorbing and no longer commanded all one's energies and attention. Also, he made it very clear that he was using the example of sex only to describe the approximation of total preoccupation in the moment. Sexually, the involvement was unconscious—in life, it was necessary to achieve a similar degree of concentration and absorption in the moment purposefully and consciously.

As I say, he did not speak of these things in relation to me, particularly or personally, at the time, but when I asked him if he thought I should do any of these exercises he merely smiled and said that when a man was in a vegetable garden he would eat vegetables for a number of reasons: because he was hungry, because he was greedy, or because he was attracted to the vegetables for some other reason. It depended on the man and his need or desire for vegetables; the vegetables, on the other hand, if eaten, would always nourish the eater—even to the point of making him ill if he did not know when to stop.

XVI

ON MY LAST DAY IN Paris, Mr. Gurdjieff did finally refer to
my reasons for coming to see him and, more specifically, to
my condition or "state" at the time I arrived. He said that
our reunion had been a good and necessary thing for me and
that he was glad that I had come to him. As to my "state" he
said that, before discussing it in detail, he would have to
know, for sure, that I would be able to come back to Paris
fairly soon. While I had no way of knowing how difficult this
might be, I assured him that I would return in about a
month, vowing privately that I would get to Paris even if I
had to get there without proper leave papers.

Thus assured, he said that my "state" or "condition" was,
perhaps unfortunately, natural to me for a great many
reasons, including the fact that I had been, as he had told
me in the past, "poisoned for life" by him and by his
teaching. He added, however, that although such states
might be natural enough to me they would be considered
unnatural by the general run of people and might also be
considered as illnesses, although such states were actually a
form of what he called "nervous over-exposure"—when I was
very tired (and he said this was true of many people) my
"skin" became, as it were, thin. I lost that protective coating
or "shell" which all human beings acquire naturally in the
course of the growing years. He said that it could be a very
good thing to be able to "shed one's shell" or "protective
coating" at will, but that it was necessary to learn when and
how to do this and not to be at the mercy of having it
happen under stress.

He gave me various "secret" exercises to do ("secret" in
the sense that they were designed for me alone and could be
harmful if revealed to, and used by, others), and two or
three definite injunctions. One of them was that I was to
drink, privately, a certain amount of hard liquor every day
—depending upon my particular "state" of the moment,
which I would have to learn to judge accurately, and he said
that he had insisted on my drinking a great deal while in
Paris in order that he would have the opportunity to observe

me and determine my chemical reaction to hard liquor. The next injunction was that I was to take a certain medicine daily and was to report to him when I next saw him on my reactions to it, and he gave me several dozen pills. He stressed the fact that I was not to take any other medicine, under any circumstances, but that if I should be forced to take anything else I should discontinue his medicine at once.

He said that it was very unfortunate for me that I had to return to the army at just that moment—that if he were able to keep me with him for from three to six months he would be able to teach me how to control and use my nervous system and my "states" properly, but that since I could not stay with him I would have to learn to do this by myself, which, he warned, might take many years. He also warned me that the exercises he was giving me were not only secret but also dangerous and that, under normal circumstances, he would not permit anyone to do them without supervision. He then said that I must remember that when he used the word "dangerous" he meant that they could result in death, which would seem very attractive to me under certain circumstances when I would be "at the mercy" of a nervous "state". He made me write down the various exercises and "rules" he had given me and said that I should memorize them—"burn them in your brain"—as quickly as possible then destroy the notes I had made.

The last specific warning he gave me was that my sense of well- being which I had had ever since seeing him in Paris would only last for about a week or ten days after which there would be a general let-down; therefore, it was important that I work very hard during that short period of time in order to consolidate the temporary gains I had made, also in an effort to "cushion" the let-down, which might be very severe.

After this last session with him, Mr. Gurdjieff told me that he was very sorry there was nothing more he could do at the moment but that I was not to forget my promise to return to Paris as soon as I could, and definitely within a month. "This promise of yours," he said, "very important. May be difference between hope and no hope for you."

XVII

BEFORE I LEFT Paris, there was one last dinner, during which Gurdjieff indulged in one of his favourite pastimes: urging one of the people present to tell an "anecdote" about one of Gurdjieff's encounters with a would-be student. The man who told the story at dinner was a self-styled *raconteur,* and the story itself is a typical example of what many people thought of as Gurdjieff's devious, and infuriating, methods.

The story concerned an Englishwoman, wealthy and well known, who approached Mr. Gurdjieff when he was, according to his custom, sitting at the Café de la Paix in Paris, surrounded by a number of his followers. The English lady introduced herself and was invited by Gurdjieff to join him at his table. She stated her business in a forthright manner: She had been told that Gurdjieff knew "the secret of life" and she had come purposely to find him and to find out from him just what that secret was. As an inducement, she showed him a cheque for the sum of £1,000.0.0 payable to him and which she promised to give him when the secret had been revealed to her.

Gurdjieff showed his usual interest in the cheque and then agreed to demonstrate the secret of life for the lady. He got up from the table, walked up to a well-dressed "lady" who was generally to be seen walking the sidewalk in front of the Café de la Paix—it was her "beat" or station—and with a profound bow, asked her if she would do him the honour of permitting him to buy her a drink. The lady had seen him many times and did not seem to think of him as a potential client, but having nothing better to do at the moment, she accepted his invitation although she did seem a little suspicious of his numerous companions. He held her chair for her, and then sat down opposite her, asked her what she would like to drink and ordered it. Something expensive.

When she had received her drink, Gurdjieff again thanked her for honouring him with her presence and then said that he had seen her many times, knew her to be a woman of good sense and many accomplishments, for which

reasons he had decided to explain something to her. He
began by telling her that, in spite of her knowledge and her
experience, he would wager that she could not possibly
guess who he was and where he was from. The lady
suggested that he was probably from some part of Russia,
but Gurdjieff assured her that he was not and that what
seemed to be his Russian accent was merely part of his
disguise. Not only, he went on, was he not from Russia, he
was not even from this planet—the planet Earth.

The lady did not make any comment on hearing this but
merely looked at her drink, then at him, and then at the
assembled group, and seemed to decide that she would put
up with his conversation in return for the drink.

Gurdjieff continued by saying that he came from a planet
which was unknown to her, unknown in fact to anyone on
the planet Earth and that his planet was named "Karatas".

As the lady still made no comment, Gurdjieff launched
into one of his long, wordy explanations, this time concerning the difficulties—for the inhabitants of the planet
Karatas—involved in living on the planet Earth. One of the
greatest difficulties for beings like himself was the question
of food, as most food produced on the Earth was completely
unsuitable for organisms from other planets. For this
reason, he continued, it was necessary for him, at great
expense and with great difficulty, to have special food flown
from the planet Karatas daily.

The lady finished her drink and was about to leave, a look
of complete boredom on her face, when Gurdjieff ordered her
another drink and assured her that he would not keep her
much longer and that she would be adequately compensated
for her time. Reassured, she stayed on but still refused to
comment on his obvious flight of fancy. She did scrutinize
his companions closely, her expression plainly suggesting
that she had inadvertently become involved with a group of
"nuts".

Gurdjieff then asked her if she would like to see some of
the food which he imported daily from Karatas, and she
shrugged her shoulders. He then produced a paper bag from
which he took a few cherries. He said that while this "food"

resembled a plant that also grew on the planet Earth it was, in reality, quite different. The lady finished her second drink and continued to stare at him.

"Would you be so gracious and so kind," he went on, "as to do me the great honour of tasting this superb fruit and telling me how it seems to you? What it resembles?"

Without a word the woman took two cherries from Gurdjieff's hand, put them into her mouth and ate them slowly. She removed the pits and dropped them into a saucer on the table. With undisguised sarcasm, she then stared at him and said, slowly and distinctly: "It seems to me that they are cherries." She then held out her hand.

Gurdjieff quickly pressed a few banknotes into her hand, stood up, made another obeisance in her direction, escorted her back to the sidewalk, bade her farewell and thanked her again for having rendered him a great service. She took a long look at all of his companions, shrugged her shoulders and walked slowly away, pocketing the money he had given her.

Gurdjieff then turned to the English lady, smiled at her and said, simply: "What you have seen is the secret of life."

The Englishwoman gave him a look of disgust, called him a charlatan and left, upon which Gurdjieff roared with laughter and returned to his writing. Inconceivable as it may seem, the Englishwoman returned to the Café de la Paix later that day, gave him the cheque, thanked him for what he had done for her and later became an ardent follower of his "system".

The laughter was general following this story, but one person present asked, quite seriously, why it was that knowledge — Gurdjieff's kind of knowledge — had to be presented in such a curious, devious, secret fashion—why could it not be made generally available to everyone, thereby benefiting everyone and improving the world in every way.

Typically, Gurdjieff avoided any discussion of his "devious" methods, but made a pronouncement about knowledge.

"Like almost all people," he said, "you not understand nature of knowledge. Knowledge, like very fine French

champagne, is rare. There exists only a certain amount—
and is impossible produce more. If you give everyone in
world one drop of champagne, nothing would be changed, no
one would appreciate it. But for people who understand
French champagne, when they drink, they appreciate; also
they have money to buy this. But even if everyone had
enough money for such drink, even so they would not buy.
While what I say is true — that existing amount of
knowledge is limited; receptivity for such knowledge is also
limited." He refused to say anything further, and that
person only remarked that he was as mystified as before.

XVIII

I DID GET TO Paris within a month to see Mr. Gurdjieff again—but during that period I came to feel that he had somehow known beforehand exactly what was going to happen to me before I saw him again. The details are of no particular interest, but among the "highlights" of that period are the facts that the predicted let-down was severe, I was hospitalized (where, oddly enough, my treatment at first consisted of having to drink a good deal of Cognac daily) and was, of course, unable to take his medicine for more than about ten days. In any case, I was not troubled about the medicine because I had had absolutely no reaction to it. I did continue to do the exercises that Gurdjieff had prescribed for me and I did, certainly, go through a "dangerous" period—a kind of self and world-evaluation that seemed to shake my foundations—and during that period the predicted "death-wish" was very strong indeed. One saving grace during that month was that, sceptically, I wondered just how suggestible I had been when I was with Gurdjieff in Paris. Was I, as it were, unconsciously producing the climaxes that he had predicted might happen? The question, even though unanswerable, did serve to help me maintain some sort of balance and objectivity, and I was not especially concerned with finding an answer to it.

When I arrived in Paris again, I telephoned Mr. Gurdjieff and he made an appointment to meet me at a café later that morning. After we had met and while we were drinking coffee, we were approached by an elderly woman who proceeded to have a long conversation with Mr. Gurdjieff in Russian. I understood enough of their conversation to gather that it was primarily concerned with problems of health, finance, and the difficulty of obtaining sufficient food in Paris at that time. The black market, I knew, was flourishing, and while food was available, it was tremendously expensive.

At the conclusion of the conversation, the woman opened a package, wrapped in newspaper, and held up a small oil painting for us to look at. Mr. Gurdjieff asked her various questions about it: when she had painted it, and so forth, and finally bought it from her for several thousand francs. She thanked him effusively and I gathered that, thanks to his purchase, she would be able to afford to eat for a few more days.

When she left us, Gurdjieff sighed, handed the painting to me, asking me to carry it back to his apartment and hang it in the hall which was already lined with similar paintings—from the baseboard to the ceiling. When I had hung the picture, he asked me if I remembered Jane Heap ("Miss Keep", as he called her). I said that I did, of course, and he said: "You know, Miss Keep not have any sympathy for my paintings. Last time she come here, I ask her what she think of my paintings, and she tell me: 'Mr. Gurdjieff, you have everything here, except art'. Miss Keep not appreciate what I do."

I could not help being amused by Jane's remark, but was interested in what he was going to say about it. He promptly went into a long harangue about art and the creative impulse, pointing out that it was particularly difficult for an artist to make money during the war, and that it was equally difficult now that the war was just about over. He went on to say that he did not collect art for his love of it, nor did he do it only from generosity and a desire to help the unfortunate artists. He said that it was very important . . . for that old lady . . . that someone should buy her art . . . because, in spite of what Miss Keep, or I, or anyone else, might feel about the quality of her painting, she had painted her pictures with her being—her real heart—and that it was very bad for any such creativity not to find an outlet; that is to say, a public, a buyer.

"I also get benefit from her art," he continued. "For in my house many people see her paintings and paintings of such other unfortunate people and they tell I have worst collection of paintings in Paris—perhaps in all world. I already unique to most people who know me, but in my collection of bad art people see that I am still more unique . . . in another way, unique."

After this "joke", he said, more seriously. "But, in truth,

people could learn from this old lady. Unlike many people who know I generous and will help others, she never ask for money, but always only wish money for painting. She already understand what some 'intellectual' people not understand. If receive money, should give something for it."

After this lecture we prepared lunch and our first drink was, contrary to custom, a toast to the health and prosperity of the little old lady artist.

XIX

THIS VISIT TO SEE Gurdjieff, made from the hospital with the assistance of an understanding military doctor, was very much like the previous one except that Gurdjieff dwelt on my condition at more length than he had before. He said that my non-reaction to the medicine he had given me only proved one thing to him—that I had an enormous, natural resistance to drugs, and should, therefore, avoid taking them whenever possible. As to drinking, he recommended that I continue to drink, but "consciously"—in the sense that I should learn to gauge accurately the needs of my system for alcohol. He insisted that I had such a need, but that it was periodic, and predicted that if I gauged the need properly I would go through periods where I would drink— or would need to drink—a good deal, and also sometimes through long periods when I would not need to drink at all; in fact, at such times, I would find that liquor might even be harmful for me. "As you grow." he added, "must remember that body can, without your awareness, make many changes in chemistry; may come time when you should never drink at all. Must try to live in tune with physical self and be conscious of all changes in own chemistry."

When he spoke of the various exercises he had given me, he made me tell him in detail how often I had done each one and also describe my reactions to each of them. He then told me to discontinue all of them and gave me two new exercises, again secret ones. When I began to make notes, he told me to tear up the paper and to stop writing. "These exercises you must learn in your heart, for ever," he said, "for in future there will be a time when you will need them and you will have nothing—not even a piece of paper. So must now memorize these exercises as the most important thing in your life, I tell truth when I say this—will be time in future when without such exercises you will die. Even with exercises will be very difficult for you to live."

I did not need any further admonitions, but in any case, he made me repeat these complicated exercises to him in complete detail several times before I returned to my unit. (I

was not returning to the hospital; I had been discharged but
given an extra three or four days to get back to my regular
unit via Paris.)

The day I was to leave, Mr.Gurdjieff said that I would
probably never see him again. "As you can see with own
eyes," he said, "I now very tired and I know that when I
finish this last book my work will be done. So now I can die,
because my task in life is coming to an end." He looked at
me gravely and continued: "This also mean that I can do
nothing more for you ever. I know that now, in your heart,
you already think about possibility of staying with me here
in Paris after you get out of army, but you must forget this. I
cannot help you any more, and besides you belong in your
own country—America. So when you get out of army do not
come back here but go home where you belong and where
you will find much work for self, and many experiences."

Somehow, it was not a moment for emotion. He was very
serious, very impersonal, and spoke without any visible
feelings—it was almost as if he had been thinking aloud. He
spoke of his death with such detachment and so convincing-
ly that it was as if he was speaking of someone else. So, with
no feelings or demonstrations, he finished talking and we
went in to the usual enormous lunch, with many guests. As
we ate, he told a great many stories and once again, he and I
laughed a great deal. He urged one of his students to tell me
the story of a visit with him to the American Embassy in
Paris because of some complications over the question of
obtaining a visa for Mr. Gurdjieff. It seemed that a group of
students had gone with him to the Embassy, armed with
various documents with which they hoped to prove that he
had urgent reasons for going to the United States. They
were all told to wait when they had arrived, and after a very
short waiting period, Mr. Gurdjieff got up and walked
around the office distributing boiled sweets (from a bag he
carried in his pocket) to all of the stenographers and clerks.
This "sweet-giving" resulted in considerable pandemonium
in the office, and, of course, the official who was to review
his application appeared in the middle of it. Even so, the
visa was obtained, but only after several interviews and at

great cost to the nervous system of those who had accompanied Gurdjieff.

Mr. Gurdjieff roared with laughter at this story and said
it proved that the world was mad. All he had done was
generously to offer sweets to some charming American girls
and it had almost cost him his visa.

At the end of lunch, Gurdjieff's mood changed very
suddenly, and when he rose from the table, I was worried
about him. In the course of a few minutes he had begun to
look very ill. In spite of this, one of the women at the table,
one of the workers, leaped to her feet and rushed to his side
to ask him some question about whatever work—probably
translation — she was doing on one of his books. He
supported himself by leaning on a chair, and answered her
questions slowly and concisely. But, as he spoke, there was
a definite change in the atmosphere in the room. All of us—
and there must have been about twenty persons present—
rose from our chairs with one accord and waited silently. We
were all expecting something—I knew I was, and the tense
faces of the others indicated that we were one in this
expectancy. When he had finished speaking to the woman,
he raised one arm and made a sweeping gesture around the
room, as if to command the attention of each one of us.

"Must make announcement." he said, dramatically, and in
English. (Several nationalities were represented, but all the
people there, I knew, spoke or understood English.) "My last
book is now finished, except for work with editor." He
paused, looked around the room, as if to examine each
person, separately and intently, and then continued: "This
mean my work is through—finished. This also have very
important meaning for me. Mean at last I can die . . . "
there was another pause, but his inflexion indicated that the
sentence was not finished, " . . . but not just because book
is finished. In life is only necessary for man to find one
person to whom can give accumulation of learning in life.
When find such receptacle, then is possible die." He smiled
benevolently, and went on: "So now two good things happen
for me. I finish work and also find one person to whom can
give results my life's work." He raised his arm again, started

to move it, this time with a finger extended and pointing, around the room, and then stopped when his finger was pointing directly at me.

There was an enormous silence in the room and Gurdjieff and I looked at each other fixedly, but, even so, I was aware that one or two of the others had turned to look in my direction. The tension in the atmosphere did not lessen until Gurdjieff dropped his arm, turned, and left the room. The rest of us seemed momentarily transfixed and I finally broke the seeming trance and walked across the room. I was stopped, abruptly, near the door, by a hand on my arm. It was a woman, one of the "instructors". She held my arm tightly in her hand, looked at me with a malevolent, sneering smile on her face, and said: "You will never learn, will you?"

I pulled my arm away from her hand gently. "What does that mean?"

She laughed. "How does it feel to be chosen?" she demanded. "From the look on you face, I can tell you exactly what you are feeling. He pointed at you, didn't he? And now —with your colossal ego—you march out of the room . . . the triumphant successor."

I have to admit that I was feeling fine. I smiled back into her face, admitting to myself a feeling of genuine triumph, and said: "Your guess is as good as mine." Then I left the apartment.

I left Paris that afternoon, and returned to my army station.

XX

BACK IN THE ARMY again, I thought a great deal about my
two visits with Mr. Gurdjieff in Paris, but it must have been
two or three days after my dramatic departure from his
apartment before I even attempted to evaluate my relationship with him or the meaning of that whole finale. When I
began to re-live the "farewell" in my mind, I was forced to
admit to myself that I had, at least momentarily, felt
chosen. That, in fact, I still did. I was pleased with my
behaviour at that moment—I had learned enough from him
to be cagey about it when I had been accused by the lady—
but the feeling of triumph was not unadulterated, and I was
besieged by questions and doubts. I even went so far as to
make a list of my doubts as I tried to think back over my
entire experience with this man. The list began, more or
less, as follows:

1. It is at least possible that he was actually referring to
   me as his "successor". It was possible on many counts:
   a. It was actually true;
   b. It was intended to "expose" my ego to myself;
   c. It was intended to produce various reactions in
      the other persons present;
   d. It was a huge joke on the devout followers.
2. What about my qualifications for the post?
   a. In all honesty, I was forced to acknowledge that
      as far as I was aware, I did not honestly know in
      what his "work" consisted. How then, could I
      carry it on?
   b. In what way, if any, was I different from the
      other members of his groups? Obviously, only in
      that I had always felt like a "lone wolf" and had
      never been able to participate whole-heartedly
      in the readings or other group activities.
3. Did I want to, assuming that I could, "carry on" his
   work—whatever it was?
   a. Yes, up to a point. Groups, dances, readings, no.
      But if there was some way in which I could
      "cull", as it were, what had seemed valuable in

> him to me from what had seemed, if not
> valueless, at least "incomprehensible", I would
> like to be able to pass it on in some way.

There were more questions—in fact they went on and on
—and there were some tentative answers. My final answer
did spring, some years later, from the ones I have listed
above; at the time however, I was only confused and rather
grimly determined to put the questions out of my mind. I
realized that I had been moved, confused and perplexed by
that last meeting, and my determination resulted in the
decision that I would, somehow, manage to get to Paris once
more before returning to the United States.

The war in Europe was over, and shortly after that last
visit to Paris, the two atomic bombs were dropped on Japan,
to the horror of most of us in the European Theatre. Like all
other soldiers, I spent most of my time trying to hasten my
own departure and speed up my return to America—not too
easy because while I had a large number of "points"—more
than I needed to get back—I was not married, and I was an
officer by that time, having received a field commission.
Married men and enlisted personnel had priority. I did,
however, manage to get myself on the shipment list after
some conniving and also wrote my own travel orders,
routing myself through Paris on some sort of non-existent
"official" business—a rather common practice in those days,
as a "last fling" in Paris was practically obligatory, even
though reasonably difficult to achieve.

As a result of all this, I did see Mr. Gurdjieff again, but it
was completely unlike my previous visits. I found him,
alone, at his apartment. He opened the door for me himself
and was wearing a nightshirt, looking very sleepy. He gave
me what I can describe only as a "cold" look and asked me
what I was doing there. "Already I tell you goodbye, and
already I think you in America. Why you come?" I was very
"hurt" and said that I was on my way to America and that I
had only come to say goodbye. He looked at me then, at least
without hostility, and said: "Cannot say goodbye again—this
already done." Then he gave my hand an impersonal, final
shake. I did not say anything more, and since he had not

asked me to come in, I turned to leave. He stopped me with a gesture, and then said sharply, and with a smile on his face: "Americans drop bomb on Japan, yes?" I nodded, and he went on: "What you think of your America now?" I was going to attempt to reply, but he closed the door gently in my face.

There had been, obviously, no time for questions. And, as I faced the door, I knew there never would be. If I have ever known anything in advance, positively, in my life. I knew something then: I would never see him again. And I didn't.

At that very moment, as I walked away from his apartment, I saw one huge question looming up before me: "What did you get out of your association with Gurdjieff? How has he affected your life? What did you learn from him?" I phrased it as three questions, but it is really one. I put it aside, then, deliberately. For the moment, at least, it was totally unanswerable. It remained unanswerable for many years. Until it, inevitably, reasserted itself.

XXI

WHEN I RETURNED to America, I did become associated with some members of the New York group. Also, as he had predicted, I had a good deal of living to do and a great deal to experience on my own. But my questions, even though I did not allow them to come to the surface of my mind, were there, waiting to be answered.

The first time that I became strongly aware that they were still there was at the time of his death. My involvement with the Gurdjieff group in New York had come to a rather sudden end, and, as always, it was the attitude of his "disciples" which seemed to me the cause of my estrangement from anything having to do with his "work". In any event, someone did manage to track me down and tell me of his death and invited me to participate in a memorial funeral service which was being held in his honour in New York. I had a few doubts about my decision, but it was immediate. I did not go; it seemed to me at best an empty "honour" and he had died, as far as I was concerned, when I had last seen him in Paris.

After that momentary, and brief, re-awakening of my questions, I was able to put them away again—put them away, that is, in the sense of attempting to actually find answers to them. I could not put away all my thinking about Gurdjieff; in fact, I thought about him frequently and with considerable affection. I began to realize that at least a part of my mind was back in that old, well-established routine of reverence for him. I was, in reality, more reverent than I had ever been before. My reverence expressed itself in a kind of non-expression. I would not mention his name and would not identify myself with his work, except on the rare occasion when I saw people who knew of my association with him. But, inevitably, a part of my divided mind was, at least unconsciously, trying to answer my questions, or some part of them. There had been one major change in my thinking, however, that had come to me "out of the blue" and with that extraordinary flash of truth that frequently accompanies sudden bursts of insight. I knew that I was not,

even remotely, any kind of "successor". But even this sudden
knowledge, once the immediate convincing moment had
passed, began to trouble me. Was I, perhaps, the successor
after all, and simply refusing to admit it? The only partial
answer I could find was that, even in death, he continued to
have an enormous and troubling influence over me. I had
learned enough from him about deviousness (not in any
particularly derogatory sense), cleverness, and slyness to
find myself wriggling through and around my own doubts
and questions. Gradually however, I began to make a
serious attempt to think about him other than in a personal
sense—to dilute, as it were, the force of his still-powerful
magnetism. I began to look at him differently. But the
"light" was still too strong to do other than look at the
fringes of the man and his work. I would try to take a quick
glance at the man and the Prieuré—the nerve- and heart-
centre of his activity—but in that picture, he was still too
strong, too all-pervading. I decided to work from the outside
in. How would I, how could I, talk about him and his work to
a total stranger, for example? That proved easier, and my
"explanation", such as it was, and as I began to try to
analyse it, ran along these lines:

In addition to the Institute, in Fountainebleau, there
were so-called "Gurdjieff groups" in London, New York, and
Chicago, and perhaps elsewhere. The existense of these
"groups" was, apparently, part of a plan to disseminate his
teaching—eventually—throughout the world. There were
even small gatherings, which could not really be called
"groups" since they usually did not have permanent leaders,
in such culturally and physically remote areas as New
Mexico. In the absence of established groups with leaders
who had, at least ostensibly, the approval of Gurdjieff
himself, the meetings were confined largely to fairly regular
readings of his books which were available, before publica-
tion, in mimeographed form. In the United States, in these
outlying areas, the people involved usually had permission
from someone (such as a group leader in New York) to read
the manuscript of *All and Everything*. The reading was the
whole thing—no questions, no comments, no exercises, no

dances, etc.

The New York and London groups were more highly organized, as was, for a time, the Chicago group. In addition to readings, there were dance or gymnastic groups and even lectures or interpretations of his teaching by the "leader". The one thing—the only thing—that all of these subsidiary groups had in common was the lack of Mr. Gurdjieff's presence, and it was an important lack. The readings, given the style of his writing, had value of a kind for the simple reason that the average person, no matter how interested he or she might be in the subject, would rarely actually finish his book if they were forced to read it alone. Generally speaking, the book is practically incomprehensible on first reading. It is somehow easier to be puzzled in a group, and in most cases it was only under these circumstances that the whole book would be read. The instructions in the beginning of the book are that it is to be read three times, and some of these smaller groups have managed to achieve such a record. The book has an impact that comes only with familiarity; in fact, it begins to have something of the power that is in the man himself. But beyond the further reading, then, of his subsequent books, I do not know what future there is for the readers.

At the time I was associated with them, the larger groups, at least, subsisted not only on readings, etc., but also on the ever-present possibility that they might someday actually see Gurdjieff in person—either they would manage to get to France to see him or, especially in the case of New York, he might make a visit to see them. While a great many of these groups had faithful and even ardent followers, none of them ever seemed to be more than carbon copies of the real thing. Even so, there was an infectious quality about the man that was often communicated even through his writing. If, after a certain length of exposure, his ideas and he, himself, were not rejected, they were accepted in a very special way. He became, to his followers, a genuine prophet—some sort of Messiah, if not some sort of God. It was apparently impossible to be simply interested. In the long run, it was almost automatic to be convinced or to lose interest—I suppose this is nothing more than a magnification of ordinary religious feeling. In any event, it would be terribly boring to attend Gurdjieff meetings *without* real conviction.

What then was Gurdjieff's purpose, and how was he trying to accomplish his aims?

Before either of these questions can be discussed—let alone answered—it is probably necessary to underline the fact that he had no purpose comprehensible to the average, relatively satisfied human being. A prerequisite to any understanding of his aims and an even relative acceptance of his means was dissatisfaction with the *status quo* in a personal sense, and dissatisfaction with, or distrust of, the state of civilization as we know it. His avowed aim, as stated in his book *All and Everything* is to "destroy" all contemporary habits, opinions, preconceptions, etc., concerning human existence; such destruction being a necessary condition for the reception and acquisition of totally new concepts about the potentialities of human existence.

In one of the few "political" statements he ever made in my presence he said that unless the "wisdom" of the East and the "energy" of the West could be harnessed and used harmoniously, the world would be destroyed. There could be a good deal of truth in that statement; in any case, given political events of our time, it does not seem particularly radical or unbelievable. It is, however, perhaps less easy to believe that Gurdjieff, alone, had the key to a system or a teaching that could accomplish the harnessing of east and west. The keystone of his teaching, of course, was that no progress—no human progress, that is—can be accomplished except on an individual level. Group work is valuable only in the sense that it helps the individual to achieve individual self-perfection. The group, as a whole, does not necessarily achieve anything at all as a group.

He compared present-day human existence to a kind of larval stage in organic development; claiming that, as individuals, we have no concept of the potential capacities of human development and that every habit, custom, tradition and tenet by which civilized man lives is, bluntly, not only unproductive but even evil or, at the least, negative. He dismissed all existing religions, philosophies and other system of thought—*as practised*—as being worthless.

In view of this blanket criticism of human existence as we know it, he did not have a tremendous number of followers. But, it should be remembered, he did not want large numbers. He compared, in all seriousness, human life to any and all other organic life, plant or animal. Nature being profligate, there was, in his view, no reason to assume that a very large percentage of human individuals had any right to expect any other destiny than organic fertilizer for the general good of the planet. He did concede that humanity, unlike plants and other animals, had the possibility of achieving higher development; of, as he put it, "acquiring" a fourth body—or for the sake of convenience in terms, a soul. But he did not—even to his own followers—hold out this promise for everyone. In the same sense that each seed of every flower has the latent potentiality of producing a blossom, just in this sense does every human embryo have the potentiality of "producing" or "acquiring" a soul. In this connection, it is necessary to have in mind the number of seeds that do not even germinate.

These views are not, obviously, very flattering to the human ego, collective or individual. Even so, given my association with him, I do not find this particularly difficult to accept. There is an obvious logic in the cycles of nature in all other forms of life: why should man be excluded or in some way different? A flower in its own way, may be aware of the possibility that it has the potentiality of blooming, and perhaps the seed that does germinate suffers unimagined agonies somewhere in the process. Most individual human beings who had any relationship with—or exposure to—Gurdjieff's theories and ideas either rejected them completely or, I suppose, assumed that they, individually, had—through exposure to him—at least the possibility of "blooming"; i.e. of developing further into what he might well have called a proper human state.

In order to have anything to do with such a system of ideas, it is obviously necessary to believe in these basic concepts, and somewhere along the line to accept the view that we have only two choices: the rather general fate of being "fodder" or "fertilizer", or, the very slim chance of maturity. I say "slim chance" advisedly because, nature being nature, only a very small percentage of the whole—no matter how much they might desire it—had even the remotest possibility of growth.

If this view or estimate of the human condition has been accepted, it was then necessary—a sort of process of elimination was built in here—to accept that Gurdjieff, alone, had the method, knew the way to further development, or progress. If you have gone this far with him it becomes difficult to contend that he did not have the key. In other words, it became (or becomes) essential to believe in him in a total sense. The insidious, or compelling, aspect is that once exposed to his point of view it is almost impossible to refute or oppose it effectively. Who can say, positively, that his view of Nature and of man's place in Nature is wrong? If one looks at Nature objectively, if one studies animals, plants, birds, evolution—and finds natural logic in the various processes of growth—then on what basis does one expect man in the sense that man is, automatically or inherently, divine or, to use a simpler word, different? Gurdjieff did not deny man's potential *divinity* (although he did not use that word), he merely stated that it had to be acquired through conscious effort and what he called "intentional suffering", a process that is almost immediately regarded with suspicion by most people. The word suffering, particularly for the western world, seems to be a word that automatically denotes something that is to be avoided. Suffering, especially "intentional suffering", according to Gurdjieff, was not only not to be avoided, but as the expression implies, to be sought.

One of the most compelling arguments on his behalf was an unstated one. He was, obviously, not out to save the world; he did not care whether everyone was interested in what he had to offer. In fact, he said frequently that only a few people could be—underlining the fact that only a very few people could ever develop anyway. It is a great temptation to include oneself among the few.

Since my stay at the Gurdjieff school was for about four years beginning at a time when I was eleven years old, I do not think I can be considered as a convinced student. I have no idea whether Gurdjieff considered me or my brother or any of the other children, most of whom were there by the accidents of their birth, as students at all. We participated, as far as our capabilities would permit, in the daily work of the school but were not students in any other sense. We did not attend readings or listen to lectures on any regular basis —there was simply no rule about it and no one objected if we happened to be present. But even at my age I had a fairly good idea of how Gurdjieff induced "conscious effort" and "intentional suffering" in his pupils—or perhaps I should say how they were exposed to it. For the average person, it consisted largely in a preliminary period of joining in reasonably hard manual labour in a group. It could be anything from building a house to working in a garden and, at the beginning, it was simply hard work that was supposed to be done conscientiously. After a while, one became conscious of being thrust into somewhat frustrating circumstances having to do with the work—such as being forced to work with someone whose temperament clashed with yours; being taken off a job as soon as you became too interested in it, etc. Most of the novice students seemed to be put through a period of purposeful frustration. Inevitably, given the reputation of the school and its stated aims, they began to wonder just exactly what was being accomplished by doing physical labour, and nothing else. The frustration would usually increase because no one, including Gurdjieff, would answer their questions—they were simply told that for the time being they were to do as they were told. When they reached some kind of breaking point, they would suddenly be given an exercise—usually being told that they should observe themselves consciously while they worked and learned more about themselves. If they stayed long enough they were gradually taken into the inner circle where they attended readings or listened to lectures and participated in the exercises or gymnastics or dances, which purported to give them the opportunity to practise physical, mental, and emotional co-ordination simultaneously. After that . . . frankly, I don't know. Most of the people who stayed that long then began to have private interviews with Gurdjieff from time to time and I do not know what took place at such interviews. I do know that by that time, such people were generally convinced followers. They were convinced by the unquestionably extraordinary magnetism and perception of the man himself. As Katherine Mansfield once pointed out (see quote, page 291), " . . . he always acts at precisely the moment one needs it. That is what is so strange . . . "

There is no question but that this was so. There is no question that Gurdjieff had an unbelievable (unless you've seen it) *awareness* of other people. It was nothing so limited as mind-reading or thought-transference. He seemed to know so much about the human processes, about the underlying logic in man, that he was conscious of everything that took place within any human being he happened to observe. It is the same kind of faculty that an occasional highly trained psychiatrist seems to have to a limited degree. Gurdjieff had it to an enormous degree, and I have never known him to be wrong—in my own case or in the case of any other people I knew. It was difficult to resist such obvious learning or "power" and, in fact, there was no reason to resist it. Contrary to the reports about him, there was no evidence that he did anything to anyone that could be considered "evil". The reported "evil" only came about through outward opposition. And a great many of his students brought it on themselves. There is nothing I know of better calculated to produce "opposition" and criticism on a rather vehement level than an attitude of almost beatific secrecy. His students, with contented, superior smiles on their faces would declare publicly that they had at last found the "real thing", or a "great teaching", etc., etc., and then, upon being challenged, seemed unable to explain what it was, or how it worked. I do not think it is "inexplicable", but I think the "method" or the "teaching" or what appears to be the "value" of his work simply cannot be communicated to people who have not had some experience with it themselves. It is primarily a question of values; the people who praise him unqualifiedly make the mistake of forgetting that they did not do so until they had experienced the impact of the man through working with him for some considerable length of time. The emotional experience that most people had with Gurdjieff and his work is not something that can be explained in a logical, convincing manner. He was idolized, believed in and adored—or hated and discredited. None of these attitudes can be considered as valid, nor do they explain him. I think it is probably fair to say that he was a genuine "mystic". And what does that mean unless mysticism is of some importance?

As to the critics and denunciators of Gurdjieff—and they are too numerous to name in anything except a long bibliography—most of them fell into one of two categories: they considered themselves students, and therefore critics, of any teaching that touched on the occult; or they were disillusioned students of Gurdjieff's method. Those in the first category seem to me to pounce on him because he did not live up to their conception of orthodoxy; as for the disillusioned and "vituperative" ex-students: If I found that Christianity, for example, had failed for me, I would find it hard to blame it on the Pope or the Bible.

XXII

I BEGAN TO FEEL that I was getting somewhere in my own thinking. I had even been able to touch on my personal experience at the Prieuré with some degree of detachment. I was pushed further along in my own questions by the judgments of a few other people. There are a number of "well-informed" and "sophisticated" people (Gurdjieff would have called them, derisively, the "intelligentsia") who know something about Gurdjieff and almost all of them know, for instance, that Katherine Mansfield, A. R. Orage, and P. D. Ouspensky were associated with him at one time or another. Many of these people will say, when Gurdjieff's name is mentioned: "Oh, yes, he's the man who killed Katherine Mansfield!" That is a direct quote, and, oddly, the judgment is nearly always phrased in those exact words. Because of this rather common catch-phrase judgment of him, it seems a good place for another look at him. Let me say, first of all, that I feel no great defensive urge to clear Mr. Gurdjieff of this accusation (which is perhaps less an accusation than a handy and rather dramatic means of identifying him); in any case, I have no direct information about the Gurdjieff-Mansfield relationship. She died at the Prieuré before I was ever there, and had she died in the arms or in the custody of some other individual or group, perhaps the accusation would be directed in that direction. Also, I do not think that Gurdjieff ever *killed* anyone.

I bring up the subject of Katherine Mansfield mostly because there has been a good deal of notoriety concerning their association. The surest and quickest approach to the Mansfield-Gurdjieff relationship must, it seems to me, be through Miss Mansfield's own words. Unfortunately, perhaps, Mr. Gurdjieff left no report on the subject.

So, to quote Miss Mansfield: [1]

[1] All quotations are from *Katherine Mansfield's Letters to John Middleton Murry 1913-1922* Ed. by John Middleton Murry, Constable & Co., Ltd., London, 1951. The pages are given in each case. These quotations are reprinted by courtesy of the Society of Authors as the literary representative of the Estate of the late Katherine Mansfield.

"I am going to Fountainebleau next week to see Gurdjieff. I will tell you about it. Why am I going? From all I hear he is the only man who understands there is no division between body and spirit, who believes how they are related. You remember how I have always said doctors only treat *half*. And you have replied: 'It's up to you to do the rest.' It is. That's true. But first I must learn how. I believe Gurdjieff can teach me. What other people say doesn't matter—other people matter not at all." (p.671)

The only comment I can make on this particular letter is the rather obvious one that in the last sentence, the reference to other people seems to me to indicate an awareness of the fact that her decision will be criticized, that she knows that Gurdjieff is "suspect" to "other people" or perhaps only to John Middleton Murry. In any case, there is little question but that Gurdjieff was and is suspect if only for the reason that any teaching that is not, as it were, protected by general public or religious approval is suspect. We suspect what we cannot grasp immediately. Gurdjieff's own literary works have contributed to this "suspicion", being for the most part incomprehensible to the average reader. But to go back to Miss Mansfield:

"Mr. Gurdjieff is not in the least like what I expected. He's what one wants to find him, really. But I do feel *absolutely confident* he can put me on the right track in every way, bodily and t'other governor." (pp. 676-677)
"I believe Mr. Gurdjieff is the only person who can help me. It is great happiness to be here. Some people are stranger than ever, but the strangers I am at last feeling near, and they are my own people at last. So I feel. Such beautiful understanding and sympathy I have never known in the outside world." (p. 679)
"There is another thing here—Friendship. The real thing that you and I have dreamed of. Here it exists between women and women and men and women, and one feels it is unalterable, and living in a way it never can be anywhere else. I can't say I have friends yet. I am simply

not fit for them. I don't know myself enough to be really trusted, and I am weak where these people are strong. But even the relationships I have are dear beyond any friendships I have known." (p. 684)

"Sometimes I wonder if we 'make up' Mr. Gurdjieff's wonderful understanding. But one is always getting a fresh exapmle of it. And he always acts at precisely the moment one needs it. That is what is so strange . . . " (p. 695)

"But this place has taught me so far how unreal I am. It has taken from me one thing after another (the things never were mine) until at this present moment all I know really, really is that I am not annihilated and that I hope —more than hope—believe." (p. 698)

There is, of course, much more about Gurdjieff and the Institute in this book. I have failed to find anything in it that is "derogatory" to Gurdjieff. She does speak of the suffering and the difficulties which she encountered at the Institute from time to time but it seems to be impossible for any objective reader to conclude that Miss Mansfield did not welcome such experiences. They seemed to her to have real substance, purpose and meaning.

In addition to Miss Mansfield's "testimony" on the subject of Gurdjieff, there is a pertinent and interesting editorial note by John Middleton Murry at the conclusion of the same book:

"It is not for me to pass judgment on the Gurdjieff Institute. I cannot tell whether Katherine's life was shortened by her entry into it. But I am persuaded of this: that Katherine made of it an instrument for that process of self-annihilation which is necessary to the spiritual rebirth, whereby we enter the Kingdom of Love. I am certain that she achieved her purpose, and that the Institute lent itself to it. More I dare not, and less I must not say."

Whatever Mr. Murry's expressed intentions, surely this paragraph does pass judgment. And rather odd—or peculiar

—judgment at that. For serious-minded people, entering the "Kingdom of Love" would not appear to be undesirable—in a sense, one might say it is the most desirable thing in the world; and the same comment could also be made about "spiritual rebirth". Which leaves us with the words "that process of self-annihilation". If "self-annihilation" is meant only as a means to "spiritual rebirth", etc., then I can only commend the process. If, on the other hand, Mr. Murry is suggesting (and the general tone of the quoted paragraph leads me to the conclusion that he is) that *physical* death was what Katherine Mansfield achieved—in other words, some form of suicide—then perhaps it should be questioned. Readers can—as a great many have—make their own conclusions about this.

But . . . Of course, there is a but. Katherine Mansfield was very seriously ill when she went to the Prieuré. Her relationship with her husband, Mr. Murry, had been, at least, "difficult" for a long time, as the *Letters* indicated. Even so, I can understand that Mr. Murry would not want his wife to die. On the other hand, had Katherine Mansfield been an old woman at the time of her death, I doubt that the veiled accusation—the implication that Gurdjieff and the Institute somehow contributed to her death, or became a helpful suicidal instrument—should have been made. The whole question, therefore, seems to me to come down to something rather simple: It was unfortunate, given our general conventional outlook on life, that Katherine Mansfield, a highly talented writer, died when she was so young.

Was it really so unfortunate? Can we regret the books that were never written? Can we regret the unlived life? Perhaps we can, logically, regret these things in the case of accidents—train wrecks, automobile crashes, murders. But it is doubtful that we can have such regrets even in the case of suicide which is, at least possibly, part of the victim's make-up and character. But, if Miss Mansfield did enter the "Kingdom of Love" and achieve "spiritual rebirth" (and, please note, Mr. Murry states "I am certain that she acheived her purpose"), then my only question would be: Was there anything else for her to achieve? Does anyone who ponders such questions have an alternative that is preferable? In fact, the statement of Mr. Murry can be taken as an extranordinary Christian tribute to Mr. Gurdjieff—one that I am not at all sure he deserves.

I am less convinced than Mr. Murry that Miss Mansfield "entered the Kingdom of love" in the hereafter, which I assume is his implication. I do believe that her own testimony at least indicates that she found, not a kingdom, but a world of "friendship" and "reality" which had great meaning for her. No mean achievement.

In addition to the "testimony" of Miss Mansfield and of Mr. Murry, P. D. Ouspensky, who did not remain forever "taken in" by Gurdjieff, as his own books will testify, had this to say on the subject of Miss Mansfield and Gurdjieff: [1]

"I arrived at the Château Prieuré for the first time at the end of October or the beginning of November, 1922. ****** I remember one talk with Miss Katherine Mansfield who was then living there. This was not more than three weeks before her death. I had given her G.'s address myself. She had been to two or three of my lectures and had then come to me to say that she was going to Paris. A Russian doctor was curing tuberculosis by treating the spleen with X-rays. I could not of course tell her anything about it. She already seemed to me to be halfway to death. And I thought that she was fully aware of it. But with all this, one was struck by the striving in her to make the best use even of these last days, to find the truth whose presence she clearly felt but which she was unable to touch. I did not think that I should see her again. But I could not refuse when she asked me for the address of my friends in Paris, for the address of people with whom she would be able to talk about the things she had talked with me. And so I had met her again at the Prieuré. We sat in the evening in one of the salons and she spoke in a feeble voice which seemed to come from the void, but it was not unpleasant.

" 'I know that this is true and that there is no other truth. You know that I have long since looked upon all

[1] Ouspensky, P. D. *In Search of the Miraculous: Fragments of an Unknown Teaching.* Routledge & Kegan Paul, London, 1950.

of us without exception as people who have suffered shipwreck and have been cast upon an uninhabited island, but who do not yet know of it. But the people here know it. The others, there, in life, still think that a steamer will come for them tomorrow and that everything will go on in the old way. These already-know that there will be no more of the old way. I am so glad that I can be here.'

"Soon after my return to London I heard of her death. G. was very good to her, he did not insist upon her going although it was clear that she could not live. For this in the course of time he received the due amount of lies and slander."

In my opinion, Mr. Ouspensky, regardless of any personal disagreement I had with him and despite the fact that his books are too "intellectual" for me, is one of the—if not *the*—most detached, objective critics of Gurdjieff, as witness his statement, in this same book:

"During this period G. invited me several times to go and live at the Prieuré. There was a good deal of temptation in this. ****** At the same time I could not fail to see, as I had seen in Essentuki in 1918, that there were many destructive elements in the organization of the affair itself and that it had to fall to pieces."

In a final effort to be completely fair to Mr. Murry and to those who still assume that Mr. Gurdjieff "killed" Miss Mansfield, let us go back to the Prieuré and to Mr. Gurdjieff himself:

When I first worked at the Prieuré—in the stables—taking care of the horse and donkey, I was, as any child would have been, amused and interested by the narrow wooden staircase which led to a small platform above the stalls of the animals. There, on the ceiling over the low platform, were portraits of numerous birds and animals, all caricatures of Katherine Mansfield's friends at the Prieuré and painted, I was told, by Alexandre de Salzmann. As many of the same people who were caricatured were still students at the Prieuré, it amused me, too, to try to identify them. No one was willing to identify them for me. Also, childishly, it was entertaining to pretend to live the role of the invalid, lying on Katherine's narrow bed, smelling and hearing the animals below, and fantasying with the animal-likenesses above.

Even at the age of eleven, I had heard criticism of Gurdjieff along the lines of the "he killed Katherine Mansfield" accusation, and was greatly surprised to find all the older students, and Gurdjieff himself, speaking of her with great friendship, affection, and regret. Also, one of my first excursions outside the Prieuré grounds was with a number of my new-found friends to visit the grave of Katherine Mansfield in the small cemetery in Avon. I, for one, find it hard to believe that Katherine Mansfield could have been unhappy at the Prieuré. But that, of course, does not refute the possibility that Gurdjieff may have killed her. Gurdjieff at no time made any effort to dispel existing doubts about her death, and I assume that he was aware of the criticism. He did speak of her in my presence, but only as he would have spoken of a departed friend or relative—with affection and, it seemed to me, a good deal of "sentimentality".

I think I can say, fairly, that my position at the Prieuré was—at least to a great extent—unique. Unique in the sense that I had no 'need' to be there. I was there, in fact, against my will—in the sense that any child is at a boarding school against his will—or at least, hardly by choice. Because of this, I regarded Mr. Gurdjieff as I might have observed anyone in authority. He was, in a general way, just another adult—with more or less the same powers that any headmaster would be expected to have. The only sense in which he seemed "unusual" was that he was treated with more awe and respect than is common among, shall we say, headmasters? If comparing Gurdjieff to a "headmaster" or to "any adult" seems "naïve" or "ridiculous". I can only say that Gurdjieff did not seem any more odd to me than, for example, Jane Heap, Margaret Anderson, Gertrude Stein,

Brancusi, etc. More imposing, if you wish, but no odder.

The important point is, I think, that I had not come to the Prieuré *searching* for anything. Someone said, recently in my hearing: "Gurdjieff was for the misfits in life. He had some sort of system which appealed to the neurotic, the dissatisfied people who could not find any answers or any solace in religion, philosophy, and so forth." I have no particular quarrel with this statement. Most of the "followers" or habitués of the Prieuré were "misfits" in the sense that they were seeking some answer, some reason, and were dissatisfied with whatever had been available to them before encountering Gurdjieff. Since, as he explained constantly, dissatisfaction was practically essential for candidates for his method, I am hardly surprised.

As a child, I was not conscious of anything "unusual" about the Prieuré. While it apparently seems strange to people who have heard about Gurdjieff and his theories— life at the Prieuré did not fit in with their conceptions of what life must have been at an "Institute for the Harmonious Development of Man". Generally, at least for a child, life at the Prieuré was simple, even elemental, in the sense that our occupations had to do with growing food for our own use, keeping the place in order, and so on. To me, the students were something like a large body of caretakers and maintenance-men. We might easily have been called a corps of janitors, gardeners, or servants. My personal relationship with Mr. Gurdjieff, of course, made me aware that something more than "maintenance" work was going on—but the nature of that relationship was no more arresting or unusual than any child's relationship to an exceptional parent. He, Gurdjieff himself, was peculiar. But at that age most adults were peculiar in my eyes—and his peculiarities were only different in degree.

Also, the Prieuré was an outgoing, happy place for all children. Whatever torments may have been suffered by resident or visiting adults, they were not obvious to the children. We were treated — except by Gurdjieff — as children, and with a good deal of love, affection and warmth. Unlike the other adults, Gurdjieff was the "boss" and, as

such, entitled to exceptional behaviour and exceptional
obedience. We thought of him as a kind of god—or perhaps
an all-powerful king. Despotic, certainly, but also humorous,
kind, affectionate, and frequently very funny. More than
that—he seemed absolutely trustworthy and, to us, logical
and right. If, at eleven, I could have understood what was
supposedly taught at the Prieuré, I might have been baffled
and confused. Since I didn't, I was only aware of being in a
"good" place, with a good man. Unusual, if you wish, but so
much the better. I had a natural child's respect for his
unquestioned authority and for his eccentricities—they
merely made him that much more interesting. Also he was
unpredictable which, contrary to popular belief, was not at
all frightening. It was far more stimulating than the activity
of all the predictable adults. Although predictable, they
were incomprehensible and rather boring: most adults are, a
fact which seems to escape us except in childhood or in old
age. But with Gurdjieff, we never knew what was going to
happen next . . . and when it did, it was usually exciting
and almost always amusing; sometimes he made it a magic
world for children . . . imagine a man wild and wonderful
enough to buy two hundred bicycles and make everyone ride
them. What child could resist that alone.

If this digression seems over-long, may I justify it by
stating that I have tried to give a picture of the Prieuré as I
saw and knew it — as a child — about one year after
Katherine Mansfield's death there. And to touch on that
death once more, one important thing in the question was
Gurdjieff's own attitude towards death itself. Mr. Murry
may be quite right, in fact I think he is right, in at least part
of his judgment about the Institute when he says that the
"Institute lent itself to" her death-wish, as it were. Gurdjieff,
obviously, did not place any great value on the prolongation
of individual human life. His insistence upon the necessity
to be constantly aware of the fact of one's death could be a
dangerous thing for many people, of course. If the death-
wish is as strong as some psychologists and doctors would
have us believe, his insistence that one must "look it in the
face" could strengthen that fertile wish. But such thinking

fails to admit the perfectly obvious fact that everyone is going to die anyway, and why not admit that fact and live with it?

My opinion of Katherine Mansfield's end, partly from the letters and other opinions quoted previously, and partly from my knowledge of Gurdjieff and the Institute, is that she was — whether psychologically or physically — dying when she went to Gurdjieff for the first time. Someone other than Gurdjieff, and here is where I seem to be in agreement with Mr. Murry, might have made great efforts to save her life—or to prolong it. Gurdjieff would not have done that, and certainly, in my opinion, did not do it. But it would be hard for me to disagree with whatever it was that he did do. She died, or at least prepared for death, in a more reconciled and "happier" state than she appeared to have achieved before in her life. Who knows, definitely, that an acceptance —to some degree—of death, is not a desirable thing? I point out again, that I had no personal experience with Miss Mansfield and was not present at the time of her death— also that I am convinced that Gurdjieff's "work" in her case was only to help her struggle towards a "proper" death. Finally, let us not rob Miss Mansfield of her stature as a human being and a writer, by assuming that she had no control whatsoever in the months before her death. She chose to be there. Her letters, if nothing else, are certainly not the letters of a woman who was being gradually "killed".

XXIII

Most of the criticism of Mr. Gurdjieff and his method is curiously vindictive and personal. It is difficult for me to understand this sort of criticism for the simple reason that it never seems to take into account that there could have been any sort of personal responsibility in relation to Gurdjieff. This possibility is usually dismissed, or at least avoided, by the statement, or the implication that Gurdjieff was so "hypnotic" or so "compelling" (or that there was something in his work that made him irresistible) that people were unable to save themselves from him.

I certainly admit Gurdjieff's personal magnetism; on the other hand, he made it very difficult for most people to become group members. In one instance that I remember very clearly, Gurdjieff was approached by a middle-aged American couple for help. The man was partially paralysed, and it was implicit in their request for admission to the Prieuré that they hoped his "work" could do something about this condition. Gurdjieff made it eminently clear, in my presence, that no aspect of his work could possibly do anything about the actual physical condition of the man (except to help him to accept it), but he had no objection to their admission to the Prieuré as long as they understood that nothing there would in any way help or alleviate the paralysis. In fact, at the beginning of the interview, which took place at the Prieuré, he at first refused them permission to establish themselves there as students. It was only after he had made his conditions perfectly clear—concerning the physical ailment—that they were allowed to stay.

I got to know the couple very well during their stay there —I was thirteen at the time, and there was a period when I was assigned to the work of cleaning their rooms. This was unheard of—everyone else cleaned their own rooms—but the exception was made in their case, as a form of courtesy, since the man was confined to a wheelchair and his wife was almost always with him, pushing him around the grounds in order that he could at least observe, if not participate in, the work that was going on. They stayed at the Prieuré for

about two months, as I remember, and the wife, particularly, seemed to feel that she was "getting something" from
being there. I don't know how her husband felt about this. I
do know that when they left the Prieuré, they announced
(more accurately, she did) that they intended to continue
with his work in New York—with the New York group.

It was about nine or ten years later when I saw these
people again. They made a particular effort to find me. I was
very surprised to hear from them, and very glad to see them
—as a child I had liked them both. To my complete
astonishment, when I did see them in New York, they spoke
of Gurdjieff with enormous personal hatred in their voices. I
was so startled that I could not say very much and did not
know of any way to defend him. But I did listen to them
both, and their long hateful harangue amounted to the fact
that Gurdjieff was a "fake", a "charlatan", and a "devil",
mostly because he had not done anything about the man's
physical condition.

In my rather simple-minded way I tried to remind them
that he had warned them, specifically, and in my presence,
that there was nothing he could do about that condition, but
I might as well have tried to reason with them in a foreign
language. Hatred simply does not respond to reasoning.
This was my first experience—in connection with Gurdjieff
—in clashing head on with a totally emotional point of view;
so emotional that reason was completely disregarded. I have
come up against it since then on many, many occasion.

Why is it that even now, years after Gurdjieff's death, the
prevailing criticism of him is so entirely emotional and so
rarely based on any fact? To me it has come to underline
Gurdjieff's own words about the "savagery" of what he
called the "feeling" or "emotional" centre in man. In my own
personal experience in the world, quite apart from Gurdjieff,
I am continually appalled at the force of emotional reactions
in people and at the weakness of their reasoning power in
emotional situations. In the case of Gurdjieff, I do not think
it was his magnetism or his power that was the cause of the
confusion. I think it was the expectations of the people who
came into contact with him. I know of almost no one who

was able to approach him and evaluate him from a
detached, thinking point of view. Even the seemingly
impartial admirers (and how could they be impartial and
also admire?) would sometimes be horrified and prejudiced
against him because he was, in their view, "dirty" or
"insanitary". I, of all people, having cleaned his room for two
years as a child, knew he could be dirty and insanitary, by
western standards, but it had no more effect on me than the
fact that he was a certain age or a certain height. What did
his sanitary habits have to do with his knowledge or his
abilities as a teacher? When I have asked that question, the
reply always seems to be that a great teacher is, of
necessity, clean. This seems to me to be the equivalent of
accepting Christianity after an investigation of the bathing
habits of Jesus Christ. Or is "cleanliness next to Godliness"
after all? And does that old saw actually refer to physical
cleanliness?

I have said in this book that I have no particular desire to
defend Mr. Gurdjieff, and I suppose that statement is not
absolutely true, or at least not cut-and-dried. If there is an
implied defence of him in this criticism of some of his
followers and detractors, it is due to my impatience with the
lack of impartial reasoning on the part of such people. They
seemed to see—and then evaluate—Gurdjieff through the
emotional mist of their desires or wants or hopes and never
with clarity. Is it really all the fault of the teacher if a
student does not get straight A's?

All that Gurdjieff had to offer, as far as I know, was a
teaching that was based on a great many other teachings,
that was not necessarily *new*. If there was any novelty in it,
it was in his method of teaching. But, my question to his
critics would have to be: What made it so difficult either to
accept or reject him or his teaching? Why do they have to
become so violently, emotionally involved with it. I admit, at
once, that I was emotionally involved with Gurdjieff as a
man, and that he had enormous influence on my life; but I
am emotionally involved with practically anyone I have
known well. So why should—or how could—Gurdjieff be an
exception? And emotional involvement does not preclude my

awareness of the fact that such-and-such a person may have habits or traits that I may dislike or of which I may even "disapprove". But is my approval or affection going to be based on my observation of such things? In fact, can I take it upon myself to *approve* of anyone?

Of course, I have emotional reactions to people. But such reactions do not have the slightest effect on their individuality, or the "totality" of such people. They exist, as they are, in whatever way they choose—or happen to be led—which is something I cannot alter, even if I should wish to do so. The only thing I can do is to accept or reject such people in a personal sense. Life seems to me to be a predatory business by its very nature, and if a person is not "useful" (in the sense that there is some mutual, valuable exchange—on *whatever* level) to another person, why have a relationship with such a person? Cold-blooded? If you wish, but isn't the very expression "cold-blooded" a purely emotional one? If it were possible, I would do practically anything for my fellow man (why not?), but this should not be taken as an "altruistic" statement. Altruism, itself, is often a questionable motive, and usually an emotional one. In my periods of "loving the world" and feeling "altruistic" I have found, to my sorrow, that there isn't anything I can do for anyone else anyway. Certainly not in any *helpful* sense. I can share their lives, but only as long as such sharing is a mutually profitable (or enjoyable, or rewarding) process. Is there another way to live with people?

XXIV

WHATEVER PROTESTATIONS I may have made to the contrary, it is probably impossible for me to stand back, impartially, and evaluate my own experience with Gurdjieff. I became so involved in the life of the Prieuré and with him as a child that such an evaluation would amount to asking a fish how his life had been affected by living in the water. Even so, I will make an attempt.

First of all, it seems important to emphasize the fact that I was primarily involved with, and interested in, the individual man—not his teaching; at least not in an intellectual sense. On the other hand, I think it was impossible to be associated with him in any way and not be affected by whatever he was teaching—he embodied his teaching. If I am aware of any single, permanent result of Gurdjieff in myself, it is a consciousness of total paradox. The duality of man's nature (whether manifested in myself or in someone else) seems to be, thanks to Gurdjieff, a condition that I am never able to forget. The only simple example—and it is fairly complicated, at that—that I can give is that there seems to be a part of me which has never, and will never, grow up in the ordinary sense of those words. I attribute this to Gurdjieff because it seems to me that one of his aims was to encourage the retention of a certain child-like naïveté in people. In his own writings he speaks of the necessity of "being able to preserve intact both the wolf and the sheep" in one's self. Roughly translated, this process, in my opinion, amounts to preserving "credulity" (or "innocence" or "naïveté") at the same time as one acquires "experience" (or "worldliness" or "scepticism").

Gurdjieff often said that it was necessary to "have all illusion" and "all disillusion" in life, and when he first said that to me when I was still a child, I took it to mean that a given person must, eventually, destroy all his illusions. In the course of time, it has come to mean something else. It is not so much a description of a process, as I now see it, as a description of a state of being that must be sustained. If one can retain the ability to "have illusions" it is then possible, no matter how cynical one's intellect might have become, to experience life, and to approach people, with an extreme receptivity. It amounts to the retention in oneself of what might be called "total gullibility".

To put this on a more personal, and understandable, basis, I would say that I believe that everyone always tells the truth. Even when I know they are lying, I believe they are telling the truth. If this seems like a contradictory or paradoxical statement, I would point out that "believing" and "knowing" are two different things and should not be confused. The ensuing struggle—the conflict between belief and knowledge—within oneself becomes a means to an end which somehow produces an open mind and a path to "understanding" which lies somewhere between belief and knowledge. The value in it, for me, is that in the conflict I am forced to evaluate not only another person, but, inevitably, myself. Thanks to just this process, I am *involved* in life, in other people.

If this process seems pointless, or inexplicable, there is very little I can say about it that will make it any clearer or give it any meaning. It seems to come down to the necessity of believing in people, *per se*, however they may happen to manifest themselves; and also continuing to rediscover the fact that life (or nature) is full of wonder—permanently startling.

One of the great difficulties in writing about Gurdjieff, or in trying to "explain" him, is that most people take him and his work so *seriously*. Whether for or against him, they are seriously so. I suppose that the fundamental "seriousness" of the subject—how to perfect oneself into real manhood (or however one might wish to describe his work)—calls for a certain gravity. But, again paradoxically perhaps, Gurdjieff's strong belief in the "total" man and in the development of all the facets of one's being, seems to me to presuppose that one must at the same time realize how ridiculous the whole process is. This "seriousness" which, in his disciples, often amounted to reverence, is the main reason that he has been the centre of controversy in those circles professing interest in him. His "philosophy" is, almost always, criticized as being "bogus" or "satanic", and defended as being a "true way", if not *the* true way. Somewhere in the controversy lies the apparently unnoticed or forgotten fact that Gurdjieff was, above everything, a *man*—in the perfectly ordinary sense that we are all men. As for his teaching, it was by his own admission based on various old and secret "teachings", and not invented by him. Also, by his own definition, he was a "troublemaker". Because of his personal struggles to keep his own duality alive—that duality and the resulting conflict which are apparently essential, in his view, to human progress—there must have been periods when he took himself too "seriously", too. Even so, he recovered, and his saving grace as a man and a teacher, was his sense of humour with its resultant perspective.

While it is difficult to give any general examples of Gurdjieff's *method* of teaching, I do remember one instance which, when I think back on it, seems to me to embody a great many aspects of the manner in which he worked:

At one time, and as a part of a general discussion on the "deterioration of knowledge and science" in the modern world, Gurdjieff brought up the subject of astrology. He claimed that many centuries ago it had been a "really genuine science" and very different from the present-day conception of astrology. As an example of the way in which it had been "civilized and misinterpreted" he said that the astrological signs were originally "invented" to synthesize the particular characteristics against which a given individual would have to fight—or to struggle—in the course of life on earth.

He said that an individual born under the sign and influence of Aries, the Ram, should—properly—remember that the Ram was a symbol of the characteristics of his nature against which he should struggle in order to achieve harmony and balance within himself.

Scorpio, in this interpretation (the female kills the male when mating has been accomplished), could generally be interpreted as a "killing" sign, although he did not mean killing in a physical sense. He went on to point out that

Pisces and Gemini were the two obvious dual signs, but that they represented two different kinds of duality. In Pisces, it is warring duality—two fishes, tied together (as they are sometimes depicted in old engravings and drawings) but struggling to break the bond between themselves—in other words, Pisceans have to struggle against a self-divisive tendency in their own natures. Gemini, on the contrary, represented a merging duality, and the struggle was against ingrowingness and towards separation. Sagittarius has to struggle against destructiveness (the arrow aimed against the world) . . . and so on. The straightforward simple method being to find out what your sign symbolized in your mind and relate it to your natural characteristics.

Gurdjieff did not discuss all the signs in detail, but suggested that once one could discover, *for oneself,* what the sign symbolized or represented in the way of characteristics (or compulsions) in one's self, then one would have to remind oneself that such a synthesis represented those elements against which one would have to fight throughout life—what might be called the "built-in obstacles" in one's own nature that were part of the key to "self-perfection" or growth; the *necessary* obstacles standing in the path to development. He added that, as was usual in all great, ancient sciences, the lesson was never clearly stated, but could only be learned with effort, and that a great part of the problem in astrology was the individual's particular interpretation of the meaning of his sign for himself. Going back to Aries, as a convenient example, he said that it was not only that persons born under this sign would have to struggle against their tendency to "ram" (or batter) in various circumstances and situations, but that it would also depend upon their interpretation of "ramming" and their personal analysis and understanding of the ways in which this compulsive characteristic was manifested. The sign, in other words, was a key—an indication—for all persons born under it, but since each person differed individually, it would be necessary for them to find out for themselves in what particular ways the sign manifested in their individuality.

He warned that in the particular, individual search and analysis of such characteristics, a clue usually could be found if one was able to observe, objectively, the characteristics within oneself to which one is inordinately attached. He said that while it was very hard to observe one's personal prejudices and "pleasing characteristics" with real objectivity, it was nevertheless necessary to do so in order to evaluate oneself correctly. In this, other people could be useful, as through them it was possible to observe the effects (upon them) of one's own *recurring,* individual manifestations. One way to discover those things within ourselves to which we are attached, which we like and of which we are proud (although perhaps quite unconsciously), is the frequency of their repetition in outward manifestations—in dealings with other people. Such recurrent manifestations could be the first clue to our "vanities", which in turn should be interpreted in relation to the characteristics of our astrological sign.

In an attempt to give an easily comprehensible, hypothetical example, and a very obvious one, he said that if a given individual should observe that in his dealings with other people he manifested a certain, persistent, recurring insistence on "having his own way", and that such a person turned out to be someone who was born under the sign of Aries, the implication is fairly obvious. Learn how, consciously, not to insist. If a Piscean was also "insisting" in this sense, the insistence might be interpreted as a "one-sided" insistence; and it might be necessary to learn, consciously, to "insist" with the other half of one's nature.

If a person born under the sign of Aries can learn not to insist in his dealings with other people (assuming that he has found he does so), he will at least have learned the possibility of not being insistent in his own self-struggles towards growth or development. Any *recurring* manifestation (any unconscious habit) is, of necessity, a form of blindness in that the repetitive manifestations, by its very operation, prevents conscious activity.

In relating this rather general conversation to Gurdjieff's "work" or his "method" I could only conclude, personally, that it is a fairly clear example of his teaching — fundamentally, the discussion seemed to me to emphasize the need to produce constant struggle within oneself which, generally, was the basis of his method—anything to keep the pot boiling. Anything, including astrology.

The simplest guidepost that he gave in this discussion of astrology and the signs of the Zodiac was to watch for those things in oneself which one "loves"—whether they were physical, emotional, or mental manifestations, compulsions, habits, or characteristics (he gave a choice of terms). If you "loved" your hands as a physical feature—this was a clue of a kind; something to do with the use or function of the hands. If you "loved" or "cherished" your propensity for eloquence, this was another clue. If you loved or were proud of the fact that you were always "honest" . . . another clue. And so on. Not much in the way of answers, but as he admonished repeatedly, there are no answers except the ones that one finds for oneself.

As a concluding statement about Gurdjieff, as a teacher, I would say that he was, without question, fanatic in the sense that, however conscious he might have been, his sense of dedication to the dissemination of his method must necessarily be considered compulsive. (He gave his birthday as January 1, in case anyone wishes to practise astrology with that date in mind.) Considering him as compulsive, automatically produces a sense of paradox. His method was based on becoming "conscious" as opposed to being "led" or "pulled" or "compelled", and one is, therefore, logically forced to ask: Why then did he teach? Would a totally conscious man—conscious, for instance, of the fact that he could only fulfil—or solve—his own destiny (if that is possible)—devote his life to an attempt to teach others? I can only reiterate my conviction that he absolutely had to be a teacher, that he was, therefore, some sort of self-created, inevitable Messiah —which, it seems to me, brings him down to a very human level. However detached he may have been, how *involved* he must have been to *have to teach*.

Also, as if blindly drawn by some magnetic pull—some force larger than himself, his primary teaching activity, in the long run, was in America. This seems to me immensely suitable—where else is the search for God, for an authority, for guidance, so openly expressed, so desperately "needed"? There was real interest, of course, also in France and England, Germany and Russia, but it seems significant that, for the most part, his really ardent adherents are in the United States. *Seek, and ye shall find.* A teacher, as Gurdjieff would have been the first to point out, *needs* pupils. He seems to me to have done a unique piece of work for those who happened to *need* him. It was, obviously, a special need. Equally obvious, he was a "special" man. As a final quote from Gurdjieff himself: "Is very important to find proper vocation in life. Only in this way possible fulfil one's destiny." Unquestionably, he found the proper vocation, *for him.* I can only assume that he also fulfilled his destiny.

EPILOGUE

A FEW DAYS after completing the preceding manuscript, I re-read, thanks to a fortuitous accident, the following passages from *Tertium Organum:* [1]

"In all living nature (and perhaps also in that which we consider as dead) *love* is the motive force which drives the creative activity in the most diverse directions.

"In springtime with the first awakening of love's emotions the birds begin to *sing,* and *build nests.*

"Of course a positivist would strive to explain all this very simply: singing acts as an attraction between the females and the males, and so forth. But even a positivist will not be in a position to deny that there is a good deal more of this singing that is necessary for 'the continuation of the species'. For a positivist, indeed, 'singing' is merely 'an accident', a 'by-product'. But in reality it may be that this singing is *the principal function of a given species,* the realization of its existence, the purpose pursued by nature in creating this species; and that this singing is *necessary,* not so much to attract females, as for some general harmony of nature which we only rarely and imperfectly sense.

"Thus in this case we observe what appears to be a collateral function of love, from the standpoint of the individual, may serve as a principal function of the species.

"Furthermore, there are not fledglings as yet: there is even no intimation of them, but 'homes' are prepared for them nevertheless. Love inspired this orgy of activity, and instinct directs it, because it is expedient from the standpoint of the species. At the first awakening of love this work begins. One and the same desire creates a new generation and those conditions under which this new generation will live. One and the same desire urges forward creative activity in all directions, brings the pairs together for the birth of a new generation, and makes

[1] P. D. Ouspensky, *Tertium Organum.* Routledge & Kegan Paul, London, 1951 (pp. 170-173).

them *build* and *create* for this same future generation.

"We observe the same thing in the world of men: there too love is the creative force. And the creative activity of love does not manifest itself in one direction only, but in many ways. It is indeed probable that by the spur of love, *Eros,* humanity is aroused to the fulfilment of its *principal function,* of which we know nothing, but only at times by glimpses hazily perceive.

"But even without reference to the purpose of the existence of humanity, within the limits of the knowable we must recognize that all the creative activity of humanity results from love. *Our* entire world revolves around love as its centre.

"Love unfolds in a human being traits of his which he never knew in himself. In love there is much both of the Stone Age and of the Witches' Sabbath. By anything less than love many men cannot be induced to commit a crime, to be guilty of a treason, to reanimate in themselves such feelings as they thought to have killed out long ago. In love is hidden an infinity of egoism, vanity and selfishness. Love is the potent force that tears off all masks, and men who run away from love do so in order that they may preserve their masks.

"If creation, *the birth of ideas,* is the light which comes from love, then this light comes from *a great fire.* In this eternally burning fire in which humanity and all the world are being incessantly purified, all the forces of the human spirit and of genius are being evolved and refined; and perhaps indeed, from this same fire or by its aid a new force will arise which shall deliver from the chains of matter all who follow where it leads.

"Speaking not figuratively, but literally, it may be said that love, being the most powerful of all emotions, unveils in the soul of man all its qualities patent and latent; and it may also unfold those *new* potencies which even now constitute the object of occultism and mysticism—the development of powers in the human souls so deeply hidden that by the majority of men their very existence is denied." **********

"In love the most important element is *that which is*

not, which *absolutely* does not exist from the usual worldly, materialistic point of view."

Not only do these words of Ouspensky's strike a deeply responsive chord in me—they have the ring of final truth—they also explain, to me, the causes of the conflict that at one time existed between Ouspensky and Gurdjieff. When Ouspensky was first interested in Gurdjieff's "ideas", Gurdjieff told him that if he, Gurdjieff, "knew as much" as Ouspensky, he would be a very great teacher indeed. The statement seemed to me a puzzling one, even after Gurdjieff had explained to me many times that "knowledge is a *passing* presence".

While Ouspensky knew, in his mind, that "Love is the potent force that tears off all masks, and men who run away from love do so in order that they may preserve their masks", Gurdjieff *understood* it. The difference between knowledge and understanding, in our time, is something akin to the difference between knowing how to make a hydrogen bomb and using it. Gurdjieff used everything he knew because he understood what he knew. Ouspensky, in a comparative sense, could only communicate on an intellectual level—his books, as reading, are far more interesting and readable than any book Gurdjieff has ever written. This fact, however, does not automatically give them more *content.*

There may be many of Gurdjieff's "disciples" who could, or do, feel that they have been maligned by my recollections of Gurdjieff's life. I am not apologizing to them for my observations of their behaviour—the behaviour of human beings under the impact of an unquestionably extraordinary human being who *loved* them is not predictable, nor is it important.

What I *knew* as a child, I am beginning to *understand* as an adult. Gurdjieff *practised* love in a form that is unknown to almost everyone: without limits.

In the Gurdjieffian sense, "to be or not to be" is not a soul-searching question. It is a preliminary statement concerning a necessary decision. Having known Gurdjieff, there is only one possible answer and, therefore, no question at all.